CompTIA®
Linux+™
Practice Tests
Exam XK0-005
Third Edition

Steve Suehring

A Wiley Brand

Acknowledgments

Thank you to Kenyon Brown, Kim Wimpsett, and the team responsible for bringing this title to and through the publication process.

About the Author

Steve Suehring is an associate professor of Computing and New Media Technologies at the University of Wisconsin–Stevens Point. Prior to joining the faculty at UWSP, Steve worked in industry for many years. Steve has written several technical books. More information is available at `www.braingia.org` or follow him on Twitter: `@stevesuehring`.

About the Technical Editor

Jason W. Eckert is an experienced technical trainer, systems architect, software engineer, and best-selling author in the technology industry. With 45 industry certifications, over 30 years of technology and programming experience, 4 published apps, and 25 published textbooks covering UNIX, Linux, security, Windows Server, Microsoft Exchange Server, PowerShell, BlackBerry Enterprise Server, and video game development, Mr. Eckert brings his expertise to every class that he teaches at triOS College. He was also named 2019 Outstanding Train-the-Trainer from the Computing Technology Industry Association (CompTIA). For more information about Mr. Eckert, visit `jasoneckert.net`.

Contents

Introduction

This book provides practice questions for the CompTIA Linux+ certification Exam XK0-005. The questions are multiple choice, and the difficulty levels vary. The balance of questions closely mirrors the exam objective weighting in emphasis of certain technologies.

How to Get Linux+ Certified

Tests are administered by CompTIA's global testing partner, Pearson VUE. For more information on taking the exam, visit the CompTIA website at www.comptia.org. You can also visit Pearson VUE at www.pearsonvue.com.

How to Use This Book and the Interactive Online Learning Environment and Test Bank

This book is intended as a supplement to *CompTIA Linux+ Study Guide Exam XK0-005, 5th Edition*. Ideally, you already own that title and can use the practice questions in this book as you work through the objectives.

This book contains 1,000 questions related to technologies that have been identified by CompTIA as necessary for an individual to obtain Linux+ certification. If you have the requisite skills and experience, then you can attempt the questions within the book, looking up answers as needed. The book can also be used to identify areas where you may need to seek out additional experience and knowledge.

The online test bank at www.wiley.com/go/sybextestprep includes all the questions from the book. Take these practice exams just as if you were taking the actual exam (without any reference material). If you get more than 90 percent of the answers correct, you're ready to take the certification exams.

Like all exams, the Linux+ certification from CompTIA is updated periodically and may eventually be retired or replaced. At some point after CompTIA is no longer offering this exam, the old editions of our books and online tools will be retired. If you have purchased this book after the exam was retired, or are attempting to register in the Sybex online learning environment after the exam was retired, please know that we make no guarantees that this exam's online Sybex tools will be available once the exam is no longer available.

Go to www.wiley.com/go/sybextestprep to register and gain access to this interactive online learning environment and test bank with study tools.

Linux+ Certification Exam Objectives: (XK0-005)

Exam objectives can be found at www.comptia.org/certifications/linux.

How to Contact the Publisher

If you believe you've found a mistake in this book, please bring it to our attention. At John Wiley & Sons, we understand how important it is to provide our customers with accurate content, but even with our best efforts an error may occur. In order to submit your possible errata, please email it to our Customer Service Team at wileysupport@wiley.com with the subject line "Possible Book Errata Submission."

Chapter

1

System Management (Domain 1.0)

1. Which command is used to load a module and its dependencies automatically?

    A. `modprobe`

    B. `lsmod`

    C. `insmod`

    D. `rmmod`

2. Which option given at boot time within the GRUB2 boot entry configuration will boot the system into single-user mode?

    A. `single-user`

    B. `su`

    C. `single`

    D. `root`

3. What is the command to display the default target on a computer running `systemd`?

    A. `systemctl defaults`

    B. `update-rc.d defaults`

    C. `systemctl runlevel`

    D. `systemctl get-default`

4. Which command is used to obtain a list of USB devices?

    A. `usb-list`

    B. `lsusb`

    C. `ls-usb`

    D. `ls --usb`

5. Which command can be used to obtain a list of currently loaded kernel modules?

    A. `insmod`

    B. `modlist`

    C. `ls --modules`

    D. `lsmod`

6. When running with a Unified Extensible Firmware Interface (UEFI) system, to which partition will the EFI system partition typically be mounted?

    A. `/etc/efi`

    B. `/efi`

    C. `/sys/efi`

    D. `/boot/efi`

7. Assuming that a USB disk contains a single partition and is made available on /dev/sdb, which command mounts the disk in /media/usb?

   A. `mount /dev/sdb1 /media/usb`

   B. `usbconnect /dev/sdb0 /media/usb`

   C. `mount /dev/sdb0 /media/usb`

   D. `usbmount /dev/sdb1 /media/usb`

8. What is one reason a device driver does not appear in the output of `lsmod`, even though the device is loaded and working properly?

   A. The use of `systemd` means drivers are not required for most devices.

   B. The use of an `initrd.img` means support is enabled by default.

   C. The system does not need a driver for the device.

   D. Support for the device has been compiled directly into the kernel.

9. Which option to `rmmod` will cause the module to wait until it's no longer in use to unload the module?

   A. `-test`

   B. `-b`

   C. `-w`

   D. `-unload`

10. Which command will output a new GRUB configuration file and send the output to the correct location for booting?

   A. `update-grub`

   B. `update-grub boot > /boot/grub.cfg`

   C. `grub-rc.d`

   D. `grub-boot`

11. What is the maximum number of primary partitions available on an MBR partitioning system?

   A. Two

   B. Four

   C. One

   D. Five

12. When working with disk partitions through a tool like `fdisk`, you see the type 0x82. Which type of partition is this?

   A. Linux

   B. Linux swap

   C. NTFS

   D. FAT

13. Which file should you edit when using GRUB2 in order to define or set options like the timeout?

    A. `/etc/default/grub`

    B. `/etc/grub/boot`

    C. `/etc/boot/grub.d`

    D. `/grub.d/boot`

14. Which option for the `grub2-mkconfig` command sends output to a file instead of STDOUT?

    A. `-stdout`

    B. `--fileout`

    C. `-o`

    D. `-f`

15. Of the following choices, which size would be most appropriate for the `/boot` partition of a Linux system?

    A. At least 1 GB.

    B. Between 100 MB and 200 MB.

    C. `/boot` should not be partitioned separately.

    D. Less than 5 MB.

16. Which of the following commands initializes a physical disk partition for use with LVM?

    A. `lvmcreate`

    B. `pvcreate`

    C. `vgextend`

    D. `pvs`

17. Which of the following commands installs GRUB into the MBR of the second SATA disk?

    A. `grub2-install /dev/hdb2`

    B. `grub2-install /dev/sda2`

    C. `grub2-config /dev/sda`

    D. `grub2-install /dev/sdb`

18. Which command is used to create a logical volume with LVM?

    A. `pvcreate`

    B. `lvmcreate`

    C. `lvcreate`

    D. `volcreate`

19. What is the logical order for creation of an LVM logical volume?

    A. Physical volume creation, volume group creation, logical volume creation

    B. Physical volume creation, logical volume creation, volume group creation

    C. Logical volume creation, physical volume creation, volume group creation

    D. LVM creation, format, partition

20. Which command should be run after making a change to the `/etc/default/grub` file?

    A. `grub`

    B. `grub-mkconfig`

    C. `grub-inst`

    D. `reboot`

21. Which command is used to change details of a logical volume?

    A. `lvmcreate`

    B. `pvcreate`

    C. `lvchange`

    D. `lvmscan`

22. A hard drive is reported as `hd(0,0)` by the GRUB Legacy configuration file. To which of the following disks and partitions does this correspond?

    A. `/dev/hdb2`

    B. `/dev/hda0`

    C. `/dev/disk1`

    D. `/dev/sda1`

23. Which of the following commands installs GRUB into the master boot record (MBR) of the first SATA drive?

    A. `grub-install /dev/hda`

    B. `grub-install /dev/sda`

    C. `grub-install /dev/hd0,0`

    D. `grub -i /dev/hda`

24. Which option given to a `yum` command will install a given package?

    A. `update`

    B. `configure`

    C. `install`

    D. `get`

25. After a new hard drive is inserted into the system, what is the correct order to make the drive ready for use within Linux?

    A. Use `fdisk` to create partitions, and then mount the partitions.

    B. Mount the partitions.

    C. Use `fdisk` to create partitions and mount `-a` to mount all the newly created partitions.

    D. Use `fdisk` to create partitions, then format the partitions using a command such as `mkfs`, and then mount the partitions.

26. When working with an `rpm` package file and using `rpm2cpio`, by default the output is sent to which location?

  A. STDOUT

  B. The file `cpio.out`

  C. The file `a.out`

  D. The file `/tmp/cpi.out`

27. Which of the following describes a primary difference between `ext2` and `ext3` filesystems?

  A. `ext3` was primarily a bug-fix update to `ext2`.

  B. `ext3` includes journaling for the filesystem.

  C. `ext3` completely changed the tools needed for management of the disks.

  D. `ext3` has no significant differences.

28. According to the Filesystem Hierarchy Standard (FHS), what is the correct location for add-on application software packages?

  A. `/etc`

  B. `/var`

  C. `/tmp`

  D. `/opt`

29. Which option to the `mount` command will mount all filesystems that are currently available in `/etc/fstab`?

  A. -f

  B. -d

  C. -a

  D. -m

30. Which option of the `systemctl` command will change a service so that it runs on the next boot of the system?

  A. enable

  B. startonboot

  C. loadonboot

  D. start

31. Which option to `xfs_metadump` displays a progress indicator?

  A. -g

  B. -p

  C. -f

  D. -v

32. The system is running out of disk space within the home directory partition, and quotas have not been enabled. Which command can you use to determine the directories that might contain large files?

A. du

B. df

C. ls

D. locate

33. Which file contains information about the filesystems to mount, their partitions, and the options that should be used to mount them?

A. /etc/filesystems

B. /etc/mounts

C. /etc/fstab

D. systemd.mount

34. According to the FHS, what is the proper mount point for removable media?

A. /etc

B. /srv

C. /tmp

D. /media

35. How many SCSI devices are supported per bus?

A. 7 to 15

B. 2 to 4

C. 12

D. 4

36. Which option to umount will cause the command to attempt to remount the filesystem in read-only mode if the unmounting process fails?

A. -o

B. -r

C. -f

D. -v

37. Which of the following represents the correct format for the /etc/fstab file?

A. <directory> <device> <type> <options>

B. <device> <type> <options>

C. <device> <type> <options> <directory> <dump> <fsck>

D. <device> <directory> <type> <options> <dump> <fsck>

38. Which of the following commands is used to identify the UUID for partitions?

    A. `blkid`

    B. `partprobe`

    C. `find`

    D. `cat`

39. The `xfs_info` command is functionally equivalent to which command and option?

    A. `xfs_test -n`

    B. `xfs_list`

    C. `tunexfs -i`

    D. `xfs_growfs -n`

40. Which of the following commands will create a `btrfs` filesystem on the first SATA drive?

    A. `mkfs /dev/sda1`

    B. `mkfs.btrfs /dev/sda`

    C. `mkfs.btr2fs /dev/sda1`

    D. `mkfs -b /dev/sda`

41. Which command and option can be used to determine whether a given service is currently loaded?

    A. `systemctl --ls`

    B. `telinit`

    C. `systemctl status`

    D. `sysctl -a`

42. Which command can be used to change the partitioning scheme for a disk, such as to change the size of existing partitions without deleting them?

    A. `resize2fs`

    B. `parted`

    C. `mkfs`

    D. `rfdisk`

43. Which of the following commands will mount a USB device at `/dev/sdb1` into the `/mnt/usb` directory, assuming a VFAT filesystem for the USB drive?

    A. `mount -t vfat /dev/sdb1 /mnt`

    B. `usbmount /dev/sdb1 /mnt/usb`

    C. `mount -t vfat /dev/sdb1 /mnt/usb`

    D. `mount -t usb /dev/sdb1 /mnt/usb`

44. Which option within `gdisk` will change the partition name?

   A. n

   B. b

   C. v

   D. c

45. Which command on a `systemd`-controlled system would place the system into single-user mode?

   A. `systemctl stop`

   B. `systemctl isolate rescue.target`

   C. `systemctl single-user`

   D. `systemctl runlevel one`

46. Which options to `fsck` can be used to check all filesystems listed in `/etc/fstab` while excluding the root partition?

   A. -NR

   B. -AR

   C. -X

   D. -C

47. Which option in `/etc/fstab` sets the order in which the device is checked at boot time?

   A. options

   B. dump

   C. fsck

   D. checkorder

48. Which file is used to indicate the local time zone on a Linux server?

   A. /etc/timez

   B. /etc/timezoneconfig

   C. /etc/timezone

   D. /etc/localtz

49. Within which directory will you find files related to the time zone for various regions?

   A. /etc/timezoneinfo

   B. /etc/zoneinfo

   C. /var/zoneinfo

   D. /usr/share/zoneinfo

50. Which option best describes the following, gathered with the `ls -la` command?

    ```
    lrwxrwxrwx. 1 root root 35 Jul 8 2014
    .fetchmailrc -> .configs/fetchmail/.fetchmailrc
    ```

    A. It is a file called `.fetchmailrc` that is linked using a symbolic link.
    B. It is a file called `.configs/fetchmail/.fetchmailrc` that is owned by `lrwxrwxrwx`.
    C. It is a directory called `.fetchmailrc` that is owned by user Jul.
    D. It is a local directory called `.configs/fetchmail/.fetchmailrc`.

51. Which environment variable controls the format of dates and times, such as a 12-hour or 24-hour formatted clock?
    A. `LOCALE_DATE`
    B. `DATE_FORMAT`
    C. `LC_TIME`
    D. `LC_DATE`

52. Which of the following encodings provides a multibyte representation of characters?
    A. ISO-8859
    B. UTF-8
    C. ISO-L
    D. UFTMulti

53. Which command can be used to view the available time zones on a system?
    A. `tzd`
    B. `/etc/locale`
    C. `timedatectl`
    D. `tzsel`

54. Which option to `lspci` is used to display both numeric codes and device names?
    A. `-numdev`
    B. `-n`
    C. `-nn`
    D. `-devnum`

55. Which of the following values for the `LANG` variable will configure the system to bypass locale translations where possible?
    A. `LANG=COMPAT`
    B. `LANG=NONE`
    C. `LANG=C`
    D. `LANG=END`

56. If you need to temporarily reconfigure all locale variables and settings for a given session, which environment variable can be used?

A. LC_LIST

B. LC_GLOBAL

C. LC_ALL

D. ALL_LOCALE

57. Which of the following commands will set the systemwide time zone to 'America/Los_Angeles'?

A. ln -sf /usr/share/zoneinfo/America/Los_Angeles /etc/localtime

B. ln -sf America/Los_Angeles ; /etc/localtime

C. ln -sd /etc/localtime /usr/share/timezone/America/Los_Angeles

D. ln -sf /etc/localtime /usr/share/zoneinfo/America/Los_Angeles

58. Which locale-related variable is used for currency-related localization?

A. LC_MONE

B. LC_CURRENCY

C. LC_MONETARY

D. LC_CURR

59. Which command is used to query and work with the hardware clock on the system?

A. hwc

B. ntpdate

C. systime

D. hwclock

60. Which option to the date command can be used to set the date and time?

A. date -f

B. date -t

C. date --change

D. date -s

61. Which function of the hwclock command will set the hardware or BIOS clock to the current system time?

A. -w

B. -s

C. -a

D. -m

62. Which of the following commands sets the hardware or BIOS clock to UTC based on the current system time?

A. hwclock --systohc --utc

B. hwclock --systohc --localtime

C. hwclock --systohc

D. hwclock --systoutc

63. Which of the following commands shows the current default route without performing DNS lookups on the IP address(es) involved?

A. netstat -rn

B. netstat -n

C. netstat -r

D. netstat -f

64. A Serial ATA (SATA) disk will use which of the following identifiers?

A. /dev/hdX

B. /dev/sataX

C. /dev/sdX

D. /disk/sataX

65. Which of the following commands adds a default gateway of 192.168.1.1 for interface eth0?

A. route add default gateway 192.168.1.1 eth0

B. eth0 --dg 192.168.1.1

C. route add default gw 192.168.1.1 eth0

D. route define eth0 192.168.1.1

66. Which option for the host command will query for the authoritative name servers for a given domain?

A. -t ns

B. -t all

C. -ns

D. -named

67. Which option for the ping command enables you to choose the interface from which the ICMP packets will be generated?

A. -i

B. -I

C. -t

D. -a

68. Which of the following commands queries for the mail servers for the domain `example.com`?

  A. `dig example.com mx`

  B. `dig example.com`

  C. `host -t smtp example.com`

  D. `dig example.com smtp`

69. Which of the following addresses represents the localhost in IPv6, such as you might find in `/etc/hosts`?

  A. `0:1`

  B. `::1`

  C. `127:0:1`

  D. `:127:0:0:1`

70. Which command can be used to listen for netlink messages on a network?

  A. `ip monitor`

  B. `netlink -a`

  C. `ip netlink`

  D. `route`

71. Which of the following configuration lines in `/etc/nsswitch.conf` causes a lookup for group information to first use local files and then use LDAP?

  A. `group: files ldap`

  B. `lookup: group [local ldap]`

  C. `group: [local ldap]`

  D. `group: localfiles ldap`

72. Which of the following `dig` commands sends the query for `example.com` directly to the server at 192.168.2.5 rather than to a locally configured resolver?

  A. `dig example.com @192.168.2.5`

  B. `dig -t 192.168.2.5 example.com`

  C. `dig -s 192.168.2.5 example.com`

  D. `dig server=192.168.2.5 example.com`

73. Which of the following commands will enumerate the `hosts` database?

  A. `getent hosts`

  B. `gethosts`

  C. `nslookup`

  D. `host`

74. Which of the following configuration lines will set the DNS server to 192.168.1.4 using /etc/resolv.conf?

   A. dns 192.168.1.4

   B. dns-server 192.168.1.4

   C. nameserver 192.168.1.4

   D. name-server 192.168.1.4

75. Which of the following commands adds a route to the server for the network 192.168.51.0/24 through its gateway 192.168.22.1?

   A. route add -net 192.168.51.0 netmask 255.255.255.0 gw 192.168.22.1

   B. route add -net 192.168.51/24 gw 192.168.22.51

   C. route -net 192.168.51.0/24 192.168.22.1

   D. route add 192.168.51.1 -n 192.168.22.0//255.255.255.0

76. Which of the following commands shows network services or sockets that are currently listening along with sockets that are not listening?

   A. netstat -a

   B. netlink -a

   C. sockets -f

   D. opensock -l

77. When partitioning a disk for a mail server running Postfix, which partition/mounted directory should be the largest in order to allow for mail storage?

   A. /etc

   B. /usr/bin

   C. /mail

   D. /var

78. Which of the following commands will change the default gateway to 192.168.1.1 using eth0?

   A. ip route default gw 192.168.1.1

   B. ip route change default via 192.168.1.1 dev eth0

   C. ip route default gw update 192.168.1.1

   D. ip route update default 192.168.1.1 eth0

79. Which of the following commands displays the Start of Authority information for the domain example.com?

   A. dig example.com soa

   B. dig example.com authority

   C. dig example.com -auth

   D. dig -t auth example.com

80. Assume that you want to enable local client services to go to hosts on the network without needing to fully qualify the name by adding the domain for either `example.com` or `example.org`. Which option in `/etc/resolv.conf` will provide this functionality?

    A. `search`

    B. `domain`

    C. `local-domain`

    D. `local-order`

81. Which of the following commands prevents traffic from reaching the host 192.168.1.3?

    A. `route add -host 192.168.1.3 reject`

    B. `route -nullroute 192.168.1.3`

    C. `route add -null 192.168.1.3`

    D. `route add -block 192.168.1.3`

82. Which of the following commands will emulate the `ping` command in Microsoft Windows, where the ping is sent for four packets and then the command exits?

    A. `ping -n 4`

    B. `ping -t 4`

    C. `ping -p 4`

    D. `ping -c 4`

83. You need to prevent local clients from going to a certain host, `www.example.com`, and instead redirect them to localhost. Which of the following is a method to override DNS lookups for the specified host?

    A. Add a firewall entry for the IP address of `www.example.com` to prevent traffic from passing through it.

    B. Delete `www.example.com` from the route table using the `route` command.

    C. Add a null route to prevent access to the IP address for `www.example.com`.

    D. Add an entry for `www.example.com` in `/etc/hosts` to point to 127.0.0.1.

84. Which of the following commands should be executed after running `ip route change`?

    A. `ip route flush cache`

    B. `ip route reload`

    C. `ip route cache reload`

    D. `ip route restart`

85. Which option should be used to send a DNS query for an SPF record with `dig`?

    A. `-t txt`

    B. `-t spf`

    C. `-t mx`

    D. `-t mailspf`

86. When you're viewing the available routes using the `route` command, one route contains flags UG while the others contain U. What does the letter G signify in the route table?

   A. The G signifies that the route is good.

   B. The G signifies that the route is unavailable.

   C. The G signifies that this is a gateway.

   D. The G signifies that the route is an aggregate.

87. Which of the following commands requests a zone transfer of `example.org` from the server at 192.168.1.4?

   A. `dig example.org @192.168.1.4 axfr`

   B. `dig example.org @192.168.1.4`

   C. `dig example.org @192.168.1.4 xfer`

   D. `dig example.org #192.168.1.4 xfer`

88. Which yum option displays the dependencies for the package specified?

   A. `list`

   B. `deplist`

   C. `dependencies`

   D. `listdeps`

89. Which of the following commands can be used to display the current disk utilization?

   A. `df`

   B. `du`

   C. `diskutil`

   D. `diskuse`

90. You are working with a legacy CentOS 5 system and need to re-create the initial RAM disk. Which of the following commands is used for this purpose?

   A. `mkinitrd`

   B. `mkramdisk`

   C. `mkdisk --init`

   D. `mkfs.init`

91. Which of the following commands is used to display the currently loaded modules on a running system?

   A. `ls -mod`

   B. `lsmod`

   C. `tree`

   D. `mod --list`

92. Which of the following commands creates a list of modules and their dependencies?
   A. lsmod
   B. depmod
   C. modlist
   D. listmod

93. Which option to sysctl displays all values and their current settings?
   A. -a
   B. -b
   C. -d
   D. -c

94. Which of the following commands installs a kernel module, including dependencies?
   A. lsmod
   B. modprobe
   C. modinst
   D. instmod

95. Which command is used to determine the modules on which another module depends?
   A. modinfo
   B. modlist
   C. modprobe
   D. tracemod

96. Which of the following commands inserts a module into the running kernel but does not resolve dependencies?
   A. lsmod
   B. modinstall
   C. insmod
   D. moduleinst

97. Which option to modprobe will remove a module and attempt to remove any unused modules on which it depends?
   A. -v
   B. -r
   C. -d
   D. -f

98. Within which of the following directories will you find blacklist information for modules loaded with modprobe?

    A. /etc/blacklist

    B. /etc/modprobe.d

    C. /etc/blacklist.mod

    D. /etc/modprobe

99. When working with a CentOS 6 system, which command is used to create the initial RAM disk?

    A. mkinit

    B. dracut

    C. mkraminit

    D. mkinitfs

100. If you'd like a value set with the sysctl command to take effect on boot, within which file should you place the variable and its value?

    A. /etc/sysctl.cfg

    B. /etc/sysctl.conf

    C. /lib/sysctl

    D. /var/sysctl.conf

101. Which of the following options to modprobe will show the dependencies for a module?

    A. --show-deps

    B. --show-depends

    C. --deps

    D. --list-depends

102. Which options for the rpm command will display verbose output for an installation along with progress of the installation?

    A. -ivh

    B. -wvh

    C. --avh

    D. --ins-verbose

103. When working with UEFI, which of the following commands changes the boot order for the next boot?

    A. efibootmgr -c

    B. efibootmgr -b -B

    C. efibootmgr -o

    D. efibootmgr -n

104. Which bootloader can be used to boot from ISO with ISO9660 CD-ROMs?

   A.   ISOLINUX

   B.   EFIBOOT

   C.   ISOFS

   D.   BOOTISO

105. When using UEFI, which of the following files can be used as a bootloader?

   A.   `shim.uefi`

   B.   `shim.efi`

   C.   `shim.fx`

   D.   `efi.shim`

106. Which of the following commands, executed from within the UEFI shell, controls the boot configuration?

   A.   `bootcfg`

   B.   `bcfg`

   C.   `grub-install`

   D.   `grcfg`

107. Which of the following can be identified as an initial sector on a disk that stores information about the disk partitioning and operating system location?

   A.   Minimal boot record (MBR)

   B.   Master boot record (MBR)

   C.   Init sector

   D.   Master partition table (MPT)

108. When using PXE boot, which file must exist within `/tftpboot` on the TFTP server for the system that will use PXELINUX for its bootloader?

   A.   `pxelinux.tftp`

   B.   `pxelinux.boot`

   C.   `pxelinux.conf`

   D.   `pxelinux.0`

109. Which option to `grub-install` will place the GRUB images into an alternate directory?

   A.   `--boot-dir`

   B.   `-b`

   C.   `-boot`

   D.   `--boot-directory`

110. When using a shim for booting a UEFI-based system, which of the following files is loaded after `shim.efi`?

    A. `grubx64.cfg`

    B. `grub.conf`

    C. `grubx64.efi`

    D. `efi.boot`

111. Part of the EXT tools, which option to the `mke2fs` command sets the type of filesystem to be created?

    A. `-f`

    B. `-a`

    C. `-t`

    D. `-e`

112. Which file is used to store a list of encrypted devices that are to be mounted at boot?

    A. `/etc/cryptdev`

    B. `/etc/crypttab`

    C. `/etc/encrtab`

    D. `/etc/fsencrypt`

113. Which command will search for a package named `zsh` on a Debian system?

    A. `apt-cache search zsh`

    B. `apt-get search zsh`

    C. `apt-cache locate zsh`

    D. `apt-search zsh`

114. Within which directory will you find the repositories used by `yum`?

    A. `/etc/yum.conf`

    B. `/etc/repos`

    C. `/etc/yum.conf.d`

    D. `/etc/yum.repos.d`

115. You are performing an `xfsrestore`. The `xfsdump` was executed with a block size of 4M. Which option do you need to invoke on `xfsrestore` in order for it to successfully use this dump?

    A. `-b 4M`

    B. `-g 1M`

    C. `-i 1M`

    D. `-k 1028K`

116. You see the word `defaults` within `/etc/fstab`. Which options are encompassed within the defaults?

A. `ro, exec, auto`

B. `rw, suid, dev, exec, auto, nouser, async`

C. `rw, exec, auto, nouser, async`

D. `rw, exec, nouser, async, noauto, suid`

117. Which of the following options to `xfsdump` sets the maximum size for files to be included in the dump?

A. `-p`

B. `-s`

C. `-z`

D. `-b`

118. Which partition type is used to indicate a software RAID array, such as an array built with `mdadm`?

A. 0xmd

B. -x-

C. 0xRD

D. 0xFD

119. When working with World Wide Identifiers (WWIDs), within which directory on a Red Hat server will you find symlinks to the current `/dev/sd` device names?

A. `/dev/disk/wwid`

B. `/dev/wwid`

C. `/dev/disk/by-id`

D. `/dev/sd.wwid`

120. Which of the following commands displays information about a given physical volume in an LVM setup?

A. `pvdisp`

B. `pvlist`

C. `pvdisplay`

D. `pvl`

121. When viewing information in `/dev/disk/by-path` using the command `ls -l`, which of the following filenames represents a LUN from Fibre Channel?

A. `/dev/fc0`

B. `pci-0000:1a:00.0-fc-0x500601653ee0025f:0x0000000000000000`

C. `pci-0000:1a:00.0-scsi-0x500601653ee0025f:0x0000000000000000`

D. `/dev/fibre0`

122. Which of the following commands displays path information for LUNs?

   A. `luninfo -a`

   B. `ls -lun`

   C. `multipath -l`

   D. `dm-multi`

123. Which command is used to remove unused filesystem blocks from thinly provisioned storage?

   A. `thintrim`

   B. `thtrim`

   C. `fstrim`

   D. `fsclean`

124. When using `tune2fs` to set an extended option such as `stripe_width`, which command-line option is needed to signify that an extended option follows?

   A. `-extend`

   B. `-E`

   C. `-e`

   D. `-f`

125. Which option to `mdadm` is used to create a new array?

   A. `--create`

   B. `--start`

   C. `--begin`

   D. `--construct`

126. Information about logical volumes can be found in which of the following directories?

   A. `/dev/lvinfo`

   B. `/dev/map`

   C. `/dev/mapper`

   D. `/dev/lvmap`

127. Which option to `mdadm` watches a RAID array for anomalies?

   A. `--mon`

   B. `--watch`

   C. `--monitor`

   D. `--examine`

128. When running `mdadm` in monitor mode, which option within `/etc/mdadm.conf` sets the destination for email if an issue is discovered?

   A. `MAILTO`

   B. `MAILADDR`

   C. `MAILFROM`

   D. `MAILDEST`

129. When using the `ip` command, which protocol family is used as the default if not otherwise specified?

    A. `tcpip`

    B. `ip`

    C. `inet`

    D. `arp`

130. Which command is used for setting parameters such as the essid, channel, and other related options for a wireless device?

    A. `ifconfig`

    B. `iwconfig`

    C. `wlancfg`

    D. `ifcfg`

131. Which of the following commands shows network sockets and their allocated memory?

    A. `ss -m`

    B. `mpas`

    C. `mem`

    D. `free`

132. Which option to the `ss` command shows the process IDs associated with the socket?

    A. `-l`

    B. `-a`

    C. `-p`

    D. `-f`

133. On a Debian system, within which directory hierarchy will you find configuration information and directories to hold scripts to be run when an interface is brought up or taken down?

    A. `/etc/netconf`

    B. `/etc/netconfig`

    C. `/etc/net.conf.d`

    D. `/etc/network`

134. Which of the following characters are valid for hostnames in `/etc/hosts`?

    A. Alphanumerics, minus, underscore, and dot

    B. Alphanumerics, minus, and dot

    C. Alphanumerics and dot

    D. Alphanumerics

135. Which of the following configuration lines in `/etc/resolv.conf` enables debugging?

    A. `debug`

    B. `options debug`

    C. `option debug`

    D. `enable-debug`

136. The system contains an NFS mounted filesystem that has become unreachable. Which option should be passed to `umount` in order to force the unmounting of the filesystem?

    A. `-nfs`

    B. `--fake`

    C. `-f`

    D. `-n`

137. Which of the following commands will send the output of the `grub2-mkconfig` command to the correct location for booting?

    A. `grub2-mkconfig --output=/boot/grub2/grub.cfg`

    B. `grub2-mkconfig --file=/boot/grub2.menu`

    C. `grub2-mkconfig --file=/boot/grub.lst`

    D. `grub2-mkconfig --output=/boot/menu.lst`

138. Which PXE Linux binary file is required for booting from HTTP or FTP?

    A. `lpxelinux.0`

    B. `pxelinux.http`

    C. `netpxlinux.0`

    D. `netpxe.0`

139. The file `/etc/grub2.cfg` is typically a symbolic link to which file?

    A. `/boot/grub.conf`

    B. `/boot/grub2/grub.cfg`

    C. `/boot/grub2.conf`

    D. `/etc/sysconfig/grub2.cfg`

140. Which of the following describes a difference between `vmlinuz` and `vmlinux`?

    A. `vmlinuz` is used for zOS systems, and `vmlinux` is used for x86 architecture.

    B. `vmlinuz` is used for 64-bit systems, and `vmlinux` is used for 32-bit systems.

    C. `vmlinuz` is compressed, whereas `vmlinux` is not.

    D. `vmlinuz` contains additional binary code for certain systems.

141. Which of the following is the location in which kernel modules are stored?

    A. `/usr/modules`

    B. `/modules`

    C. `/usr/lib/modules/{kernel-version}`

    D. `/usr/modules/{kernel-version}`

142. Which `rpm` option can be used to verify that no files have been altered since installation?

    A. `-V`

    B. `-v`

    C. `--verbose`

    D. `--filesum`

143. Which of the following is not typically used to store shared libraries?

    A. `/lib`

    B. `/etc/lib`

    C. `/usr/lib`

    D. `/usr/local/lib`

144. Which of the following commands updates the package cache for a Debian system?

    A. `apt-get cache-update`

    B. `apt-cache update`

    C. `apt-get update`

    D. `apt-get upgrade`

145. You need to update the configuration files for package repositories. Within which directory are details of the current package repositories stored on a Debian system?

    A. `/etc/apt.list`

    B. `/etc/sources.list`

    C. `/etc/apt/sources.list.d/`

    D. `/etc/apt.d/sources.list`

146. Which of the following commands is used to change the keyboard layout settings?

    A. `keybrdctl`

    B. `keyctl`

    C. `localectl`

    D. `localemap`

147. Which of the following directories contains configuration files related to networking?

    A. `/etc/netdevices/`

    B. `/etc/netcfg/`

    C. `/etc/config/network/`

    D. `/etc/sysconfig/network-scripts/`

148. You need to change the label that has been applied to a filesystem. The filesystem is formatted as EXT4. Which EXT tool can be used to change the label?

    A. `e2label`

    B. `e4label`

    C. `fslabel.ext4`

    D. `fslabel`

149. Which command should be used to make changes to the choices made when a Debian package was installed?

- **A.** dpkg-reconfigure
- **B.** dpkg -r
- **C.** dpkg --reconf
- **D.** apt-get reinstall

150. Which option for yum performs a search of the package cache?

- **A.** seek
- **B.** query
- **C.** --search
- **D.** search

151. Assume you need to add a kernel module with a custom command, such as to specify options at load time. Within which file could you add this configuration?

- **A.** /etc/modprobe-cfg
- **B.** /etc/modprobe.conf
- **C.** /etc/modprobe.cf
- **D.** /etc/modprobe.cfg

152. Which command option for rpm can be used to show the version of the kernel?

- **A.** rpm kernel
- **B.** rpm -q kernel
- **C.** rpm search kernel
- **D.** rpm --list kern

153. Which command is used to install a kernel into the /boot directory, using the files from /usr/lib/kernel?

- **A.** kernel-ins
- **B.** ins-kernel
- **C.** install-kernel
- **D.** kernel-install

154. Which option in /etc/yum.conf is used to ensure that the kernel is not updated when the system is updated?

- **A.** exclude=kernel*
- **B.** exclude-kernel
- **C.** updatekernel=false
- **D.** include-except=kernel

155. When using `fdisk` to partition a disk, you have two partitions created for the system but still have leftover space, also called unallocated space, on the drive. What is another name used to refer to unallocated space?

    A. Highly available

    B. Redundant

    C. Raw device

    D. Partition forward

156. Which command searches for and provides information on a given package on a Debian system, including whether the package is currently installed?

    A. `dpkg -i`

    B. `dpkg -s`

    C. `apt-cache`

    D. `apt-info`

157. Which of the following installs a previously downloaded Debian package?

    A. `dpkg -i <package name>`

    B. `apt-install <package name>`

    C. `apt-slash <package name>`

    D. `dpkg -U <package name>`

158. You need to obtain information about a package installed on an OpenSUSE system that uses the `zypper` command. Which of the following options to the `zypper` command displays information about the package?

    A. `inf`

    B. `getInfo`

    C. `info`

    D. `i`

159. Which type of storage would be the most appropriate format to store a large object as a single file in a cloud environment?

    A. File

    B. ext2

    C. cifs

    D. Blob

160. You need to find available packages on a Fedora system managed by the `dnf` package system. Which option to the `dnf` command looks for a given package?

    A. `search`

    B. `info`

    C. `find`

    D. `locate`

161. Which of the following real filesystems can be resized using `resize2fs`?

    A. `nfs`

    B. `xfs`

    C. `ext3`

    D. `cifs`

162. Which subcommand to the `virsh` command is used to connect to the hypervisor?

    A. `plug`

    B. `hypervisorconnect`

    C. `conhyper`

    D. `connect`

163. You need to determine if ASCII and Unicode are supported on the system. Which option to the `iconv` command shows the available character sets on a given system?

    A. `--showchar`

    B. `--show`

    C. `--list`

    D. `--all`

164. Which of the following best describes the `/dev/` filesystem?

    A. The `/dev/` filesystem is used for storing device information for connected devices.

    B. The `/dev/` filesystem is used for configuration files.

    C. The `/dev/` filesystem is used for development.

    D. The `/dev/` filesystem is used to list devices for compilation into the kernel.

165. Which of the following files shows the currently mounted filesystems?

    A. `/etc/fstab`

    B. `/proc/mounts`

    C. `/fs`

    D. `/root/mounts`

166. When working with a Microsoft Windows–based filesystem, you see that it is mounted as a CIFS mount. What does CIFS stand for?

    A. Common Information File Sharing

    B. Common Internet File System

    C. Cloned Internet File Sharing

    D. Created In Five Seconds

167. When using `sed` for a substitution operation, which option must be included so that the substitution applies to the entire line rather than just the first instance?

A. g

B. a

C. r

D. y

168. Which option to the `blkid` command purges the cache to remove devices that do not exist?

A. -p

B. -a

C. -g

D. -m

169. While you can use `blkid` to obtain the UUIDs for filesystems in order to facilitate storage space monitoring and disk usage, which location on the filesystem also shows this information?

A. /dev/diskbyuuid

B. /dev/uuid

C. /dev/fs/uuid

D. /dev/disk/by-uuid

170. In a scripting scenario, you need to enable legacy locations for things like networking. Which file can be used for storing network configuration?

A. /etc/netdev

B. /etc/networking

C. /etc/sysconfig/network

D. /etc/sysconfig/netdev

171. You are attempting to use `rmdir` to remove a directory, but there are still multiple files and other directories contained within it. Assuming that you're sure you want to remove the directory and all of its contents, what are the command and arguments to do so?

A. rm -f

B. rm -rf

C. rmdir -a

D. rmdir -m

172. Which of the following commands will provide the usernames in a sorted list gathered from the /etc/passwd file?

A. cat /etc/passwd | awk -F : '{print $1}' | sort

B. sort /etc/passwd | cut

C. echo /etc/passwd

D. cat /etc/passwd | awk '{print $1}' | sort

173. What will be the result if the touch command is executed on a file that already exists?

    A. The access timestamp of the file will change to the current time when the touch command was executed.

    B. The file will be overwritten.

    C. There will be no change.

    D. The file will be appended to.

174. Which option to both mv and cp will cause the command to prompt before overwriting files that already exist?

    A. -f

    B. -Z

    C. -r

    D. -i

175. Which file contains the current list of partitions along with their major and minor numbers and the number of blocks?

    A. /dev/disk

    B. /dev/partitions

    C. /proc/disk

    D. /proc/partitions

176. Assuming a block storage device used for virtualization of sda, which file can be used to view the number of read I/O requests for the device?

    A. /proc/sys/sda

    B. /proc/sys/sda/stat

    C. /sys/block/sda/stat

    D. /sys/disk/sda/stat

177. The current hierarchy on the server contains a directory called /usr/local. You need to create an additional directory below that called /usr/local/test/october. Which command will accomplish this task?

    A. mkdir -p /usr/local/test/october

    B. mkdir /usr/local/test/october

    C. mkdir -r /usr/local/test/october

    D. mkdir -f /usr/local/test/october

178. What command is used to bring a command to foreground processing after it has been backgrounded with an &?

    A. bg

    B. fore

    C. 4g

    D. fg

179. You are using the Vi editor to change a file, and you need to exit. You receive a notice indicating "No write since last change." Assuming you want to save your work, which of the following commands will save your work and exit Vi?

  A. :wq

  B. :q!

  C. dd

  D. x

180. When using a multipath device managed by multipathd and found in /dev/disk/by-multipath, what is the name given to the identifier for that device that is globally unique?

  A. UUID

  B. WWID

  C. GUID

  D. DISKID

181. You have attempted to stop a process using its service command and also using the kill command. Which signal can be sent to the process using the kill command in order to force the process to end?

  A. -15

  B. -f

  C. -9

  D. -stop

182. When editing with Vi, which command changes into insert mode and opens a new line below the current cursor location?

  A. f

  B. a

  C. o

  D. i

183. While recovering from a kernel panic and using the console, you are having difficulty working with the console due to continual messages being displayed on the console itself. Which option to dmesg can be used to disable logging to the console?

  A. -o "no logging console"

  B. -D

  C. -Q

  D. -F

184. Which option to rmmod forces the module to be unloaded?

  A. -f

  B. -a

  C. -w

  D. -h

185. Which command-line option modifies the behavior of depmod such that only newer modules are added when comparing modules.dep?

   A. -A

   B. -B

   C. -C

   D. -D

186. Which command prints device and partition information in a tree-like structure, including partition size and current mount status?

   A. fsck

   B. lsblk

   C. blkshow

   D. shblk

187. You need to create a script for use with the parted command. When using the parted command to obtain a list of partitions, which additional option formats the output such that it can be more easily parsed by a script?

   A. -p

   B. -s

   C. -m

   D. -v

188. Which command is used to create an Ethernet bridge?

   A. bridgecon

   B. brctl

   C. bridgeman

   D. BridgeManager

189. Which kill signal can be sent in order to restart a process?

   A. -HUP

   B. -RESTART

   C. -9

   D. -SIG

190. Which command will move all files with a .txt extension to the /tmp directory?

   A. mv txt* tmp

   B. move *txt /temp

   C. mv *.txt /tmp

   D. mv *.txt tmp

191. When using `nslookup` interactively, which of the following commands changes the destination to which queries will be sent?

   A. dest

   B. server

   C. queryhost

   D. destination

192. Another administrator made a change to one of the local scripts stored in `/usr/local/bin` and used for administrative purposes. The change was also immediately reflected in the copy of the script in your home directory. However, when you examine the file with `ls`, it appears to be a normal file. What is the likely cause of such a scenario?

   A. The file was executed after edit.

   B. The administrator copied the file to yours.

   C. Your file is a hard link to the original.

   D. The file has been restored from backup.

193. Which option to `ln` creates a symlink to another file?

   A. -sl

   B. -s

   C. -l

   D. --ln

194. When using `ls -la` to obtain a directory listing, you see an object with permissions of `lrwxrwxrwx`. What type of object is this?

   A. It is a directory.

   B. It is a symlink.

   C. It is a temporary file.

   D. It is a local file.

195. On a system using SysVinit as part of the basic boot process, in which directory are startup and shutdown scripts for services stored?

   A. /etc/init-d

   B. /etc/init

   C. /etc/sysV

   D. /etc/init.d

196. Which option to the `cp` command will copy directories in a recursive manner?

   A. -v

   B. -R

   C. -Z

   D. -i

197. Which option to `df` displays the output in human-readable format?

    A. -h

    B. -m

    C. -j

    D. -s

198. Which command creates a TCP connection to the server `www.example.com` on port 80?

    A. nc www.example.com 80

    B. nc www.example.com

    C. nc www.example.com:80

    D. nc:80 www.example.com

199. Which option to the `file` command specifies that `file` should examine compressed files?

    A. -a

    B. -z

    C. -w

    D. -b

200. Which option to Vim enables editing of binary or executable files?

    A. -a

    B. -b

    C. -c

    D. -d

201. When using the `rmdir` command, which option also removes child directories?

    A. -c

    B. -p

    C. -m

    D. -a

202. Emptying or clearing a block device is sometimes accomplished by writing zeroes to the device. Which file is used for this purpose?

    A. /dev/format

    B. /dev/go

    C. /dev/zero

    D. /tmp

203. Which option to `zip` updates files within the archive but does not add files?

    A. -a

    B. -f

    C. -d

    D. -e

204. Which of the following will execute a job through `cron` at 12:15 a.m. and 12:15 p.m. every day?

    A. `0,12 15 * * *`

    B. `15 0,12 * * *`

    C. `15 * * * 0/12`

    D. `*/12 * * * 15`

205. Which file is used to provide a list of users that can add and delete `cron` jobs?

    A. `/etc/cron.job`

    B. `/etc/cron.allow`

    C. `/etc/cron.users`

    D. `/etc/crontab`

206. Which of the following commands schedules a series of commands to execute one hour from now?

    A. `atq +1hr`

    B. `at now + 1 hour`

    C. `atq`

    D. `at -1`

207. Which of the following best describes the `/proc` filesystem?

    A. `/proc` contains information about files to be processed.

    B. `/proc` contains configuration files for processes.

    C. `/proc` contains information on currently running processes, including the kernel.

    D. `/proc` contains variable data such as mail and web files.

208. Which option to `fdisk` provides a list of partitions on a given device?

    A. `-s`

    B. `-l`

    C. `-e`

    D. `-d`

209. Within which directory would you find a list of files corresponding to the users who have current `cron` jobs on the system?

    A. `/var/spool/cron/crontabs`

    B. `/var/spool/jobs`

    C. `/etc/cron`

    D. `/etc/cron.users`

210. Which command deletes an `at` job with an ID of 3?

    A. `atq`

    B. `at -l`

    C. `atrm 3`

    D. `rmat 3`

211. Which of the following is used as a system-wide `cron` file?

    A. `/etc/cron.d`

    B. `/etc/cron.sys`

    C. `/etc/crontab`

    D. `/etc/cron.tab`

212. Within which directory will you find scripts that are scheduled to run through `cron` every 24 hours?

    A. `/etc/cron.daily`

    B. `/etc/cron.weekly`

    C. `/etc/cron.hourly24`

    D. `/etc/crontab`

213. The system that you're working with recently had a hard drive failure, resulting in degraded storage. A new hard drive has been installed and Linux has been restored from backup to the drive. However, the system will not boot and instead shows a `grub >` prompt. Within the `grub >` prompt, which command will show the current partitions as seen by GRUB?

    A. `ls`

    B. `showPart`

    C. `partitionlist`

    D. `ps`

214. A legacy PATA disk is used to boot the system. You recently added an internal DVD drive to the computer, and now the system will no longer boot. What is the most likely cause?

    A. The BIOS has identified the DVD drive as the first disk, and therefore the system can no longer find the Linux partition(s).

    B. The hard drive became corrupt when the DVD drive was installed.

    C. The hot swap option has not been enabled in the BIOS.

    D. The DVD drive is not detected by the computer and needs to be enabled first in the BIOS and then in Linux prior to installation.

215. Which of the following will run a command called `/usr/local/bin/changehome.sh` as the `www-data` user when placed in `/etc/crontab`?

    A. `1 1 * * * www-data /usr/local/bin/changehome.sh`

    B. `www-data changehome.sh`

    C. `*/1 www-data changehome.sh`

    D. `* * */www-data /usr/local/bin/changehome.sh`

216. Which command and option are used to update a Debian system to the latest software?

    A. `apt-update`

    B. `apt-get upgrade`

    C. `dpkg -U`

    D. `apt-cache clean`

217. You need to write a script that gathers all the process IDs for all instances of Apache running on the system. Which of the following commands will accomplish this task?

   A. ps auwx | grep apache

   B. pgrep apache

   C. processlist apache

   D. ls -p apache

218. Which command can be run to determine the default priority for processes spawned by the current user?

   A. prio

   B. nice

   C. renice

   D. defpriority

219. Which of the following commands shows the usage of inodes across all filesystems?

   A. df -i

   B. ls -i

   C. du -i

   D. dm -i

220. Which command will list the cron entries for a given user as denoted by <username>?

   A. crontab -l -u <username>

   B. crontab -u <username>

   C. cron -u <username>

   D. cronent -u <username>

221. You are having difficulty with an interface on the server, and it is currently down. Assuming that there is not a hardware failure on the device itself, which command and option can you use to display information about the interface?

   A. ifconfig -a

   B. ifup

   C. netstat -n

   D. ifconfig

222. Which option to the traceroute command will use TCP SYN packets for the path trace?

   A. -T

   B. -t

   C. -s

   D. -i

223. When troubleshooting an issue where SSH connections are timing out, you think the firewall is blocking SSH connections. Which of the following ports is used for Secure Shell communication?

    A. TCP/23

    B. TCP/25

    C. TCP/22

    D. TCP/2200

224. Which options for `netcat` will create a server listening on port 8080?

    A. `netcat -p 8080`

    B. `nc -l -p 8080`

    C. `nc -p 8080`

    D. `nc -s 8080`

225. Which of the following commands displays the Start of Authority information for the domain `example.com`?

    A. `dig example.com soa`

    B. `dig example.com authority`

    C. `dig example.com -auth`

    D. `dig -t auth example.com`

226. When configuring a local NTP server role, to what server address can you set the server's NTP client?

    A. `127.0.0.1`

    B. `192.168.1.100`

    C. `ntp.example.com`

    D. `pool.ntp.org`

227. A developer has created an application and wants to take advantage of `syslog` for logging to a custom log file. Which facility should be used for an application such as this?

    A. `syslog`

    B. `kern`

    C. `local#`

    D. `user`

228. You are troubleshooting a DNS problem using the `dig` command and receive a "status: NXDOMAIN" message. Which of the following best describes what NXDOMAIN means?

    A. NXDOMAIN means you have received a non-authoritative answer for the query.

    B. NXDOMAIN means the domain or host is not found.

    C. NXDOMAIN indicates a successful query.

    D. NXDOMAIN signifies that a new domain record has been added.

229. Which of the following commands can be used to restart the CUPS service after a configuration change on a server running `systemd`?

A. `systemctl restart cups.service`

B. `systemctl restart cups`

C. `systemctl reboot cups.target`

D. `systemctl restart cups.target`

230. You need to temporarily prevent users from logging in to the system using SSH or other means. Which of the following describes one method for accomplishing this task?

A. Run `touch /etc/nologin`.

B. Disable `sshd`.

C. Remove `/etc/login`.

D. Add a shadow file.

231. When expiring a user account with `usermod -e`, which of the following represents the correct date format?

A. `YYYY-MM-DD`

B. `MM/DD/YYYY`

C. `DD/MM/YY`

D. `MM/DD/YY HH:MM:SS`

232. Which of the following commands can be used to stop a given service, such as `httpd .service`, from starting on boot with a `systemd`-based system?

A. `systemctl disable httpd.service`

B. `systemctl stop httpd.service`

C. `systemd disable httpd.service`

D. `systemd enable httpd.service boot=no`

233. Which of the following commands searches the entire filesystem for files with the `setuid` bit set?

A. `find ./ -perm suid`

B. `find / -perm 4000`

C. `find / -type suid`

D. `find / -type f -perm setuid`

234. You are upgrading the kernel that has been previously compiled on the same server. Which of the following commands incorporates the contents of the existing kernel configuration into the new kernel?

A. `config --merge`

B. `make oldconfig`

C. `merge config`

D. `int configs`

235. Which of the following commands should you execute after making changes to `systemd` service configurations in order for those changes to take effect?

    A. `systemd reload`

    B. `reboot`

    C. `systemctl daemon-reload`

    D. `systemctl reboot`

236. As a system administrator, you need to change options for `automount`. Which of the following files is the default configuration file for the `autofs` automounter?

    A. `/etc/autofs`

    B. `/etc/auto.master`

    C. `/etc/autofs.conf`

    D. `/etc/automounter.conf`

237. Which of the following directory hierarchies contains information such as the WWN for Fibre Channel?

    A. `/sys/class/wwn`

    B. `/sys/class/fc_host`

    C. `/sys/class/fclist`

    D. `/sys/class/fc/wwn`

238. Which option to the `rsync` command provides archive mode?

    A. `-r`

    B. `-o`

    C. `-a`

    D. `-f`

239. When compiling software such as with the `gcc` compiler, which of the following is the recommended name for a file containing commands and relationships used with the `make` command?

    A. `Makefile`

    B. `makefile`

    C. `make.file`

    D. `Makefile.txt`

240. You have downloaded a source file with the extension `.gz`. Which of the following commands will uncompress the file?

    A. `unzip`

    B. `gunzip`

    C. `dezip`

    D. `uncomp`

241. Which target for `make`, typically included in the `makefile` for most projects, will place compiled files into their final destination and perform other operations such as making the appropriate files executable?

A. `list`

B. `distclean`

C. `run`

D. `install`

242. When creating a local package repository, which option within the `.repo` file in `/etc/yum.repos.d/` is used to set the URL for the repository?

A. `url`

B. `repourl`

C. `httpurl`

D. `baseurl`

243. When running the `lsblk` command, there is no separate partition listed for `/boot`. From which partition is the system likely booted?

A. There is a `/boot` partition under the `/` partition.

B. The `/boot` partition is hidden.

C. The system has not yet built the `/boot` partition.

D. The `/boot` partition does not show up with `lsblk`.

244. Which of the following commands displays the currently open ports and the process that is using the port?

A. `netstat -a`

B. `lsof -i`

C. `ps auwx`

D. `netlist`

245. Which option to the `wget` command logs output?

A. `-r`

B. `-o`

C. `-b`

D. `-k`

246. When executed on a `systemd`-enabled server, the `service status` command is equivalent to which command?

A. `systemd status`

B. `journald status`

C. `service-systemd status`

D. `systemctl status`

247. Which signal to the `kill` command can be used to signal that BIND should reload, including its configuration?

   A.   -15

   B.   -1

   C.   -9

   D.   -2

248. You are troubleshooting a daemon process and have started the daemon manually from the command line so that it does not fork into the background. Which key combination can be used to terminate the daemon?

   A.   Ctrl+A

   B.   Ctrl+B

   C.   Ctrl+C

   D.   Ctrl+D

249. Which service command is used to shut down a service?

   A.   shutdown

   B.   stop

   C.   norun

   D.   runstop

250. Which subcommand with `hostnamectl` can be used to set the type of machine on which it is running?

   A.   set-machine

   B.   machine-type

   C.   set-type

   D.   chassis

251. Which option to the `curl` command sets the local filename to which the output will be saved?

   A.   -f

   B.   -o

   C.   -O

   D.   -l

252. Which of the following commands searches a server for files with the `setgid` bit enabled?

   A.   find / -perm 4000

   B.   find ./ -perm setgid

   C.   grep setgid *

   D.   find / -perm 2000

253. You need to redirect output for a long-running process but do not need to see or capture the output. To which location can you redirect output so that it does not consume disk space?

  A. A regular file

  B. /dev/null

  C. /dev/random

  D. A network interface

254. Which target for the `service` command will cause a daemon to reread its configuration files without restarting the daemon itself?

  A. read

  B. load

  C. start

  D. reload

255. You have executed a daemon process manually from the command line and now need to suspend the process. Which key combination can be used for this purpose?

  A. Ctrl+S

  B. Ctrl+C

  C. Ctrl+Z

  D. Ctrl+B

256. You have been asked to recommend a simple command-line-based text editor for a beginning user. Which of the following should you recommend?

  A. Vi

  B. Nano

  C. nc

  D. ShellRedirect

257. You need to ensure that a service does not start on a `systemd` system. Which `systemctl` command should be used for this purpose?

  A. disable

  B. delete

  C. mask

  D. norun

258. Which command can be used to print using a specially formatted string?

  A. printf

  B. echo

  C. print

  D. here

259. You need to copy a file to a remote system, but that remote system does not have FTP or any other file-sharing services running. You have the ability to SSH into the server. Which of the following commands can be used for this purpose?

 A. scp

 B. ncftp

 C. go

 D. xfer

260. Which of the following describes a method for changing the sort order when using the top command such that the highest memory utilizers will be shown at the top of the list?

 A. Within top, type **o** and then select mem.

 B. Within top, press Shift+F, scroll to %MEM, press **s** to select, and then press Q to quit.

 C. Within top, press S and then select %MEM.

 D. Within top, press Shift+S, select %MEM, then press Q to quit.

261. Which option to the fsck command causes it to run the check even if the filesystem is apparently marked as clean?

 A. -f

 B. -m

 C. -a

 D. -c

262. One of your customers needs to transfer a large file and is asking for FTP to be enabled on the server. Thinking of security, what options can you offer that are more secure?

 A. USB

 B. Email (SMTP)

 C. SSL

 D. SFTP

263. You need to extract files from a backup created with an older version of HPUX. The tar command does not seem to work for these files. Which of the following may be able to extract from this backup?

 A. gzip

 B. bzip2

 C. cpio

 D. hpb

264. You believe that the system has been broken into and files may have been changed. After taking the system offline and unmounting one of the affected partitions, what could you do next?

 A. Use dd to make an image of the partition to preserve it.

 B. Create a backup using tar.

 C. Examine the partition with fdisk.

 D. Use mkfs to reformat the partition.

265. Which option to the `zip` command causes the command to traverse directories?

A. -g

B. -m

C. -r

D. -a

266. You are working on a Debian system and need to set ownership on a file such that the user used to execute Apache can write to the file. What command can you use to determine which user Apache is running as?

A. `ps auwx | grep apache`

B. `ls -a`

C. `free | grep httpd`

D. `monapache`

267. When scripting for build automation, you need to run a configure script prior to running the `make` command. Which of the following will execute the configure script, assuming that it's in the same directory as the script invoking it?

A. `configure`

B. `./configure`

C. `../configure`

D. `/configure`

268. Which command can be used to change the size of a logical volume when using Logical Volume Manager?

A. `vgs`

B. `lvresize`

C. `vgcreate`

D. `lvs`

269. Which file contains information about RAID arrays on a Linux system?

A. `/proc/mdstat`

B. `/raidstat`

C. `/var/raidinfo`

D. `/etc/raid.txt`

270. When working with `mdadm`, which command-line argument is used to specify things like striping and parity?

A. `--layout`

B. `-R`

C. `--level`

D. `-x`

271. Which command displays Desktop Management Interface information?

    A. `dmidump`

    B. `dlad`

    C. `dmid`

    D. `dmidecode`

272. SSHFS is an example of which type of filesystem use?

    A. Attachment

    B. Disk

    C. RAID

    D. FUSE

273. Which of the following best describes `.rpmnew` and `.rpmsave` files?

    A. The `.rpmnew` file contains RPM files and their hashes while `.rpmsave` contains a list of saved hashes.

    B. The `.rpmnew` file contains new RPM files available for download while `.rpmsave` contains a list of files that have been saved locally.

    C. The `.rpmnew` file contains a list of RPM files that have changed since the last save while `.rpmsave` is a backup of the last `.rpmnew` file.

    D. The `.rpmnew` file contains a new configuration file for a package when local changes exist to the configuration file while `.rpmsave` contains the local configuration file when a new file is included in the package.

274. You are using the `top` command to monitor processes and you notice that the `nc` command is consuming a lot of CPU cycles. Which command can be used to change the priority of the command?

    A. `renice`

    B. `nice`

    C. `ps`

    D. `top`

275. Which command is used to create a packaged application to be distributed with Flatpak?

    A. `flatpak-builder`

    B. `flatpak-create`

    C. `flatpak-pack`

    D. `flatpak-compile`

276. Which background process runs to maintain the list of snap packages available on an Ubuntu system?

    A. `snapper`

    B. `snapperd`

    C. `snapdaemon`

    D. `snapd`

277. Which tool is used to create a sandboxed AppImage package?

   A. `appimagetool`

   B. `apptool`

   C. `ocon`

   D. `app-ocon`

278. Which network-related tool combines elements of both ping and traceroute?

   A. `tcpdump`

   B. `wireshark`

   C. `mtr`

   D. `nmcli`

279. Which option to `resolvectl` specifies the protocol?

   A. `-f`

   B. `-x`

   C. `-p`

   D. `-m`

280. Which command shows the background processes related to the current shell?

   A. `jobs`

   B. `htop`

   C. `pidof`

   D. `-m`

281. Which of the following commands displays Media Access Control (MAC) to IP address association?

   A. `arp`

   B. `-x`

   C. `-p`

   D. `-m`

282. As root, you run the command cd ~ followed by pwd to print the working directory. What is the expected output?

   A. `/home`

   B. `/root`

   C. `/sbin`

   D. `/bin`

283. Which command can be used to determine a file type?

   A. `file`

   B. `xz`

   C. `lsof`

   D. `prep`

284. When running the `ps` command you notice that a process has a Z in the state field. What does Z represent?

    A. Sleeping

    B. Running

    C. Stopped

    D. Zombie

285. You need to kill a process using its name rather than its process id. Which command can be used for this purpose?

    A. `pkill`

    B. `pend`

    C. `pterminate`

    D. `kp`

286. You need to change directory one level up from the current directory. Which command accomplishes this task?

    A. `cd .`

    B. `cd ~`

    C. `mv ~`

    D. `cd ..`

Chapter

2

System Operations and Maintenance (Domain 2.0)

1. You need to delete a user from the system, including their home directory. Which of the following utility commands accomplishes this task?

   A. `userdel`

   B. `userdel -r`

   C. `userdel -R`

   D. `deluser`

2. You need to enable the web server (running as the `www-data` user and group) to write into a directory called `/home/webfiles`. Which commands will accomplish this task in the most secure manner?

   A. `chgrp www-data /home/webfiles ; chmod 775 /home/webfiles`

   B. `chmod 777 /home/webfiles`

   C. `chgrp www-data /home/webfiles ; chmod 711 /home/webfiles`

   D. `chmod 707 /home/webfiles`

3. Assume that passwords must be changed every 60 days. Which command will change the date of the user's last password change without the user actually changing the account password?

   A. `chage -f`

   B. `chage -W`

   C. `chage -l`

   D. `chage -d`

4. What is the order in which user configuration files are located on login to a Bash shell?

   A. `.bash_login, .profile, /etc/profile`

   B. `.bash_profile, .bash_login, .profile`

   C. `.profile, .bash_login, .bash_profile`

   D. `.bash_login, .bash_profile, .profile`

5. Within which directory should you place files to have them automatically copied to a user's home directory when the user is created?

   A. `/etc/userhome`

   B. `/etc/templateuser`

   C. `/etc/skel`

   D. `/home/skel`

6. Which bash parameter or option will cause the shell to be executed without reading the initialization files?

   A. `--no-rc`

   B. `--no-init`

   C. `--norc`

   D. `--rc-none`

7. You need to create a function that will be available each time you log in to the system. Within which file should this function be placed?

   A. .bash_profile

   B. .rc

   C. /etc/profile

   D. .bash_run

8. Assuming X forwarding has been enabled on the SSH server, which environment variable is used to set the location for newly spawned windows from within an SSH session?

   A. DISPLAY

   B. XTERMINAL

   C. XTERM

   D. XDISP

9. Which of the following options in the SSH configuration file needs to be enabled so that X sessions can be sent over an SSH connection?

   A. X11Connect yes

   B. X11Forwarding yes

   C. ForwardX yes

   D. XForward yes

10. Which file contains user information such as username and real name and is readable by all users of the system?

   A. /etc/pass

   B. /etc/shadow

   C. /etc/passwd

   D. /etc/userinfo

11. Which of the following commands changes a group called DomainAdmins to DomainUsers?

   A. groupmod -n DomainUsers DomainAdmins

   B. groupchg DomainAdmins DomainUsers

   C. chgroup DomainAdmins DomainUsers

   D. group -N DomainAdmins DomainUsers

12. When running useradd, which option needs to be specified in order for the user's home directory to be created?

   A. -h

   B. -m

   C. -x

   D. -a

13. Which of the following commands locks out password-based login for a user but does not prevent other forms of login?

A. usermod -L

B. userdel -r

C. useradd -h

D. userlock

14. Which of the following commands produces a report listing the last password change date for all users on the system?

A. passwd -a

B. passwd -S

C. passwd -a -S

D. passwd --all

15. Which file contains a list of usernames, UIDs, and encrypted passwords?

A. /etc/passwd

B. /etc/shadow

C. /etc/encpass

D. /etc/grouppass

16. Which command is used to change a user's home directory to /srv/data/username and move the contents at the same time?

A. usermod -d /srv/data/username -m

B. homedir -m /srv/data/username

C. userex -m /srv/data/username

D. userchg /m /srv/data/username -d

17. Which option to useradd will add groups for a user?

A. -g

B. -x

C. -l

D. -G

18. Which option to useradd creates a system user rather than a normal user?

A. -r

B. -s

C. -a

D. -S

19. Which file contains encrypted password information for groups?

A. `/etc/group`

B. `/etc/gshadow`

C. `/etc/gsecure`

D. `/etc/group.conf`

20. Which of the following best describes a valid use of the `groupdel` command?

A. You may force group deletion with the `-f` option.

B. If a user's primary group is to be deleted, that user must be deleted first or have their primary group changed.

C. Groupdel can be run at any time, regardless of group membership.

D. The `-r` option for `groupdel` will recursively change users' GIDs after group deletion.

21. Which of the following commands displays the UID, primary group, and supplemental groups for a given user?

A. `id`

B. `getid`

C. `passwd`

D. `chage`

22. Which option to the `usermod` command is used to change a given user's real name?

A. `-R`

B. `-n`

C. `-d`

D. `-c`

23. A user needs to work with printers and printer-related items. Which of the following commands adds the user (called `username` in the options) to the appropriate group for this purpose?

A. `usermod -aG printerusers username`

B. `usermod -aG lpadmin username`

C. `usermod -gA lpadm username`

D. `usermod -a lpadm username`

24. You need to examine who is currently logged in to the system. Which of the following commands will display this information?

A. `listuser`

B. `fuser`

C. `ls -u`

D. `w`

25. Within the following entry in /etc/shadow, to what does the number 15853 refer?
mail:*:15853:0:99999:7:::

   A. The UID of the mail user

   B. The number of files owned by mail

   C. The date of the last password change (since 1/1/1970)

   D. The number of days until the account expires

26. Which of the following commands displays a listing of who is logged in to the server along with the date and time that they logged in?

   A. whois

   B. who

   C. loggedin

   D. curusers

27. Which of the following commands adds a group?

   A. groupadd

   B. addgrp

   C. grpadd

   D. creategroup

28. Which of the following commands enables the sticky bit for a user on a file called homescript.sh?

   A. chmod +sticky homescript.sh

   B. chmod 755 homescript.sh

   C. chmod u+t homescript.sh

   D. chown u+sticky homescript.sh

29. The umask reports as 022. What is the permission that will be in effect for a newly non-executable created file?

   A. u+rw, g+r, w+r

   B. 755

   C. 644

   D. a+r

30. Which of the following best describes the relationship between UIDs and GIDs on a Linux system when an authentication server is being configured?

   A. The UID and GID are the same across the system for a given user.

   B. Each user has a UID and GID that are the same and are created when the user is created.

   C. The UID represents the user, while the GID is a globally unique user ID.

   D. There is no direct relationship between UID and GID.

31. When you're configuring a server for an SNMP server role, which ports need to be allowed through the firewall for SNMP traffic?

    A. Ports 23 and 25

    B. Ports 110 and 143

    C. Ports 80 and 443

    D. Ports 161 and 162

32. You need to look at information on logins beyond what was captured by the current log file for the last command. Which option to the last command can be used to load information from an alternate file?

    A. `-a`

    B. `-t`

    C. `-e`

    D. `-f`

33. When creating a certificate authority server role, which of the following commands generates a private key for use with SSL and places it into the file `/etc/ssl/example.com.private`?

    A. `openssl genrsa -out /etc/ssl/example.com.private`

    B. `openssl generate-private > /etc/ssl/example.com.private`

    C. `openssl genpriv > /etc/ssl/example.com.private`

    D. `openssh genkey -out /etc/ssl/example.com.private`

34. Which of the following options within an OpenSSH server configuration is used to determine whether the root user can log in directly with an SSH client?

    A. `PermitRootLogin`

    B. `AllowRoot`

    C. `RootLogin`

    D. `PermitDirectRootLogin`

35. Which option to `ssh` creates a port forwarding to which remote clients can also connect?

    A. `-L`

    B. `-R`

    C. `-P`

    D. `-E`

36. Which subcommand of `openssl` is used to create a Certificate Signing Request (CSR) for Secure Sockets Layer (SSL)/Transport Layer Security (TLS)?

    A. `req`

    B. `csr`

    C. `gencsr`

    D. `newcsr`

37. Within which directory should scripts and other files to run at login be stored?

A. `/etc/login`

B. `/etc/profile`

C. `/etc/bash.defs`

D. `/etc/profile.d`

38. Using udev to configure a network adapter for use with a firewall so that it has a specific and consistent name, you edit the udev rules file. Which option within the rules file ensures that the device will always have a name of `eth0`?

A. `ATTR-NAME="eth0"`

B. `NAME="eth0"`

C. `DEV_NAME="eth0"`

D. `NAME_DEV="eth0"`

39. You are configuring a database service and need to open the default port for MySQL on the firewall. Which port is the default for MySQL?

A. 6592

B. 25

C. 389

D. 3306

40. When configuring Apache for a web server role, which of the following directives tells the server the location of the SSL private key?

A. `SSLKeyFile`

B. `SSLCertificatePrivateKey`

C. `SSLCertificateKeyFile`

D. `SSLPrivateKey`

41. Which of the following commands will correctly change the group ownership of the file called `a.out` to users?

A. `chgrp users a.out`

B. `chgrp a.out users`

C. `groupchg a.out users`

D. `grpchg users a.out`

42. Which option to `umask` will display the permissions to be used in a POSIX format?

A. `-P`

B. `-p`

C. `-S`

D. `-v`

43. Which option to chown recursively changes the ownership?

   A. -f

   B. -R

   C. -a

   D. -m

44. Which option to chgrp will change group ownership of all files within a given directory?

   A. -directory

   B. -d

   C. -R

   D. -V

45. When sourcing a file in bash, which chmod command would be necessary to provide the minimum privileges in order for the file to be sourced correctly, assuming that your current user owns the file?

   A. chmod 600

   B. chmod 755

   C. chmod 777

   D. chmod 400

46. Which of the following commands removes an expiration from an account?

   A. sudo chage -l username

   B. sudo chage -E -1 username

   C. sudo chage -E now username

   D. sudo chage --noexpire username

47. You need to determine whether LDAP integration is working correctly. In order to do so, you would like to obtain a list of users, as read by /etc/nsswitch.conf. Which command can be used for this purpose?

   A. getuser

   B. getent

   C. usermod

   D. userlist

48. A command has the following listing obtained with ls -la:

-rwsr-xr-x 1 suehring suehring 21 Nov 2 13:53 script.sh

What does the s denote within the user permissions in the listing?

   A. The suid bit has been set for this program.

   B. This is a symlink.

   C. The file will not be executable.

   D. The file is a special system file.

49. Which system logging facility is used for messages from the kernel?

    A. `syslog`

    B. `kernel`

    C. `kern`

    D. `system`

50. What is the name of the `systemd` service that provides logging facilities?

    A. `systemd-journald`

    B. `systemd-loggingd`

    C. `systemd-syslog`

    D. `systemd-logger`

51. Which configuration option in `/etc/logrotate.conf` will cause the log to be emailed to `admin@example.com` when the log rotation process runs for the selected log?

    A. `mail admin@example.com`

    B. `sendmail admin@example.com`

    C. `maillog admin@example.com`

    D. `logmail admin@example.com`

52. You are deploying an Exim server and need to work with the firewall to ensure that the proper incoming ports are open. Which protocol and port should you allow inbound for normal SMTP traffic?

    A. TCP/23

    B. TCP/25

    C. TCP/110

    D. TCP/143

53. Which port(s) and protocol(s) should be opened in a firewall in order for the primary and secondary name servers to communicate for a given domain?

    A. `udp/53`

    B. Both `tcp/53 and udp/53`

    C. `tcp/53`

    D. `udp/53 and tcp/503`

54. When examining open ports on the server, you see that TCP port 3000 is listed with no corresponding protocol name, such as `smtp`, `imaps`, and so on. In which file would you find a list of port-to-protocol translations that could be customized to add this new port?

    A. `/etc/ports`

    B. `/etc/p2p`

    C. `/etc/ppp`

    D. `/etc/services`

55. On which port does ICMP operate?

   A. TCP/43

   B. UDP/111

   C. UDP/69

   D. ICMP does not use ports.

56. Which of the following commands displays account information such as expiration date, last password change, and other related details?

   A. `usermod -l`

   B. `userinfo -a`

   C. `chageuser -l`

   D. `chage -l`

57. Which command is used to create a public/private key pair for use with SSH?

   A. `ssh -k`

   B. `ssh-keygen`

   C. `ssh-genkey`

   D. `ssh -key`

58. Within which file should you place public keys for servers from which you will accept key-based SSH authentication?

   A. `~/.ssh/authorized_keys`

   B. `~/.ssh/keys`

   C. `~/.ssh/keyauth`

   D. `~/.sshd/authkeys`

59. You need to execute a command as a specific user. Which of the following commands enables this to occur?

   A. `sudo -u`

   B. `sudo -U`

   C. `sudo -s`

   D. `sudo -H`

60. Which option in `/etc/sudoers` will cause the specified command to not prompt for a password?

   A. `PASSWORD=NO`

   B. `NOPASSWD`

   C. `NOPASSWORD`

   D. `NOPROMPT`

61. Which of the following commands will display kernel parameters related to resource limits such as CPU time, memory, and other limits for the currently logged-in user?

   A. `reslimit`

   B. `limitres -a`

   C. `ulimit -a`

   D. `proclimit -n`

62. When working with TCP wrappers, which line within the `/etc/hosts.deny` file will prevent any host within the 192.168.1.0/24 network from accessing services that operate from `xinetd`?

   A. `BLOCK: 192.168.1.0/24`

   B. `REJECT: 192.168.1.0`

   C. `ALL: 192.168.1.0/255.255.255.0`

   D. `NONE: 192.168.1/255.255.255.0`

63. You are using an RSA-based key pair for SSH. By default, what is the name of the private key file in `~/.ssh`?

   A. `id_rsa`

   B. `id_rsa.priv`

   C. `id_rsa.key`

   D. `rsa_key.priv`

64. Which option to the `su` command will execute a single command with a non-interactive session?

   A. `-s`

   B. `-u`

   C. `-c`

   D. `-e`

65. When working with digital signatures, after specifying the key server, which option to gpg is used to specify the key to send to the key server?

   A. `key-name`

   B. `keyname`

   C. `send-key`

   D. `sendkey`

66. Which of the following commands should be used to edit the `/etc/sudoers` file?

   A. Any text editor such as Vi or emacs

   B. `editsudo`

   C. `visudo`

   D. `visudoers`

67. Which file can be used to store a server-wide cache of hosts whose keys are known for SSH?

  A. `/etc/sshd_known_hosts`

  B. `/etc/ssh_known_hosts`

  C. `~/.ssh/known_hosts`

  D. `/root/ssh_known_hosts`

68. Which option within `/etc/sshd/sshd.conf` (or `/etc/ssh/sshd_config`) can be changed to prevent password-based authentication?

  A. `PasswordAuthentication`

  B. `Passwords`

  C. `AllowPass`

  D. `AllowPasswords`

69. Which of the following commands generates a GnuPG key pair?

  A. `gpg --gen-key`

  B. `gpg --key`

  C. `gpg --send-key`

  D. `gpg --create-key`

70. Which file is used as the default storage for public keyrings for gpg?

  A. `publickeys.gpg`

  B. `pubring.gpg`

  C. `public.gpg`

  D. `pubkeys.gpg`

71. Which option to the `su` command is used to obtain the normal login environment?

  A. `-u`

  B. `-U`

  C. `-`

  D. `-login`

72. Which option enables SSL configuration for a given website or server?

  A. `SSLEngine`

  B. `SSLDirect`

  C. `SSLEnable`

  D. `SSLConnect`

73. When using the `net` command in an Active Directory single sign-on (SSO) environment, which option enables authentication using Kerberos?

A. `-b`

B. `-k`

C. `-l`

D. `-a`

74. Within which directory are individual configuration files stored for the Pluggable Authentication Module (PAM) mechanism?

A. `/etc/pamd`

B. `/etc/pam`

C. `/etc/pam.d`

D. `/etc/pam.conf.d`

75. On which port does the `slapd` LDAP daemon listen for connections?

A. 389

B. 3389

C. 3306

D. 110

76. Which PAM module prevents logins from accounts other than root when the file `/etc/nologin` exists?

A. `pam_login.so`

B. `pam_preventlogin.so`

C. `pam_nologin.so`

D. `pam_logindef.so`

77. Which PAM module is responsible for normal or standard password authentication?

A. `pam_auth.so`

B. `pam_login.so`

C. `pam_unix.so`

D. `pam_standardlogin.so`

78. Which PAM module provides a mechanism for checking and enforcing the strength of passwords in order to enforce a password policy?

A. `pam_passwdstr.so`

B. `pam_cracklib.so`

C. `pam_libpasswd.so`

D. `pam_strpass.so`

79. Which format should the certificate and key be in for a Postfix TLS configuration?

   A. PKCS

   B. PEM

   C. TLS

   D. SSL

80. Which `iptables` chain is used to create a port redirect?

   A. `REDIRECT`

   B. `PREROUTING`

   C. `PORTREDIR`

   D. `ROUTING`

81. Which of the following commands saves the current set of `iptables` rules into a file?

   A. `save-iptables`

   B. `iptables-create`

   C. `iptables-save`

   D. `ipt-save`

82. Which of the following commands lists the current `iptables` rules while not attempting to resolve host or port names?

   A. `iptables -L`

   B. `iptables -List -no-resolve`

   C. `iptables -a`

   D. `iptables -nL`

83. Which of the following directories contains configuration files for the `fail2ban` system?

   A. `/etc/fail2ban.cfg`

   B. `/etc/fail2ban.d`

   C. `/etc/f2b`

   D. `/etc/fail2ban`

84. Within an OpenSSH configuration, which option disables the use of empty passwords?

   A. `DisableEmptyPass`

   B. `PermitEmptyPasswords`

   C. `EmptyPasswordAuth`

   D. `PermitPasswordLength`

85. Which of the following commands sets the default policy for the INPUT chain to discard packets that don't have a specific rule allowing them?

   A. `iptables INPUT DROP`

   B. `iptables chain INPUT policy DROP`

   C. `iptables -P INPUT DROP`

   D. `iptables POLICY=DROP CHAIN=INPUT`

86. When configuring VPN service through a firewall, on which port and protocol does Open-VPN listen?

   A. ICMP/1194

   B. UDP/1194

   C. TCP/1194

   D. VPN/1194

87. Which of the following best describes the difference between the DROP and REJECT targets in iptables?

   A. Both DROP and REJECT do the same thing.

   B. DROP silently discards packets, while REJECT sends back an ICMP acknowledgment.

   C. REJECT silently discards packets, while DROP sends back an ICMP acknowledgment.

   D. DROP sends back a direct message, and REJECT sends a redirect.

88. Which of the following partial iptables rules sets up a configuration that limits log entries to three per minute?

   A. -m limit 3 -j LOG

   B. -m limit --limit 3/minute --limit-burst 3 -j LOG

   C. -m limit --limit 3

   D. -m limit --limit-minute 3 --burst 3 -j LOG

89. Which of the following partial iptables rules allows incoming ICMP traffic?

   A. -A INPUT -p ICMP -j ACCEPT

   B. -A IN -P ICMP

   C. -A INPUT -P ACCEPT-ICMP

   D. -A IN -P ICMP -j ACCEPT

90. Which of the following partial iptables rules blocks all traffic from source IP 192.168.51.50?

   A. -A INPUT -p ALL 192.168.51.50 -j ACCEPT

   B. -A INPUT -p ALL -s 192.168.51.50 -j DROP

   C. -A INPUT -p ALL -s 192.168.51.50 -j BLOCK

   D. -A INPUT -p ALL -f 192.168.51.50 -j DISCARD

91. Which of the following partial iptables rules will allow all hosts to connect to TCP port 2222?

   A. -A INPUT -p TCP -s 0/0 --destination-port 2222 -j ACCEPT

   B. -A TCP -s ALL -p 2222 -j ACCEPT

   C. -A INPUT -p TCP -s *.* --destination-port 2222 -j ALLOW

   D. -A INPUT --destination-port */* -j ACCEPT

92. Which of the following commands enables forwarding such as would be used for NAT?

    A. `echo "1" > /proc/sys/net/ipv4/nat`

    B. `echo "1" > /proc/sys/net/ipv4/ip_forward`

    C. `iptables --enable-forwarding`

    D. `ip-forward --enable`

93. Within a jail configuration for `fail2ban`, which configuration option sets the name and location of the log file to monitor for failures?

    A. `logpath`

    B. `monitor`

    C. `logfile_mon`

    D. `monitor_log`

94. Which command sends a copy of the public key identity to another server for use with SSH?

    A. `ssh-key`

    B. `ssh-copy-key`

    C. `ssh-sendkey`

    D. `ssh-copy-id`

95. Which option in `/etc/sudoers` sets the destination address for administrative and security emails related to `sudo`?

    A. `mail`

    B. `mailto`

    C. `secmail`

    D. `adminmail`

96. Which port should be allowed through a firewall for NTP communication?

    A. Port 139

    B. Port 161

    C. Port 123

    D. Port 194

97. You are looking for files related to the SSL configuration on the server. After looking in `/etc/ssl`, within which other directory might the files reside?

    A. `/etc/sslconfig`

    B. `/usr/share/ssl`

    C. `/etc/pki`

    D. `/etc/private`

98. Which OpenSSH configuration directive is used to specify the users who will be allowed to log in using SSH?

   A. `AllowUsers`

   B. `PermitUsers`

   C. `UsersAllowed`

   D. `AllowedUsers`

99. Which option within a `LOG` target for `iptables` sets a string that will be prepended to log entries?

   A. `--log-prefix`

   B. `--prepend`

   C. `--log-prepend`

   D. `--log-str`

100. Within the SELinux configuration, which option controls whether the policy will be targeted or strict?

   A. `SEPOLICY`

   B. `SELINUXTYPE`

   C. `SETARGET`

   D. `SELINUXPOLICY`

101. Which of the following best describes the status of SELinux when the command `getenforce` returns `Permissive`?

   A. A `Permissive` return means SELinux is enabled but rules are not enforced, although DAC rules are still in effect.

   B. A `Permissive` return means SELinux is not enabled.

   C. A `Permissive` return means SELinux is enabled, although rules are not enforced and DAC rules are not in effect.

   D. A `Permissive` return means SELinux is using an enforcing policy.

102. Which of the following describes the primary difference between the configuration files `ssh.conf` and `sshd.conf` (typically found in `/etc/sshd/` or `/etc/ssh/`)?

   A. `sshd.conf` is the configuration file for the system SSH, and `ssh.conf` is the options configuration file.

   B. `sshd.conf` is the configuration file for the system SSH daemon, and `ssh.conf` provides system-wide client SSH configuration.

   C. `sshd.conf` is used when SSH will be disabled, and `ssh.conf` is used when SSH is enabled.

   D. `sshd.conf` is the first configuration file read for a client connection, while `ssh.conf` is the first configuration read for a server configuration.

103. When you're working with PAM, a module that is marked as `required` has failed. Which of the following describes what happens to the other modules in that realm?

   A. Processing stops immediately when a failure of a required module occurs.

   B. Processing stops after all required modules are processed.

   C. Processing continues until another required module is encountered.

   D. Processing continues through other modules but ultimately fails.

104. What is the UID of the root account?

   A. 1000

   B. 0

   C. 100

   D. 65535

105. Using a system such as Google Authenticator to provide multifactor authentication is an example of which type of token?

   A. Hardware

   B. Software

   C. Virtual-based

   D. Usage-based

106. Within which directory are the predefined zones for `firewalld`?

   A. `/etc/firewalld/`

   B. `/usr/lib/firewalld/zones/`

   C. `/usr/firewalld/zones/`

   D. `/etc/firewall/zones`

107. You need to set a bootloader password for GRUB. To do so, which of the following configuration options should be set in `/boot/grub/grub.conf`?

   A. `login`

   B. `prompt`

   C. `boot-passwd`

   D. `password`

108. Assuming that the output from the `sestatus` command indicates that SELinux is in `Permissive` mode, which of the following commands is used to change the mode to `Enforcing`?

   A. `setenforce en`

   B. `setenforce 1`

   C. `setenforce on`

   D. `setenforce --enable`

109. Your organization uses `ssh-agent` for authentication assistance with SSH. Which command can be used to add a private key to `ssh-agent`?

  A. `ssh-privkey`

  B. `ssh-agent-key`

  C. `ssh-add`

  D. `ssh-addkey`

110. When working with access control lists (ACLs), which of the following commands is used to display information about the access control list for a given file?

  A. `getfacl`

  B. `getacl`

  C. `acldisp`

  D. `showacl`

111. You need to provide a special username and other parameters related to a specific host to which you connect using SSH. To which file should you add this information?

  A. `~/.ssh/hosts`

  B. `~/.ssh/known_hosts`

  C. `~/.ssh/config`

  D. `~/.ssh/hostconfig`

112. You are using `chmod` in order to change several web-related files so that the web server/public can read them. Which option should you add to the `chmod` command in order for the permissions to inherit to other files?

  A. `-R`

  B. `-v`

  C. `-i`

  D. `-M`

113. Which option to `setsebool` writes the current values to disk so that they will be applied at next reboot?

  A. `-A`

  B. `-P`

  C. `-D`

  D. `-M`

114. When working with AppArmor, within which directory are profiles and application permissions located?

  A. `/etc/apparmor/`

  B. `/etc/apparmor.d/`

  C. `/etc/appa.d/`

  D. `/etc/armor.d/`

115. When using Kerberos authentication, which of the following commands shows the ticket cache?

    A. `ktix`

    B. `ktel`

    C. `kcache`

    D. `klist`

116. Which of the following options to the `ls` command displays ownership and permission information?

    A. `-m`

    B. `-l`

    C. `-b`

    D. `-f`

117. Which option to `getsebool` returns the entire list of SELinux booleans?

    A. `-a`

    B. `-b`

    C. `-c`

    D. `-d`

118. Which AppArmor command uses `netstat` to determine the network-related processes that do not have AppArmor profiles?

    A. `aa-profiles`

    B. `aa-netstat`

    C. `aa-unconfined`

    D. `aa-netlist`

119. Which group can be used to restrict access to execute the `su` command?

    A. `super`

    B. `admins`

    C. `wheel`

    D. `runsu`

120. You need to change the SELinux security context of a file. Which of the following commands should be used for this purpose?

    A. `setcontext`

    B. `sesecon`

    C. `chcon`

    D. `setcon`

121. Which of the following is an advantage of using an SSL-based VPN client?

A. The transport may be able to get around firewalls that otherwise block VPN traffic.

B. The use of SSL makes default configuration easier.

C. The use of SSL means keys do not need to be configured.

D. The use of SSL makes no difference.

122. When configuring PKI on a Red Hat system, which options are available as hashing algorithms when RSA is used as a key type?

A. SHA256withRSA

B. MD4

C. SHA2048

D. SHAwithEC

123. Which of the following passwords can be used to secure a system such that it will not boot, even if the attacker has physical access to place a USB boot disk in the computer?

A. GRUB password

B. UEFI/BIOS password

C. Root password

D. SHA1 password

124. Which option to the `restorecon` utility can be used to view the current contexts without making changes?

A. -n

B. -r

C. -g

D. -p

125. You need to view the SELinux contexts for various processes on the system. Which of the following commands will accomplish this task?

A. showcon

B. proccon

C. lcon -Z

D. ps -Z

126. Which PAM module can be used to lock accounts after failed login attempts?

A. pam_lock

B. pam_tally2

C. pam_loginlock

D. pam_watchlog

127. Which of the following commands places all AppArmor profiles into complain mode?

   A. `aa-complain /etc/apparmor.d/*`

   B. `aa-enable -complain /etc/apparmor.d/*`

   C. `aa-enable -complain /etc/apparmor/*`

   D. `aa-complain /etc/apparmor/*`

128. Which option within the `sshd_config` file sets per-user configuration?

   A. `UserConf`

   B. `Match User`

   C. `Per-User`

   D. `Conf User`

129. Which option to the `firewall-cmd` command sets the current runtime configuration to be available on next reboot of the computer?

   A. `--set-perm`

   B. `--make-perm`

   C. `--runtime-to-permanent`

   D. `--current-to-persistent`

130. When working with `ufw`, you need to allow SSH traffic. Which of the following commands facilitates this scenario?

   A. `ufw allow tcp/22`

   B. `ufw enable ssh`

   C. `ufw allow ssh`

   D. `ufw enable tcp/21-22`

131. Which of the following is the name for the firewall control software associated with Netfilter?

   A. `iptables`

   B. `ipt`

   C. `netfw`

   D. `netfilterfw`

132. When you're copying files using `scp`, which port needs to be open in the firewall?

   A. TCP/21

   B. TCP/22

   C. TCP/20 and TCP/21

   D. UDP/53

133. You are viewing the contents of a directory with the `ls` command but do not see files that begin with a single dot (`.`). Which option to `ls` shows those files?

   A. `-a`

   B. `-b`

   C. `-c`

   D. `-d`

134. Which option to `ssh` specifies the private key to use for authentication?

   A. `-m`

   B. `-i`

   C. `-k`

   D. `-a`

135. You have found that the owner of the Apache process is `www-data`. Assuming that the file does not have read privileges, what command will change the ownership of a file, given as `<filename>`, such that `www-data` can write to the file?

   A. `chown www-data <filename>`

   B. `chown apache-www-data <filename>`

   C. `chmod www-data +w <filename>`

   D. `chmod www-data.apache <filename>`

136. When using `sudo` in a scripted environment, which option can be used to specify a noninteractive mode?

   A. `-f`

   B. `-m`

   C. `-n`

   D. `-l`

137. Which command is used to turn off AppArmor profiles?

   A. `aa-disable`

   B. `aa-turnoff`

   C. `aa-enable -d`

   D. `aa-off`

138. Which command and option are used to view the SELinux security context of a given file?

   A. `ls -context`

   B. `file -Z`

   C. `ls -Z`

   D. `sel -context`

139. Digital signatures can be provided in Linux through which of the following commands?

   A. gds

   B. gpg

   C. dmc

   D. gds2

140. You need to make a change to the global behavior of AppArmor. To avoid editing the profiles directly, which directory contains common settings that can be changed instead?

   A. /etc/apparmor.d/configs

   B. /etc/apparmor/globals

   C. /etc/apparmor/edits

   D. /etc/apparmor.d/tunables

141. Which of the following directories contains configuration for UFW?

   A. /etc/ufwd

   B. /etc/ufw.d

   C. /etc/ufw

   D. /etc/ufirewall

142. Which software can be used in connection with iptables in order to more effectively block traffic from entire network ranges?

   A. ipblock

   B. ipset

   C. iplist

   D. ipcoll

143. You have created a public key and private key for use with SSH. The contents of which key should be copied to a remote host in order to enable authentication?

   A. The public key.

   B. The private key.

   C. Both the public and private keys.

   D. Neither the public nor the private key. It must be generated on the remote host.

144. What is the octal notation to specify that a directory should have read+write+execute permissions for the owner and read+execute permissions for the group and other?

   A. 711

   B. 644

   C. 755

   D. 777

145. Which option to `sestatus` shows the context of a file?

    A. `-f`

    B. `-v`

    C. `-m`

    D. `-a`

146. Which option to `chage` sets the maximum days that a password is valid?

    A. `-v`

    B. `-m`

    C. `-M`

    D. `-d`

147. Which option within an SSH server configuration enables authentication using Kerberos?

    A. `UseKerberos`

    B. `KerberosAuthentication`

    C. `EnableKerberos`

    D. `KerberosEnable`

148. You are working with `iptables-save` to examine the contents of tables in a scripted environment. Which option to `iptables-save` can be used to specify the table name rather than outputting information for all tables?

    A. `-t`

    B. `-a`

    C. `-s`

    D. `-i`

149. Ports below what number are considered to be the well-known ports?

    A. 256

    B. 512

    C. 1024

    D. 65535

150. Which PAM module is responsible for enforcing limits such as the maximum number of logins and CPU time used?

    A. `pam_enforce.so`

    B. `pam_limittest.so`

    C. `pam_max.so`

    D. `pam_limits.so`

151. When using LDAP for authentication, what will be logged with the `loglevel` set to 0×10 in a `slapd.conf` configuration file?

    A. No debugging

    B. Trace debugging

    C. Stats logging

    D. Packets sent and received

152. On which port does LDAP over SSL listen for connections?

    A. 389

    B. 443

    C. 636

    D. 3128

153. Which of the following PAM modules can be used for authorization and authentication scenarios using external files?

    A. `pam_fileauth.so`

    B. `pam_listfiles.so`

    C. `pam_filesauth.so`

    D. `pam_fileauth.so`

154. Which option to `ssh-keygen` sets the type of key that will be created?

    A. `-k`

    B. `-t`

    C. `-e`

    D. `-i`

155. You are attempting to remove a software package from a Debian system. Which command removes the package?

    A. `apt-cache remove-update`

    B. `apt-cache remove`

    C. `apt-get remove`

    D. `apt-get delete`

156. Which of the following configuration options sets a hard limit of 25 processes for a user called suehring in `/etc/security/limits.conf`?

    A. `suehring hard proc 25`

    B. `suehring hard nproc 25`

    C. `suehring proc 25 hard-limit`

    D. `proc 25 suehring hard`

157. Which command is used to configure kernel parameters for a new GPU driver added to the system?

   A. gpuctl

   B. gpuload

   C. sysconfig

   D. sysctl

158. Which type of module interface for PAM is used to set a policy such as the time of day that a user can log in?

   A. auth

   B. account

   C. password

   D. policy

159. Which command can be used to set file attributes such as making a file immutable?

   A. chr

   B. fattr

   C. chattr

   D. fop

160. Which range of UIDs is typically used by service accounts?

   A. 1 to 999

   B. 1 to 100

   C. 32,768 to 65,535

   D. 1,000 to 1,999

161. Which message type(s) should be queried when looking for SELinux access denials or violations?

   A. AVC

   B. DEN

   C. AVC,USER_AVC

   D. STOP,VIOL

162. Which option is used to display information about current file attributes?

   A. lsfile

   B. lsattr

   C. showfile

   D. exattr

163. Which of the following describes a key difference between a self-signed certificate and a certificate issued by a trusted certificate authority?

    A. A self-signed certificate is valid for only 30 days.

    B. A self-signed certificate will be automatically trusted by clients when attempting to connect.

    C. A self-signed certificate will need to be manually trusted by clients when attempting to connect to a service that uses the certificate.

    D. There is no practical difference between a self-signed certificate and one issued by a trusted certificate authority.

164. Which of the following software packages can be used to scan a host for rootkits?

    A. rkfind

    B. wxps

    C. tmroot

    D. Chkrootkit

165. Within which file is the default umask set?

    A. `/etc/profile`

    B. `/etc/umask`

    C. `/defaults/umask`

    D. `/etc/user.defs`

166. After recovering from kernel panic, you would like to look at what might have happened. Which of the following files contains the kernel ring buffer messages?

    A. `/var/log/dmesglog`

    B. `/var/log/start.log`

    C. `/var/log/kern.log`

    D. `/var/log/bootlog.txt`

167. Which of the following commands is used to examine the `systemd` journal or log file?

    A. `journallist`

    B. `ctlj`

    C. `journalctl`

    D. `jctl`

168. Assuming that the `$ModLoad imudp` configuration option has been set in the `/etc/rsyslog.conf` configuration file for `rsyslogd`, which of the following additional options is necessary to configure the port on which the server will listen?

    A. `$Port 514`

    B. `$UDPServerRun 514`

    C. `$Listen 514`

    D. `$UDPListen 514`

169. Which option in `journald.conf` controls the maximum file size for individual journal logs?

    A. `SystemMaxFileSize`

    B. `MaxFile`

    C. `LogFileSize`

    D. `LogSize`

170. Which option within a `logrotate` configuration file disables compression of the log file?

    A. `compressoff`

    B. `limitcompress`

    C. `nocompression`

    D. `nocompress`

171. Which of the following files should be used to display a message to users prior to logging in locally?

    A. `/etc/loginmesg`

    B. `/etc/logmessage.txt`

    C. `/etc/issue`

    D. `/etc/banner`

172. Which file contains a message that is displayed after successful login?

    A. `/etc/loginbanner`

    B. `/etc/issue`

    C. `/etc/motd`

    D. `/etc/message`

173. When working with System Security Services Daemon (sssd), which command is used to discover and join an Active Directory domain for a single sign-on (SSO) authentication scenario?

    A. `joinad`

    B. `adjoin`

    C. `realm`

    D. `realm-ad`

174. You need to provide SSL certificates for several hosts within your organization, some of which are public-facing. Which type of certificate should be used for this purpose?

    A. Wildcard certificate

    B. Self-signed certificate

    C. Certificate-in-escrow

    D. Unchained certificate

175. Within which file are values related to password aging defined on a system that uses `/etc/shadow`?

    A. `/etc/shadow.defaults`

    B. `/etc/shad.defs`

    C. `/etc/login.defs`

    D. `/etc/shadow.conf`

176. When working with nftables to maintain a stateful firewall, which connection state represents a packet or session that has not yet been established?

    A. `new`

    B. `unseen`

    C. `clear`

    D. `conn_new`

177. Which file sets the global or default values for the `ssh` command client behavior?

    A. `/etc/ssh/config`

    B. `/etc/ssh/client_config`

    C. `/etc/ssh/ssh_config`

    D. `/etc/ssh/sshd_config`

178. When using dynamic port forwarding with SSH, which type of proxy is used?

    A. Squid

    B. Internal

    C. Curb

    D. Socks

179. Which polkit function is used to create a rule?

    A. `addRule()`

    B. `createRule()`

    C. `NewRule()`

    D. `ruleAdd()`

180. You need to relabel after changing SELinux policies. Which of the following commands triggers the autorelabel process?

    A. `autorel`

    B. `touch /.autorelabel`

    C. `selinux -rel`

    D. `systemd-relabel`

181. Which command can be used to create a new SELinux policy using a logfile of actions that have been denied by SELinux policy ?

    A. `updatese --log`

    B. `selinux --audit`

    C. `audit2allow`

    D. `genserules --log`

182. You have used `getenforce` to verify that the current mode is Enforcing and need to change certain rules in real time. Which command can be used for this purpose?

    A. `systemd-selinux`

    B. `sechange`

    C. `semanage`

    D. `setsepol`

183. Assuming a Fedora system, which command can be used to change the policy, such as changing from minimum to targeted?

    A. `setse --policy`

    B. `system-selinux`

    C. `selinux-change`

    D. `system-config-selinux`

184. Which of the following is the correct syntax to remove the group ID (SGID) bit on a directory using the `chmod` command?

    A. `chmod group-sgid directory`

    B. `chmod g-s directory`

    C. `chmod sgid -r directory`

    D. `chmdo -r gs directory`

185. When using `pkexec` with PolicyKit, which option specifies the user under which the program will be executed?

    A. `--username`

    B. `--account`

    C. `--user`

    D. `--login`

186. Which of the following is the correct syntax to enable port forwarding so that connections to local port 5150 will be sent to www.example.com on port 80?

    A. `-L www.example.com:80->5150`

    B. `-L 5150:www.example.com:80`

    C. `-L 5150->www.example.com:80`

    D. `-F 5150->www.example.com:80`

187. Which of the following represents an accurate statement about stateless firewalls?

    A. Stateless firewalls have three zones: internal, external, and DMZ.

    B. Stateless firewalls are the only type available in Linux.

    C. Stateless firewalls examine packet headers to connect related packets.

    D. Stateless firewalls examine source and destination.

188. Which configuration option within `/etc/login.defs` sets the minimum value for a user ID (UID)?

    A. `UID_MIN`

    B. `MIN_UID`

    C. `USERID_MIN`

    D. `UID_MINIMUM`

189. Assuming that you own and operate the domain `example.com`, when viewing additional details about an SSL certificate, the valid hosts are shown as `*.example.com`. Based on this information, what can you tell about this certificate?

    A. It is a wildcard certificate.

    B. It is a self-signed certificate.

    C. It is invalid for example.com.

    D. It uses an invalid hostname.

Chapter

3

Scripting, Containers, and Automation (Domain 3.0)

1. You are writing a shell script using Bash and need to print the contents of a variable. Which of the following commands can be used to do so?

    A. echo

    B. lf

    C. sp

    D. varpt

2. Which of the following packages provides orchestration for Linux in an agentless manner?

    A. Ansible

    B. Puppet

    C. Automat

    D. vid

3. Which of the following commands can be used to execute a command with a customized environment?

    A. set

    B. env

    C. run

    D. crun

4. Which of the following commands, when used with git, retrieves the latest objects from a repository and attempts to incorporate those changes into the local working copy of the repository?

    A. fetch

    B. pull

    C. retr

    D. get

5. Which of the following best describes the concept of infrastructure as code?

    A. The management of switches and routers using compiled programs

    B. The management of servers and other systems using scripting, source code management, and automation

    C. The deployment of hardware using Agile methodologies

    D. Planning for bugs in infrastructure code and allowing time to fix them

6. Which of the following commands changes a file called script.sh, which is located in your home directory, such that it can be executed by the owner of the file and no one else?

    A. chmod 700 ~/script.sh

    B. chown +x /script.sh

    C. chmod ~/script.sh +x

    D. chmod 777 /home/script.sh

7. Which command can be used to add functions and variables to the current shell?

    A. source

    B. echo

    C. en

    D. src

8. Which of the following is the correct method for invoking the Bash shell for a script, typically found as the first line of the script?

    A. #!/BASH

    B. #!bash

    C. #!/bash

    D. #!/bin/bash

9. You need to send output from a command to a log file. Overwriting the contents of the log file is acceptable. Which of the following characters is used to redirect output in such a way as to fulfill this scenario?

    A. |

    B. <

    C. >

    D. &

10. You need to create a new empty git repository called repo. Which of the following sequences accomplishes this task?

    A. mkdir repo; cd repo; git init --bare

    B. mkdir repo; git init repo/

    C. git init repo -md

    D. git create repo/

11. Which of the following terms is used in orchestration and automation scenarios to refer to the collection of devices being managed?

    A. Device collection

    B. Inventory

    C. Machines

    D. UsableObjects

12. You need to print output from a Bash script such that single quotes appear in the outputted string. Which character should be used as an escape sequence in order to get the single quotes into the output?

    A. /

    B. '

    C. ?

    D. \

13. Which exit code indicates success for a Bash script?

   A. 0

   B. 1

   C. 2

   D. EOF

14. Which of the following commands produces output `sit sat set`?

   A. `echo s{i,a,e}t`

   B. `echo s(i,a,e)t`

   C. `echo s[i,a,e]t`

   D. `echo s/i,a,e/t`

15. Which of the following characters or character sequences begins a comment in a Bash script?

   A. `/*`

   B. `//`

   C. `#`

   D. `'`

16. Which, if any, file extension is required in order for a Bash script to execute?

   A. `.sh`

   B. `.bash`

   C. `.bat`

   D. No special extension is necessary.

17. After fetching changes for a previously cloned git repository, which git command is used to incorporate the changes from that branch into the local copy?

   A. `put`

   B. `push`

   C. `merge`

   D. `inc`

18. Which of the following best describes the role of an agent in software orchestration?

   A. An agent is software that listens for and executes commands from the server.

   B. An agent is used to migrate from one operating system to another.

   C. An agent is a hardware-based token used for authentication.

   D. An agent is not used in software orchestration.

19. Being able to deploy additional servers in response to high demand or load is an example of which type of automation?

    A. Build

    B. Compile

    C. Infrastructure

    D. Config

20. Which command can be used to indicate a local variable within a Bash script?

    A. `localvar`

    B. `ll`

    C. `local`

    D. `%local%`

21. Which git command is used to retrieve a repository from a remote server?

    A. `clone`

    B. `checkout`

    C. `co`

    D. `retr`

22. You need to echo the name of the script back to the user for usage or help output. Which positional parameter can be used for this purpose?

    A. `$me`

    B. `$1`

    C. `$myname`

    D. `$0`

23. Which of the following commands can be used to print the contents of the current shell environment?

    A. `echoenv`

    B. `printenv`

    C. `showenv`

    D. `envvar`

24. You are writing a `while` loop in a Bash script and need to compare two string values. Which operator is used for this purpose?

    A. `-ne`

    B. `=`

    C. `equal`

    D. `eq`

25. You need to create a Bash script that will loop continually and perform some commands within the loop. Which of the following lines will accomplish this task?

    A. `if [ $exit -eq "exit" ]`

    B. `while true; do`

    C. `for ($i = 0, $i++)`

    D. `continue until ($exit)`

26. Which of the following commands changes the location to which HEAD is pointing with git?

    A. `git point`

    B. `git checkout`

    C. `git change`

    D. `git load`

27. You need to declare a variable as part of the environment prior to running a Bash script. Which of the following commands accomplishes this?

    A. `dec`

    B. `create`

    C. `export`

    D. `get`

28. Which of the following commands displays the contents of the PATH variable in Bash?

    A. `echo PATH`

    B. `echo $PATH`

    C. `echo $CURPATH`

    D. `ext $PATH`

29. Which character sequence is used to execute a command within a subshell in a Bash script?

    A. `$()`

    B. `subs()`

    C. `$%`

    D. `$(~`

30. You need to make a change to the configuration of the SSH daemon across your infrastructure. Being able to do so from a central server is an example of which type of automation?

    A. Security

    B. Automated configuration management

    C. Development configuration management

    D. Usability management

31. Which option is used with the env command in order to remove a variable from the environment?

   A. -r

   B. -u

   C. -n

   D. -d

32. Within a Bash script, you need to run two commands but only run the second command if the first succeeds. Which of the following metacharacters can be used to accomplish this task?

   A. <>

   B. &

   C. &&

   D. |

33. You need to redirect the output from a command and append that output to a file. Which of the following character sequences accomplishes this task?

   A. >

   B. >>

   C. |

   D. ^

34. You need to obtain a directory listing of all files and directories except those that begin with the letter *p*. Which of the following commands accomplishes this task?

   A. ls -l !p

   B. ls -l [!p]

   C. ls -l [^p]

   D. ls -l [^p]*

35. Which of the following files is used within a git repository in order to indicate files and file patterns that should not be versioned?

   A. novers

   B. .gitignore

   C. gitignore.txt

   D. gitnover

36. You need to iterate through a directory listing and perform an operation on certain files within it. To accomplish this task, you will be using a Bash script and a looping construct. Which looping construct is most appropriate for this purpose?

   A. until

   B. do

   C. for

   D. foreach

37. You are debugging a Bash script written by a different system administrator. Within the script, you see a command surrounded by backquotes, or `` ` ``. What will be the result of surrounding the command with backquotes?

A. The command will execute and send all output to the console.

B. The command will not execute.

C. The command will execute as if the $() command substitution was used.

D. The command will execute and send all output to /dev/null.

38. Which git command displays a short history of commits along with the commit ID?

A. showhist

B. list

C. log

D. hist

39. You are committing code to a git repository and need to include a message on the command line. Which option enables this behavior?

A. -m

B. -h

C. -f

D. -l

40. Compiling software when a developer commits code to a certain branch in a repository is an example of which type of automation?

A. Infrastructure

B. Build

C. Complex

D. DevOps

41. You are working with a MySQL database and need to read in several SQL commands from a file and send them into the MySQL CLI for execution. You will be using STDIN redirection for this. Which of the following commands is correct, assuming a filename of customers.sql?

A. mysql < customers.sql

B. mysql | customers.sql

C. mysql > customers.sql

D. mysql >< customers.sql

42. You are collaborating on a coding project using git as the source code management tool. Teammates are saying that they cannot see your code, although you have been committing code regularly. Which of the following is most likely the problem?

A. You have not added commit messages.

B. You need to send the commit IDs to the teammates.

C. You have not executed git push to send the code to the server.

D. You are committing using the -h flag.

43. Which option to the chmod command performs a recursive change?

    A. -re

    B. -R

    C. -c

    D. -v

44. Which character sequence is used to indicate the default case within a case statement in a Bash script?

    A. ()

    B. *.*

    C. **

    D. *)

45. Which character sequence indicates the end of an if conditional in a Bash script?

    A. }

    B. fi

    C. end

    D. endif

46. What is the name of the default branch in a git repository?

    A. source

    B. main

    C. primary

    D. first

47. You need to use the output from a command as input for another command. Which character facilitates this scenario?

    A. >

    B. |

    C. !

    D. `

48. Which git command shows the current state of the working copy of a repository?

    A. git list

    B. git status

    C. git state

    D. git view

49. Which option to the echo command suppresses the ending newline character that is normally included?

  A. -a

  B. -n

  C. -d

  D. -y

50. Determining the version of software installed on each client node is an example of collecting information for which collection in an automated infrastructure?

  A. Inventory

  B. Group

  C. Procedure

  D. Build

51. You need to redirect STDERR from a command into a file to capture the errors. Which character sequence can be used for this purpose?

  A. >

  B. %2>

  C. 2>

  D. %%>

52. You need to make a change to your git environment because your email address has changed. Which of the following commands ensures that your new email address will be used for all subsequent commits?

  A. git config user.email

  B. git change email

  C. git config email.addr

  D. git config email.address

53. Which shell built-in command is used to display a list of read-only variables?

  A. ro

  B. readonly

  C. env-ro

  D. ro-env

54. Assume that you're using the Bash shell and want to prevent output redirects from accidentally overwriting existing files. Which command and option can be used to invoke this behavior?

  A. setoutput -f

  B. overwrite=no

  C. overwrite -n

  D. set -C

55. You have received a file that does not have a file extension. Which command can you run to help determine what type of file it might be?

A. grep

B. telnet

C. file

D. export

56. Which of the following commands will display the last 50 lines of your command history when using Bash, including commands from the current session?

A. bashhist 50

B. history 50

C. cat .bash_history

D. tail -f .bash_history

57. When using Bash, how would you execute the last command starting with a certain string, even if that command was not the last one that you typed?

A. Precede the command with ! and then the string to search for.

B. Search for the command in history.

C. Precede the command with a ? and then the string to search for.

D. This is not possible with Bash.

58. Which shell built-in command can be used to determine the location from which a given command will be run?

A. type

B. when

C. find

D. help

59. Which command is used to read and execute commands from a file in the Bash shell?

A. run

B. execute

C. source

D. func

60. You need a command to be executed on logout for all users. Within which file should this be placed (assume all users are using Bash)?

A. ~/.bash_logout

B. /etc/bash.bash_logout

C. /home/.bash_logout

D. /etc/bash_logout

61. Which of the following commands removes an environment variable that has been set?

    A. `profile --unset`

    B. `env -u`

    C. `set -u`

    D. `import`

62. When setting the shebang line of a shell script, which of the following commands will help to determine the location of the interpreter automatically?

    A. `#!/usr/bin/env bash`

    B. `#!/bin/bash`

    C. `#!env`

    D. `/bin/int bash`

63. Which of the following best describes the PS1 environment variable?

    A. PS1 is used to set the location of the `PostScript` command.

    B. PS1 is used to define the default shell prompt for Bash.

    C. PS1 is used as a per-system variable.

    D. PS1 is user-defined and does not have a default value or setting.

64. Which variable within a Bash script is used to access the first command-line parameter?

    A. `$ARG`

    B. `$0`

    C. `$1`

    D. `$ARG0`

65. Which of the following commands will print a list of six numbers beginning at 0?

    A. `list 0-5`

    B. `seq 0 1 5`

    C. `echo 0-5`

    D. `seq 0 1 6`

66. Which of the following commands will execute a script and then exit the shell?

    A. `run`

    B. `source`

    C. `./`

    D. `exec`

67. Which command within a shell script awaits user input and places that input into a variable?

    A. `exec`

    B. `get`

    C. `read`

    D. `prompt`

68. What characters are used to mark a sequence of commands as a function within a shell script?

    A. Parentheses to declare the function (optional), and curly braces to contain the commands

    B. Curly braces to declare the function, and parentheses to contain the commands

    C. Square brackets to declare the function, and curly braces to contain the commands

    D. Run quotes to denote the function

69. Which character sequence is used to terminate a `case` statement in a Bash script?

    A. end

    B. done

    C. esac

    D. caseend

70. Which option to `declare` displays output in a way that could then be used as input to another command?

    A. -o

    B. -n

    C. -p

    D. -m

71. Which characters are used to denote the beginning and end of the test portion of a `while` loop in a shell script?

    A. Parentheses ( )

    B. Curly braces { }

    C. Square brackets [ ]

    D. Double quotes " "

72. When using the `test` built-in with one argument, what will be the return if its argument is not null?

    A. false

    B. true

    C. unknown

    D. -1

73. Which environment variable is used when changing directory with the tilde character, such as `cd ~` ?

    A. HOMEDIR

    B. HOMEPATH

    C. HOME

    D. MAILPATH

74. You would like to examine the entries for a single file through the `git commit` history. Which command should be used for this purpose, assuming a filename of `nhl_scores.php`?

   A. `git log --history nhl_scores.php`

   B. `git log --follow nhl_scores.php`

   C. `git history nhl_scores.php`

   D. `git commit-history nhl_scores.php`

75. Which of the following best describes attributes of an inventory within an automated continuous integration/continuous deployment (CI/CD) infrastructure?

   A. Parameters such as the client IP address and software versions

   B. The number of client nodes

   C. The software used on the server for the orchestration

   D. The architectural pattern for deployment

76. Which operator should be used when comparing integers to determine if one is equal to another in a Bash script?

   A. `-ro`

   B. `===`

   C. `-eq`

   D. `-fe`

77. You would like to run several commands in succession but not have the output sent into the next command. Which of the following metacharacters will accomplish this task?

   A. `&`

   B. `>`

   C. `;`

   D. `|`

78. Which escape sequence is used to denote the alert or bell?

   A. `\a`

   B. `\b`

   C. `\c`

   D. `\d`

79. Which of the following is a valid variable declaration in a Bash script, setting the variable NUM equal to 1?

   A. `NUM = 1`

   B. `$NUM = 1`

   C. `NUM= 1`

   D. `NUM=1`

80. Which of the following commands will obtain the date in seconds since the epoch and place it into a variable called DATE within a shell script?

    A. DATE="$(date +%s)"

    B. DATE="date"

    C. DATE="$(date)";

    D. DATE="$date %s"

81. Which sequence is used to mark the beginning and end of the commands to execute within a for loop in a shell script?

    A. Curly braces { }

    B. The keywords do and done

    C. Semicolons ;

    D. Tabs

82. Which option to the declare command will create a variable that is read-only?

    A. -r

    B. -ro

    C. -p

    D. -x

83. Which environment variable controls the format of dates and times, such as a 12-hour or 24-hour formatted clock?

    A. LOCALE_DATE

    B. DATE_FORMAT

    C. LC_TIME

    D. LC_DATE

84. Which option to netstat displays interface information in a table-like format that might be suitable for use with scripting?

    A. -i

    B. -r

    C. -t

    D. -l

85. You are running a shell script from within your SSH session. Which key combination can be used to terminate the script?

    A. Ctrl+X

    B. Ctrl+-

    C. Ctrl+C

    D. Ctrl+Esc

86. Which of the following conditionals in a Bash script will test if the variable DAY is equal to SUNDAY?

A. `if ($DAY == "SUNDAY")`

B. `if ($DAY -eq "SUNDAY")`

C. `if [ $DAY == "SUNDAY" ]`

D. `if [ DAY = "SUNDAY" ]`

87. Which of the following commands adds `~/code/bin` to the path?

A. `PATH=~/code/bin:$PATH`

B. `PATH=/code/bin:$PATH`

C. `PATH=/home/code/bin:$PATH`

D. `PATH=PATH:~/code/bin`

88. Which option to `git merge` can be used to attempt to roll back a merge that has conflicts?

A. `--rollback`

B. `--abort`

C. `--rewind`

D. `--restart`

89. Which environment variable can be used to change the default path for a new git repository created with `git init`?

A. `GIT_DIR`

B. `GIT_HOME`

C. `GIT_DEST`

D. `GIT_LOC`

90. Which character sequence is used to add a horizontal tab using `echo` with a Bash script?

A. `\h`

B. `\t`

C. `\a`

D. `\f`

91. You need to exclude a build file, called `build.o`, from being tracked by git. Which character sequence can be used in the `.gitignore` file to exclude or ignore that file in all directories?

A. `build.o`

B. `/build.o`

C. `**/build.o`

D. `build.*`

92. Which file-globbing sequence will match all files that begin with an uppercase *A* or an uppercase *F*?

   A. `[AF]*`

   B. `[af]*`

   C. `*AF*`

   D. `AF*`

93. Assuming a remote name of `origin`, which `git` command can be used to obtain additional information about the remote?

   A. `git show origin`

   B. `git remote show origin`

   C. `git show remotes`

   D. `git remote list`

94. Which character sequence displays the number of command-line arguments that were passed to a Bash script?

   A. `$NUM`

   B. `$CLA`

   C. `$+`

   D. `$#`

95. Which environment variable can be set if you wish to automatically log users out of their shell after a certain period of inactivity?

   A. `TIMEOUT`

   B. `TMOUT`

   C. `TO`

   D. `IDLETIME`

96. You are debugging a Bash script and notice a line that contains `echo $NUM #sending $NUM to output`. What will be the result of this line when executed?

   A. It will not output anything because it is commented out.

   B. It will cause a syntax error because it is invalid syntax.

   C. It will output the contents of the NUM variable.

   D. It will output the sequence "$NUM".

97. When cloning a repository with `git clone`, you need to change the name of the remote so that it is not called `origin`. Which option can be added to `git clone` to accomplish this task?

   A. `--origin`

   B. `--remote`

   C. `--name`

   D. `--remote-name`

98. When working in a virtual server environment, which column within `iostat` output shows the amount (percentage) of time spent in an involuntary wait scenario due to the hypervisor?

    A. proc

    B. wait

    C. user

    D. steal

99. If you need to temporarily reconfigure all locale variables and settings for a given session, which environment variable can be used?

    A. LC_LIST

    B. LC_GLOBAL

    C. LC_ALL

    D. ALL_LOCALE

100. A set of commands to execute on a client node is an example of which type of infrastructure automation?

    A. Procedure

    B. Subset

    C. Agent

    D. Collection

101. Which character sequence is used to indicate the end of an individual clause within a `case` statement in a Bash script?

    A. //

    B. 'eol

    C. ;;

    D. <

102. Which of the following commands removes a currently defined aliased command?

    A. remove

    B. rm

    C. unalias

    D. delete

103. Which of the following tests will determine if a file exists in the context of a shell script?

    A. -a

    B. -e

    C. -m

    D. -i

104. Which of the following values for the LANG environment variable will configure the system to bypass locale translations where possible?

A. LANG=COMPAT

B. LANG=NONE

C. LANG=C

D. LANG=END

105. Which option to the `git config` command shows all of the configuration parameters that have been set?

A. --list

B. --show

C. -u

D. --display

106. Which character sequence should be used if you need to redirect STDERR to a file and append to the file?

A. 2>

B. 2>>

C. &>>

D. 1>>

107. When working with infrastructure as code, you have received a file with a `.yml` extension. What is the likely format for the contents of this file?

A. YAML

B. XML

C. Tab-delimited

D. Text

108. Which of the following best describes the result of the command `cat /etc/passwd | cut -d: -f1 > users.txt`?

A. The first field will be extracted from the passwd file and placed into a file called `users.txt`.

B. The second field will be extracted from the passwd file and placed into a file called `users.txt`.

C. The passwd file will be separated based on a colon and output placed into `users.txt`.

D. The passwd file will be sent to the terminal where only fields beginning with a colon will be shown and placed into a file called `users.txt`.

109. Which shell built-in can be used to move positional parameters down, where $2 becomes $1, $3 becomes $2, and so on?

A. move

B. rev

C. shift

D. dec

110. You are using `git pull` to obtain changes to a shared repository. Which option should you add to `git pull` in order to prevent autocommit so that you can look at the results of the merge first?

    A. `--pre-merge`

    B. `--no-auto`

    C. `--nc`

    D. `--no-commit`

111. Which of the following pairs indicates the beginning and end of an `until` loop in a Bash script?

    A. `do; done`

    B. `start; stop`

    C. `beg; end`

    D. `until; litnu`

112. Which exit code is used to indicate a general error within a Bash script?

    A. 0

    B. 1

    C. 256

    D. –1

113. You need to redirect `STDIN` until a certain character combination is encountered. Which of the following operators can be used for this purpose?

    A. `>STDIN`

    B. `<<`

    C. `<&`

    D. `>`

114. Assuming that a file has been previously added to a repository with `git add`, which option to the `git commit` command can be used to automatically add and commit the file?

    A. `-a`

    B. `-b`

    C. `-c`

    D. `-d`

115. Which locale-related environment variable is used for currency-related localization?

    A. `LC_MONE`

    B. `LC_CURRENCY`

    C. `LC_MONETARY`

    D. `LC_CURR`

116. Which of the following lines added to `.profile` in a user's home directory will set their time zone to Central time?

   A. `TZ=/Central ; export TZ`

   B. `TIMEZONE='America/Chicago' ; export TIMEZONE`

   C. `set TZ=/Central`

   D. `TZ='America/Chicago'; export TZ`

117. Which of the following creates an array in a Bash script?

   A. `ARRAY=(val1 val2)`

   B. `ARRAY = "val1 val2"`

   C. `ARRAY_PUSH($ARRAY,"val1","val2");`

   D. `ARRAY{0} = "val1"`

118. Which test within a shell script `while` loop will examine one value to see if it is less than another?

   A. `-less`

   B. `-lessThan`

   C. `-lt`

   D. `-lthan`

119. Assuming that a space-separated list of values has been defined as `LIST="one two three four"`, which of the following `for` loop constructs will iterate through the elements in the list?

   A. `for LIST`

   B. `for VAR in LIST`

   C. `for VAR in $LIST`

   D. `for $LIST -> $VAR`

120. Which keyword(s) is/are used to begin an alternate condition within a Bash script?

   A. `if`

   B. `else if`

   C. `elif`

   D. `elsif`

121. Within which directory does git store a local copy of the repository metadata?

   A. `.gitmeta`

   B. `gitlocalmeta`

   C. `.git`

   D. `git`

122. You need to redirect both STDERR and STDOUT to a file. Which of the following character sequences accomplishes this task?

   A. 2>

   B. 2>&1

   C. 2+1

   D. +2+1

123. Within a Bash script, you need to run two commands but only run the second command if the first fails. Which of the following metacharacters can be used to accomplish this task?

   A. <>

   B. &

   C. &&

   D. ||

124. Which of the following commands creates a new branch called project1 and points the HEAD toward that branch?

   A. git branch project1

   B. git checkout project1

   C. git checkout -b project1

   D. git create project1 -H

125. Which of the following best describes the difference between a while and an until loop in a Bash script?

   A. A while loop always executes once; an until loop does not.

   B. An until loop always executes once; a while loop does not.

   C. A while loop executes as long as a condition is true; an until loop executes until the condition is false.

   D. An until loop executes until a condition is true; a while loop executes until a condition is false.

126. Which statement can be used in a Bash script to determine if variable $num1 is greater than $num2, assuming both variables contain integers?

   A. if ["$num1" -gt "$num2"]

   B. if ["$num1" > "$num2"]

   C. if ($num1 -gta $num2)

   D. if [$num1 gt $num2]

127. Which of the following protocols is typically used for agentless infrastructure orchestration?

   A. SMTP

   B. ICMP

   C. SSH

   D. FTP

128. Which of the following character sequences expands or interpolates a variable called VAR within a Bash script?

A. VAR

B. $(VAR}

C. ${VAR}

D. *VAR*

129. You are creating a configuration file in JSON format for use with Terraform. Which of the following is the expected file extension for this configuration file?

A. .tf

B. .txt

C. .tf.json

D. .tfjs

130. Which of the following commands displays the status of a pod on a Kubernetes cluster?

A. kubectl status

B. kubectl pod status

C. kubectl status pods

D. kubectl get pod

131. Which of the following best describes the relationship between pods and containers with Kubernetes?

A. Pods and containers are the same.

B. Pods can contain multiple containers.

C. Containers can contain multiple pods.

D. There is no relationship between pods and containers.

132. When working with a network configuration, which of the following terms refers to a computer with two network interfaces?

A. Bridging

B. Dual-homed

C. Overlay

D. Forwarding

133. You are using a container image for a cloud deployment and are building a stateful application that must store data between deployments. Which type of storage should be used?

A. Ephemeral volume

B. Bridged volume

C. Container image

D. Persistent volume

134. Which of the following describes the difference between NAT and bridging in a virtualization environment?

    A. NAT uses the host adapter IP address for all network activity, while bridging enables the virtual machine to get its own IP.

    B. NAT enables the virtual machine to get its own IP, while bridging uses the host adapter IP address for all network activity.

    C. NAT is used to enable external clients to access the virtual machine, and bridging joins two virtual machines together.

    D. NAT and bridging refer to the same thing in virtualization.

135. When `cloud-init` is used for bootstrapping and deployment of an EC2 instance, which file format should be used for the configuration files?

    A. XML

    B. YAML

    C. HTML

    D. JS

136. When troubleshooting a file that is not found, you notice that the file location is linked as `../file.txt`. Which type of path has been used for this file?

    A. Virtual

    B. Symbolic

    C. Relative

    D. Absolute

137. Working with a file called `test.php` to determine line count, the output from the wc command is `14 18 293 test.php`. Which of the three digits corresponds to line count?

    A. 14

    B. 18

    C. 293

    D. None of the options are line count.

138. Which type of logging driver is the default for Docker containers?

    A. `json-file`

    B. `sql`

    C. `normal`

    D. `yaml-file`

139. Which docker command removes an image from a host node?

    A. `del`

    B. `rem`

    C. `rmf`

    D. `rmi`

140. Which of the following best describes an overlay network when used with technology such as Kubernetes?

    A. An overlay network is a newly deployed network that uses real-world IP addresses on top of existing private IP addresses.

    B. An overlay network is a virtual network used for communication between containers.

    C. An overlay network is used for IPv6 communication on top of IPv4 infrastructure.

    D. An overlay network is used for communication between wifi-enabled hosts and containers.

141. Linkerd, Consul Connect, and Istio are examples of software to provide which type of abstraction when working with Kubernetes?

    A. Service mesh

    B. Virus scanning

    C. Multifactor authentication

    D. Mapping

142. Which of the following commands will send the contents of /etc/passwd to both STDOUT and a file called `passwordfile`?

    A. `cat /etc/passwd > passwordfile`

    B. `var /etc/passwd | passwordfile`

    C. `cat /etc/passwd | tee passwordfile`

    D. `echo /etc/passwd | stdout > passwordfile`

143. What is the default delimiter used by the `cut` command?

    A. Colon

    B. Tab

    C. Space

    D. Comma

144. What option is used to change the number of lines of output for the `head` and `tail` commands?

    A. `-l`

    B. `-f`

    C. `-g`

    D. `-n`

145. Which of the following egrep commands will examine /etc/passwd to find users that are using either /bin/bash or /usr/bin/zsh for their shell environment?

    A. `grep sh /etc/passwd`

    B. `egrep '/*/.sh$' /etc/passwd`

    C. `grep '/*/.=sh$' /etc/passwd`

    D. `egrep '/*/..?sh$' /etc/passwd`

146. Which of the following commands searches each user's `.bash_history` file to determine if the user has invoked the `sudo` command?

  A. `find /home -name "bash_history" | grep sudo`

  B. `find /home -name ".bash_history" | xargs grep sudo`

  C. `find /home/.bash_history | xargs grep sudo`

  D. `find /home -type history | xargs grep sudo`

147. Which command can be used to convert lowercase letters to uppercase letters across an entire file?

  A. `du`

  B. `touc`

  C. `conv`

  D. `tr`

148. When using `sed` for a search and replace operation, which option must be included so that the substitution applies to the entire line rather than just the first instance?

  A. `g`

  B. `a`

  C. `r`

  D. `y`

149. Which Bash environment variable is used to obtain the exit status of the most recent pipeline?

  A. `$.`

  B. `$E`

  C. `$STAT`

  D. `$?`

150. Which of the following is valid syntax for creating a pull request with the `git` command?

  A. `pull-req`

  B. `pull`

  C. `request`

  D. `request-pull`

151. Which character combination sets the body of the message to `STDIN` when using the `mail` command?

  A. `<`

  B. `>`

  C. `<<<`

  D. `|`

152. Which command will find directories with names beginning with 2019 located beneath the current directory?

    A. `find ./ -name "2019"`

    B. `find ./ -type d -name "2019"`

    C. `find / -type d "2019"`

    D. `find ./ -type d -name "2019*"`

153. Which of the following best describes the difference between merging and rebasing in Git?

    A. Merging reapplies changes from the first commit of the origin master branch to create a new snapshot and commit.

    B. Rebasing reapplies changes from one branch to the other.

    C. Merging reapplies changes from one branch to the other.

    D. Rebasing uses soft links to re-create the merge history.

154. Which of the following formats are used for SaltStack configuration files?

    A. YAML

    B. JSON

    C. TXT

    D. DOC

155. Which option to `git tag` enables searching through the tags for a given repository?

    A. `-s`

    B. `-a`

    C. `-d`

    D. `-l`

156. Which of the following is most accurate when referring to host networking with virtualization or containerized applications?

    A. Host networking is necessary for service communication to the outside world.

    B. Communication is limited to localhost through inter-process communication.

    C. Communication will flow through the host network stack.

    D. Virtualization and containerized applications cannot use host networking.

157. Which command is used to obtain a pre-built docker image from a known repository?

    A. `install`

    B. `inst`

    C. `build`

    D. `pull`

158. Which of the following commands is a simple pager that is found on most Linux systems?

   A. more

   B. pg

   C. grep

   D. mr

159. Which of the following docker commands shows the current running containers?

   A. container show

   B. container ls

   C. list -containers

   D. show container

160. The default format for an OVF template uses which document standard?

   A. YML

   B. XML

   C. OVFMeta

   D. HTML

161. Which command can be used to search the contents of all files below your current location for files that contain the characters *DB*?

   A. grep -r "DB" *

   B. grep -ri "DB" *

   C. cat * | less

   D. cat *.txt | grep DB

162. Which docker command creates a container from an image and starts that image?

   A. run

   B. go

   C. make

   D. start

163. Which docker command sends an image to the Docker Hub registry or to a local registry?

   A. go

   B. send

   C. push

   D. upload

164. Which configuration option with a Docker configuration shows the ports that will be opened when the image is started?

    A. PORT

    B. EXPOSE

    C. OPEN

    D. LISTEN

165. Which of the following commands can be used to connect to a Docker container?

    A. docker telnet

    B. docker open

    C. docker go

    D. docker attach

166. Which of the following commands will provide the usernames in a sorted list gathered from the /etc/passwd file?

    A. cat /etc/passwd | awk -F : '{print $1}' | sort

    B. sort /etc/passwd | cut

    C. echo /etc/passwd

    D. cat /etc/passwd | awk '{print $1}' | sort

167. Which option for the wc command prints the number of lines given as input?

    A. -f

    B. -a

    C. -l

    D. -o

168. What is the default number of lines printed by the head and tail commands, respectively?

    A. 10 for head, 5 for tail

    B. 5 for head, 10 for tail

    C. 10 for both head and tail

    D. 3 for both head and tail

169. When using Docker compose to create a single-node multi-container application, which format is required for the configuration file?

    A. JSON

    B. YAML

    C. PDF

    D. XML

170. You have been asked to create a template for virtualization. The template will be in JSON format. Which of the following is the correct name for JSON?

    A.   Just Simple Object Nodes

    B.   JavaScript Object Notation

    C.   Java Standard Object Notation

    D.   JavaScript Standard Object Notation

171. When you're working to design a Kubernetes-based application, what is the name for a container that acts as a proxy to connect to services outside of the pod?

    A.   ProxyCloud

    B.   Ambassador

    C.   Sideload

    D.   Integration Container

Chapter

4

Troubleshooting
(Domain 4.0)

1. While troubleshooting a network service that does not appear to start, which option to the `ss` command shows the current TCP listening sockets?

   A. −lt

   B. −ct

   C. -m

   D. -f

2. You are examining a problem report where a USB disk is no longer available. Which command is used to obtain a list of USB devices?

   A. usb-list

   B. lsusb

   C. ls-usb

   D. ls --usb

3. You have lost the password for a server and need to boot into single user mode. Which option given at boot time within the GRUB configuration will start the system in single user mode to enable password recovery and/or reset?

   A. single-user

   B. su

   C. single

   D. root

4. Which of the following is a good first troubleshooting step when a hard disk is not detected by the Linux kernel?

   A. Unplug the disk.

   B. Check the system BIOS.

   C. Restart the web server service.

   D. Run the `disk-detect` command.

5. Which command and option are used to set the maximum number of times a filesystem can be mounted between running `fsck`?

   A. tune2fs −c

   B. dumpe2fs

   C. tune2fs −m

   D. setmount

6. When checking filesystems with the `fsck` command, which option skips checking of the root filesystem?

   A. −A

   B. −M

   C. −R

   D. −S

7. You have connected a USB disk to the system and need to find out its connection point within the system. Which of the following is the best method for accomplishing this task?

    A. Rebooting the system

    B. Viewing the contents of `/var/log/usb.log`

    C. Connecting the drive to a USB port that you know the number of

    D. Running `dmesg` and looking for the disk

8. How many SCSI devices are supported per bus?

    A. 7 to 15

    B. 2 to 4

    C. 12

    D. 4

9. Within which folder are systemd unit configuration files stored?

    A. `/etc/system.conf.d`

    B. `/lib/system.conf.d`

    C. `/lib/systemd/system`

    D. `/etc/sysconfd`

10. You are troubleshooting a service not starting on time. Which network unit target waits until the network is up, such as with a routable IP address?

    A. `network.target`

    B. `network-online.target`

    C. `network-up.target`

    D. `network-on.target`

11. To which file should a unit file be symlinked in order to disable the unit file?

    A. `/etc/systemd/unit.disable`

    B. `/etc/systemd/disabled`

    C. `/tmp/disabled`

    D. `/dev/null`

12. You are troubleshooting a service that does not stop correctly. During troubleshooting, you find that the command to stop the service needs to be changed. Which configuration option specifies the command to execute for stopping a service?

    A. `StopCmd`

    B. `ExecStop`

    C. `StopScript`

    D. `StopSvc`

13. You are working with a service dependency issue where a service is starting even though it depends on a different service. The unit file currently lists the dependency with `Wants=`. To what should the `Wants=` be changed to in order to make the requirement stronger between the two services?

    A. `Needs=`

    B. `LoadFirst=`

    C. `Verify=`

    D. `Requires=`

14. When troubleshooting potential collisions for a network interface, which option to the `ip` command displays additional information that includes a count of collisions?

    A. `-s`

    B. `-c`

    C. `-o`

    D. `-f`

15. Which of the following is true of Linux swap space?

    A. Swap is used to hold temporary database tables.

    B. Swap is used as additional memory when there is insufficient RAM.

    C. Swap is used by the mail server for security.

    D. Swap is used to scrub data from the network temporarily.

16. You are running a Linux instance on a cloud provider and notice slow performance. Which CPU time metric helps to determine if cycles are being used by other instances on the same hypervisor?

    A. HyperV

    B. CircleTime

    C. Steal

    D. CrossProc

17. You need to examine the hardware to determine if the processor supports virtualization. Which command can be used to display the status of virtualization support?

    A. `cpustat`

    B. `cpuinfo`

    C. `lscpu`

    D. `brcxpu`

18. When you're troubleshooting a file access issue for a user, which command can be run in order to determine if the issue is related to SELinux policy?

    A. `ls -P`

    B. `pol --info`

    C. `showpol`

    D. `ls -Z`

19. Which of the following commands can be used to help troubleshoot an application crash that may be related to system calls?

A. strace

B. systemt

C. systemd-trace

D. systemd-debug

20. Which setting should be changed in journald.conf in order to ensure that journal log files are written to disk?

A. Location=

B. Persistence=

C. Storage=

D. WriteTo=

21. As part of troubleshooting services not starting on time, you need to add a service to be started before another to an already-existing systemd unit file. What delimiter is used to separate services with the Before= and After= configuration options in a systemd unit file?

A. Comma

B. Semicolon

C. Colon

D. Space

22. When using the du command to diagnose which directories are large, you would like to summarize the output in a more human-friendly format. Which option(s) should be used?

A. --summarize

B. -uh

C. -h

D. -sh

23. Which option to tune2fs forces the operation to complete in the event of a problem such as corruption?

A. -f

B. -m

C. -x

D. -k

24. You have purchased new SSD hardware that uses the NVMe protocol, but you cannot find the disks in the normal /dev/sd* location where you have traditionally found such storage. In which location should you look for these drives?

A. /dev/nd*

B. /dev/nvme*

C. /dev/nv*

D. /dev/nvme/*

25. Which of the following commands mounts /dev/sda1 in the /boot partition?

    A. mount /dev/sda /boot

    B. mount /boot /dev/sda1

    C. mount /dev/sda1 /boot

    D. mount -dev sda1 /boot

26. Using vmstat to examine the run queues on a single processor system with four cores reveals that there are six jobs in 'r' status. Which of the following describes the current situation?

    A. There are four jobs running and two waiting in the run queue.

    B. There are six jobs running.

    C. There is one job running and there are five in the run queue.

    D. The 'r' column describes regulated processes and not the run queue.

27. Which command is used to search for physical volumes for use with LVM?

    A. lvmcreate

    B. pvcreate

    C. lvmdiskscan

    D. lvmscan

28. Which configuration option within a systemd timer unit file causes the program to execute a certain number of seconds or minutes after the system has booted?

    A. OnBootSec

    B. StartupCommand

    C. StartCmdSec

    D. CmdSec

29. You are troubleshooting an issue reported by a user and suspect it may be related to their environment variables. What command should the user run in order to view the current settings for their environment when using Bash?

    A. environment

    B. env

    C. listenv

    D. echoenv

30. Which command can be used to determine the default CPU scheduling priority for a given user?

    A. nice

    B. sked

    C. pri

    D. sched

31. Users are reporting that various programs are crashing on the server. Examining logs, you see that certain processes are reporting out-of-memory conditions. Which command can you use to see the overall memory usage, including available swap space?

    A. `tree`

    B. `pgrep`

    C. `uptime`

    D. `free`

32. You suspect that there is high CPU utilization on the system and need to perform further troubleshooting. Which command can be used to determine the current load average along with information on the amount of time since the last boot of the system?

    A. `uptime`

    B. `sysinfo`

    C. `bash`

    D. `ls -u`

33. You need to start a long-running process that requires a terminal and foreground processing. However, you cannot leave your terminal window open due to security restrictions. Which command will enable you to start the process and return at a later time to continue the session?

    A. `fg`

    B. `bg`

    C. `kill`

    D. `screen`

34. You are troubleshooting an NFS filesystem that will not unmount. Which option within the mount point's systemd mount file can be used to force the mount point to be unmounted?

    A. `NFSUmount=`

    B. `Timeout=`

    C. `Options=`

    D. `ForceUnmount=`

35. You have backgrounded several tasks using &. Which command can be used to view the current list of running tasks that have been backgrounded?

    A. `procs`

    B. `plist`

    C. `jobs`

    D. `free`

36. You suspect there is a runaway process on the server. Which command can be used to kill any process by using its name?

   A. `killproc`

   B. `killname`

   C. `killall`

   D. `kill -f`

37. You are using `top` to investigate a report of the system processing being slow. A developer reports that that the `id` column within `%Cpu(s)` output of `top` is reporting as 98.3 and they would like to know which PID is associated with that much CPU. What should you tell them?

   A. The `id` column represents the average delay for a process.

   B. The `id` column is CPU time related to user processes.

   C. The process ID will need to be found with the `ps` command to determine which PID corresponds to the `id` output.

   D. The number that corresponds to `id` represents idle time of the CPU and not the time used by a process ID.

38. When an `fsck` is running on an ext3 filesystem, the process is taking longer than expected and requiring input from the administrator to fix issues. What option could be added to `fsck` next time so that the command will automatically attempt to fix errors without intervention?

   A. `-o`

   B. `-V`

   C. `-y`

   D. `-f`

39. You are using a storage area network (SAN) that keeps causing errors on your Linux system due to an improper kernel module created by the SAN vendor. When the SAN sends updates, it causes the filesystem to be mounted as read-only. Which command and option can you use to change the behavior of the filesystem to account for the SAN bug?

   A. `mount --continue`

   B. `tune2fs -e continue`

   C. `mkfs --no-remount`

   D. `mount -o remount`

40. Which command is used to format a swap partition?

   A. `fdisk`

   B. `mkswap`

   C. `formatswap`

   D. `format -s`

41. The system is running out of disk space within the home directory partition, and quotas have not been enabled. Which command can you use to determine the directories that might contain large files?

    A. du

    B. df

    C. ls

    D. locate

42. Which option is set on a filesystem in order to enable user-level quotas?

    A. quotaon

    B. enquota=user

    C. usrquota

    D. userquota

43. Which option to quotacheck is used to create the files for the first time?

    A. -f

    B. -u

    C. -m

    D. -c

44. While troubleshooting a file permission issue, you wrote a Bash script containing an if conditional. Which of the following tests will determine whether a file exists and can be read by the user executing the test?

    A. -e

    B. -s

    C. -a

    D. -r

45. Which start-up type is the default for systemd services if no Type= or BusName= options are specified?

    A. oneshot

    B. exec

    C. simple

    D. none

46. Which command can be used as a means to elevate privileges to run a command as root?

    A. asroot

    B. elev

    C. sudo

    D. runroot

47. To which shell can a user account be set if they are not allowed to log in interactively to the computer?

   A. /bin/bash

   B. /bin/tcsh

   C. /bin/zsh

   D. /bin/false

48. When troubleshooting disk usage, which of the following commands is used to determine the amount of disk space used by systemd journal log files?

   A. journalctl --disk

   B. journalctl -du

   C. journalctl --disk-usage

   D. journalctl -ls

49. Which command can be used to determine the current time-zone setting while trouble-shooting a time-zone configuration issue?

   A. timedatectl status

   B. timedate --gettz

   C. tzdata --list

   D. timezone --show

50. Which of the following is not used as a private address for internal, non-Internet use?

   A. 172.16.4.2

   B. 192.168.40.3

   C. 10.74.5.244

   D. 143.236.32.231

51. Which of the following commands adds a default gateway of 192.168.1.1 for interface eth0?

   A. route add default gateway 192.168.1.1 eth0

   B. eth0 --dg 192.168.1.1

   C. route add default gw 192.168.1.1 eth0

   D. route define eth0 192.168.1.1

52. Which option for the host command will query for the authoritative nameservers for a given domain?

   A. -t ns

   B. -t all

   C. -ns

   D. -named

53. Which option for the `ping` command enables you to choose the interface from which the ICMP packets will be generated?

    A. `-i`

    B. `-I`

    C. `-t`

    D. `-a`

54. Which of the following commands queries for the mail servers for the domain `example.com`?

    A. `dig example.com mx`

    B. `dig example.com`

    C. `host -t smtp example.com`

    D. `dig example.com smtp`

55. You need to test SSL connectivity to a web server at `www.example.com`. Which of the following commands accomplishes this task?

    A. `rd www.example.com -L`

    B. `curSSH https://www.example.com`

    C. `openssl https://www.example.com:443`

    D. `openssl s_client -connect www.example.com:443`

56. Which command can be used to listen for netlink messages on a network?

    A. `ip monitor`

    B. `netlink -a`

    C. `ip netlink`

    D. `route`

57. Which of the following `dig` commands sends the query for `example.com` directly to the server at 192.168.2.5 rather than to a locally configured resolver?

    A. `dig example.com @192.168.2.5`

    B. `dig -t 192.168.2.5 example.com`

    C. `dig -s 192.168.2.5 example.com`

    D. `dig server=192.168.2.5 example.com`

58. Which of the following commands will enumerate the `hosts` database?

    A. `getent hosts`

    B. `gethosts`

    C. `nslookup`

    D. `host`

59. Which of the following configuration lines will set the DNS server to 192.168.1.4 using `/etc/resolv.conf`?

    A. `dns 192.168.1.4`

    B. `dns-server 192.168.1.4`

    C. `nameserver 192.168.1.4`

    D. `name-server 192.168.1.4`

60. Which of the following commands adds a route to the server for the network 192.168.51.0/24 through its gateway of 192.168.51.1?

    A. `route add -net 192.168.51.0 netmask 255.255.255.0 gw 192.168.51.1`

    B. `route add -net 192.168.51/24 gw 192.168.1.51`

    C. `route -net 192.168.51.0/24 192.168.51.1`

    D. `route add 192.168.51.1 -n 192.168.51.0//255.255.255.0`

61. Which of the following commands shows network services or sockets that are currently listening along with sockets that are not listening?

    A. `netstat -a`

    B. `netlink -a`

    C. `sockets -f`

    D. `opensock -l`

62. Which of the following represents a correct configuration line for `/etc/hosts`?

    A. `192.168.1.4 cwa.braingia.org cwa`

    B. `cwa.braingia.org cwa 192.168.1.4`

    C. `cwa.braingia.org 192.168.1.8 alias cwa`

    D. `alias cwa.braingia.org cwa 192.168.1.4`

63. Which command can be used to determine how much time a Linux command takes?

    A. `time`

    B. `cmdtime`

    C. `timeproc`

    D. `proctime`

64. Which of the following commands will change the default gateway to 192.168.1.1 using eth0?

    A. `ip route default gw 192.168.1.1`

    B. `ip route change default via 192.168.1.1 dev eth0`

    C. `ip route default gw update 192.168.1.1`

    D. `ip route update default 192.168.1.1 eth0`

65. Which option to `dumpe2fs` displays the bad blocks for a given partition?

  A. -bb

  B. -C

  C. -b

  D. -f

66. Which option to `xfs_check` is used to verify a filesystem that is stored in a file?

  A. -v

  B. -a

  C. -f

  D. -d

67. Which option within a systemd mount file specifies the filesystem to be mounted?

  A. FSPath=

  B. Path=

  C. Where=

  D. What=

68. Assume that you want to enable local client services to go to hosts on the network without needing to fully qualify the name by adding the domain for either `example.com` or `example.org`. Which option in `/etc/resolv.conf` will provide this functionality?

  A. search

  B. domain

  C. local-domain

  D. local-order

69. Which of the following commands prevents traffic from reaching the host 192.168.1.3?

  A. route add -host 192.168.1.3 reject

  B. route -nullroute 192.168.1.3

  C. route add -null 192.168.1.3

  D. route add -block 192.168.1.3

70. Which of the following describes a primary difference between `traceroute` and `tracepath`?

  A. The `traceroute` command requires root privileges.

  B. The `tracepath` command provides the MTU for each hop, whereas `traceroute` does not.

  C. The `tracepath` command cannot be used for tracing a path on an external network.

  D. The `traceroute` command is not compatible with IPv6.

71. Which of the following commands will emulate the `ping` command in Microsoft Windows, where the `ping` is sent for four packets and then the command exits?

   A. `ping -n 4`

   B. `ping -t 4`

   C. `ping -p 4`

   D. `ping -c 4`

72. Which option to `journalctl` displays log messages as they are being logged?

   A. `--tail`

   B. `--du`

   C. `-f`

   D. `-m`

73. Which of the following commands should be executed after running `ip route change`?

   A. `ip route flush cache`

   B. `ip route reload`

   C. `ip route cache reload`

   D. `ip route restart`

74. Which option should be used to send a DNS query for an SPF record with `dig`?

   A. `-t txt`

   B. `-t spf`

   C. `-t mx`

   D. `-t mailspf`

75. When troubleshooting a connectivity issue, you have found that you can reach a server via the Web but cannot ping it and suspect that there are dropped packets. Which of the following best describes a possible cause for this scenario?

   A. TCP traffic has been blocked at the firewall.

   B. The DNS lookup is failing.

   C. ICMP traffic has been blocked.

   D. There is a reject route in place.

76. When you're viewing the available routes using the `route` command, one route contains the flags UG and the others contain U. What does the letter G signify in the route table?

   A. The G signifies that the route is good.

   B. The G signifies that the route is unavailable.

   C. The G signifies that this is a gateway.

   D. The G signifies that the route is an aggregate.

77. Which of the following commands requests a zone transfer of `example.org` from the server at 192.168.1.4?

A. `dig example.org @192.168.1.4 axfr`

B. `dig example.org @192.168.1.4`

C. `dig example.org @192.168.1.4 xfer`

D. `dig example.org #192.168.1.4 xfer`

78. You are troubleshooting a disk space issue and notice that the journal files are consuming too much space. Which option within journald.conf sets a limit on how much disk space can be used?

A. `MaxDisk=`

B. `SystemMaxUse=`

C. `MaxSpace=`

D. `SpaceLimit=`

79. Although no dependencies may appear in a unit file, a service with a `Type=dbus` depends on which service?

A. `dbus.socket`

B. `dbus.run`

C. `dbus.dep`

D. `dbus.svc`

80. Which of the following commands scans the IP address 192.168.1.154 for open ports?

A. `nmap 192.168.1.154`

B. `lsof 192.168.1.154`

C. `netstat 192.168.1.154`

D. `netmap 192.168.1.154`

81. You are troubleshooting an NFS filesystem that will not mount. Which option within the mount point's systemd mount file is used to specify the type of filesystem being mounted?

A. `FSType=`

B. `Type=`

C. `App=`

D. `MountType=`

82. What is the file extension used with systemd unit files that provide time-based control of services?

A. `.svc`

B. `.cron`

C. `.sked`

D. `.timer`

83. You are using `nmap` to scan a host for open ports. However, the server is blocking ICMP echo requests. Which option to `nmap` can you set in order to continue the scan?

    A. -P0

    B. -no-ping

    C. -s0

    D. -ping-0

84. Which option within `/etc/security/limits.conf` is used to control the number of times a given account can log in simultaneously?

    A. nlogins

    B. loginmax

    C. maxlogins

    D. loginlimit

85. Which option to `nmap` sets the scan to use TCP SYN packets for finding open ports?

    A. -sS

    B. -sT

    C. -sY

    D. -type SYN

86. Which option to `tune2fs` enables the specification of various journal options such as specifying the location of the journal itself?

    A. -a

    B. -J

    C. -x

    D. -A

87. You are troubleshooting high latency and low throughput with a disk and using `iostat` to assess performance. Which option to `iostat` displays information on a per-partition basis for block devices?

    A. -a

    B. -c

    C. -d

    D. -p

88. Which of the following commands displays blocks in and blocks out as related to I/O?

    A. iorpt

    B. iptraf

    C. vmswap

    D. vmstat

89. Which of the following commands can be used to display a list of currently logged-in users along with the current load average and time since last reboot?

    A. `uptime`

    B. `w`

    C. `swap`

    D. `sysinfo`

90. You need to examine the hardware to determine the amount of memory on the system and the block size. Which command can be used for this purpose?

    A. `free`

    B. `memstat`

    C. `lsmem`

    D. `memx`

91. While troubleshooting high latency, you need to collect data on throughput. Which of the following monitoring tools can use SNMP and scripts to collect data for performance-related graphing such as throughput and bandwidth?

    A. `ptop`

    B. `pstree`

    C. Cacti

    D. Grafr

92. Which swapon option silently skips those swap partitions that do not exist?

    A. `-u`

    B. `-e`

    C. `-i`

    D. `-o`

93. Which of the following abbreviations is used to signify system time CPU percentage in the output of the `top` command?

    A. `sys`

    B. `us`

    C. `sy`

    D. `system%`

94. Which of the following commands deactivates swap space?

    A. `swapoff`

    B. `swap -off`

    C. `unmountswap`

    D. `uswap`

95. Which of the following swapon options displays information on the size of swap space along with its used space?

    A. --list

    B. -a

    C. --show

    D. -h

96. Which of the following commands displays information about a given physical volume in an LVM setup?

    A. pvdisp

    B. pvlist

    C. pvdisplay

    D. pvl

97. Which of the following commands looks for LVM physical volumes and volume groups involved in an LVM configuration?

    A. vgscan

    B. lvmscan

    C. lvlist

    D. pvlist

98. Which of the following commands is used to display a list of physical volumes involved in LVM?

    A. pvdisp

    B. pvlist

    C. pvscan

    D. pvmm

99. While troubleshooting interface errors, you need to examine the protocol family supported by an interface. When you're using the ip command, which protocol family is used as the default if not otherwise specified?

    A. tcpip

    B. ip

    C. inet

    D. arp

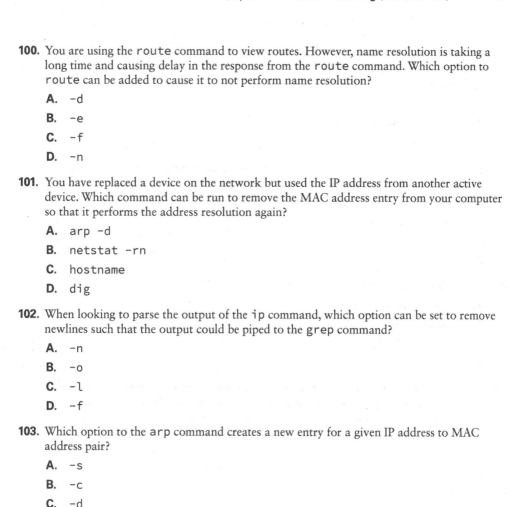

100. You are using the `route` command to view routes. However, name resolution is taking a long time and causing delay in the response from the `route` command. Which option to `route` can be added to cause it to not perform name resolution?

A. -d

B. -e

C. -f

D. -n

101. You have replaced a device on the network but used the IP address from another active device. Which command can be run to remove the MAC address entry from your computer so that it performs the address resolution again?

A. `arp -d`

B. `netstat -rn`

C. `hostname`

D. `dig`

102. When looking to parse the output of the `ip` command, which option can be set to remove newlines such that the output could be piped to the `grep` command?

A. -n

B. -o

C. -l

D. -f

103. Which option to the `arp` command creates a new entry for a given IP address to MAC address pair?

A. -s

B. -c

C. -d

D. --add

104. Which option to `tcpdump` displays a list of available interfaces on which `tcpdump` can operate?

A. -a

B. -d

C. -D

D. -i

105. Which option to `nmap` will cause it to always perform name resolution?

A. -n

B. -R

C. -b

D. -a

106. Which of the following commands provides a live `traceroute` of the route between two hosts, updating the information for each hop in near real time?

    A. `traceroute --live`

    B. `mtr`

    C. `route -update`

    D. `liveroute`

107. You are using a local RAID array and investigating a performance issue. When using `mdadm` in monitor mode, which option sets the polling interval?

    A. `--delay`

    B. `--internal`

    C. `--interval`

    D. `--poll`

108. When viewing the results of a `traceroute`, you see `!H`. To what does `!H` refer?

    A. Network unreachable

    B. Host available

    C. Host unreachable

    D. High length

109. Assuming that policy routing has been enabled in the kernel, which option to the `ping` command can be used to mark the outgoing request appropriately in order to indicate that the packet should be processed according to a particular policy?

    A. `-m`

    B. `-a`

    C. `-p`

    D. `-k`

110. When you're troubleshooting a possible issue with bad blocks on a disk, which option to `fsck` will report statistics such as CPU time used on completion of the `fsck` operation?

    A. `-s`

    B. `-r`

    C. `-l`

    D. `-f`

111. Which of the following files provides information on memory utilization, including free memory, buffers, cache usage, and several additional items?

    A. `/proc/cpuinfo`

    B. `/proc/memtime`

    C. `/proc/memuse`

    D. `/proc/meminfo`

112. Which scan mode for nmap provides an Xmas scan?

A. -sT

B. -sS

C. -sP

D. -sX

113. Which option to tcpdump sets the snapshot length of packets to capture?

A. -s

B. -l

C. -d

D. -c

114. On which port does the ping command operate for ICMP echo requests?

A. 53

B. 1337

C. 33433

D. No port

115. When running the df command, you need to change the scale such that the report shows terabytes instead of bytes. Which option will accomplish this task?

A. -ST

B. -BT

C. -j

D. -T

116. Which option to mke2fs is used to check for bad blocks during filesystem creation?

A. -a

B. -b

C. -c

D. -d

117. Which option to the ping command shows latency rather than round-trip time?

A. -L

B. -i

C. -U

D. -d

118. You suspect that bandwidth limitations may be preventing large files from transferring in a timely manner. Which of the following commands is used to measure network throughput?

A. tp

B. iperf

C. ith

D. ithrough

119. You would like to monitor interrupt usage in real time on a Linux server in order to troubleshoot communication ports usage. Which of the following commands can be used for this purpose?

A. `int`

B. `moni`

C. `itop`

D. `imon`

120. You are configuring an RDMA interface. Which of the following commands displays information about InfiniBand devices?

A. `ibmon`

B. `ibstat`

C. `rdmon`

D. `rdstat`

121. You need to increase the performance of process ID 4382 by changing its priority. Which of the following commands will accomplish this task?

A. `renice -5 -p 4382`

B. `renice 5 -p 4382`

C. `renice 100 4382`

D. `renice 4382 +5`

122. Which option to `netstat` is used to disable DNS or hostname lookups?

A. `-b`

B. `-h`

C. `-q`

D. `-n`

123. You would like to find all of the process IDs associated with the `sshd` process on an Ubuntu system. Which of the following commands accomplishes this task?

A. `ps -sshd`

B. `pidof sshd`

C. `pids sshd`

D. `ps --a=sshd`

124. Which kill signal sends a hangup to a given process?

A. 1

B. 5

C. 24

D. 30

125. Which of the following commands displays the current target runlevel on a systemd system?

    A. `ls -l /etc/systemd/system/default.target`

    B. `systemctl default-target`

    C. `systemd default-target`

    D. `ls -l /etc/systemd/system-default.target`

126. You would like to change the byte-to-inode ratio on a new filesystem in order to prevent inode exhaustion. Which option to `mke2fs` accomplishes this task?

    A. `-b`

    B. `-r`

    C. `-i`

    D. `-u`

127. Which directory contains information on FibreChannel HBA ports?

    A. `/sys/fc/ports`

    B. `/sys/class/hba`

    C. `/sys/class/fc_host`

    D. `/sys/class/fc/ports`

128. Which type of module interface for PAM is used to set a policy such as the time of day that a user can log in?

    A. `auth`

    B. `account`

    C. `password`

    D. `policy`

129. You need to create a restrictive access control list (ACL) on a server. Which policy should be the default for the `INPUT` chain within the firewall?

    A. `deny`

    B. `permit`

    C. `accept`

    D. `discard`

130. Which option to the `ls` command displays the ownership attributes, including user and group owners of a given file or directory?

    A. `-o`

    B. `-a`

    C. `-l`

    D. `-d`

131. When creating a daemon process that will be used on the local server, which of the following communication methods should be used?

   A. Localhost/network

   B. Socket

   C. Message-passing

   D. RDP

132. When using the `free` command to determine memory usage, which column shows the memory used by the kernel for things like kernel buffers?

   A. used

   B. shared

   C. buffers

   D. cache

133. Which of the following commands provides a command-line interface into Network Manager?

   A. nmc

   B. dmc

   C. nmcli

   D. netman

134. Which command displays network usage in a top-like interface?

   A. iftop

   B. iptop

   C. ptop

   D. netcap

135. You suspect saturation is affecting network performance with your Linux server. Which command can be used to help determine the amount of traffic being passed through a given interface?

   A. netp

   B. sat

   C. iptraf

   D. ipsat

136. You are looking to optimize the I/O scheduler for your Linux server. Which I/O scheduling algorithm is the default?

   A. deadline

   B. noop

   C. cfq

   D. iqueue

137. You would like to efficiently manage firewall rules such that you can define a group of IP addresses to which a single rule can be applied. Which command enables you to create a group of IP addresses?

A. `ipgroup`

B. `iptables -group`

C. `addrgroup`

D. `ipset`

138. You are receiving reports of timeouts from users attempting to SSH between servers. Which command should be used to help troubleshoot these reports?

A. `tcptraceroute`

B. `ping`

C. `telnet`

D. `ps`

139. Which command can be used to capture network traffic in `pcap` format for later analysis by a tool like Wireshark?

A. `tcpcap`

B. `pdump`

C. `tshark`

D. `pcapr`

140. You need to determine the owner of an IP address. You have attempted to use `nslookup` to determine the hostname, but there was no PTR record for the IP. Which command can be used to determine who owns the IP address?

A. `iplookup`

B. `ipowner`

C. `whois`

D. `bg`

141. Which command can be used to help diagnose latency issues with a disk?

A. `diskstat`

B. `statd`

C. `fdisk`

D. `ioping`

142. Which command can be used to trigger the kernel to update the partition table?

A. `ifdisk`

B. `partup`

C. `partprobe`

D. `uppart`

143. Which of the following commands can be used to display historical performance data across several different parameters?

    A. `sar`

    B. `kernperf`

    C. `pkern`

    D. `perfshow`

144. Which option to `sysctl` displays all of the available parameters?

    A. `-a`

    B. `-b`

    C. `-c`

    D. `-d`

145. When examining output from the `state` column of the `ps` command, there is a process with a state of D. What state is that process currently in?

    A. Debug

    B. Interruptible sleep

    C. Uninterruptible sleep

    D. Dead

146. You are troubleshooting a system startup problem that prevents the system from fully booting into a graphical user interface (GUI). Which systemd target could be used to further troubleshoot the issue?

    A. Poweroff

    B. Multiuser

    C. Reboot

    D. SafeMode

147. You are troubleshooting printer access on a Linux system. On which port does the CUPS printing daemon listen by default?

    A. 25

    B. 342

    C. 631

    D. 316

148. What is the required extension for systemd mount files?

    A. `.mount`

    B. `.service`

    C. `.fs`

    D. `.mountd`

149. Which utility can be used to find SELinux context violations?

    A.   `sestat`

    B.   `secv`

    C.   `convio`

    D.   `ausearch`

150. You have added a new RAID adapter to the system. Which command can be used to ensure that the adapter was detected by the kernel?

    A.   `showraid`

    B.   `lsadapt`

    C.   `dmesg`

    D.   `raidlist`

151. Which option is used to send a signal to a process when using `pkill`?

    A.   `-<SIGNAL>`

    B.   `-s`

    C.   `-i`

    D.   `-h`

152. You are troubleshooting a directory permission issue. The directory and all subdirectories are owned by root. Within the top-level directory there is another directory that has 755 permissions on it. However, a non-root user cannot obtain a directory listing of that subdirectory. Which of the following might be the issue?

    A.   Directory permissions from a higher-level directory do not allow a directory listing.

    B.   Directory permissions need to be 777 on the subdirectory.

    C.   The write permission is needed for the subdirectory.

    D.   The other permission needs to be 7 for the subdirectory.

153. What is the default request size for `ioping`?

    A.   4 bytes

    B.   4 KB

    C.   512 KB

    D.   1024 KB

154. Within which file can you determine the current I/O scheduler algorithm?

    A.   `/sys/block/<device>/queue/scheduler`

    B.   `/sys/block/<device>/iosch`

    C.   `/etc/iostat.cfg`

    D.   `/etc/default/ioscheduler`

155. Which option to iftop prevents hostname lookups from occurring?

    A. -d

    B. -a

    C. -t

    D. -n

156. Which command can be used within the nslookup CLI to change the server to which the query will be sent?

    A. dest

    B. server

    C. srv

    D. auth

157. What are the minimum permissions needed for a user to write into a directory for which they are not the owner and are not in a group that owns the directory?

    A. Write

    B. Read/write/execute

    C. Read/execute

    D. Write/execute

158. Which of the following protocols provides a means for authentication to occur external to the Linux system?

    A. SSL

    B. SSH

    C. LDAP

    D. AD

159. When creating a file, a user is receiving an error. The file is very large. What command can the user execute in order to determine the file size limitation?

    A. limit

    B. ulimit

    C. filelimit

    D. flimit

160. What are the minimum permissions for a Bash script so that it is executable by everyone without needing to prefix the command with the word *bash*?

    A. 755

    B. 644

    C. 777

    D. 222

161. Which option within a systemd timer unit file is used to specify when a job should run?

A. OnCalendar=

B. Time=

C. RunAt=

D. TimedEvent=

162. Which of the following abbreviations is used to signify time spent waiting for I/O in the output of the top command?

A. wi

B. io

C. wa

D. iotime%

163. Which of the following commands retrieves the current group membership list for a user?

A. groupmem

B. groups

C. lsgr

D. getgr

164. You have added a swap disk to a Linux server and have executed mkswap. However, on examination of the output from the free command, you see that the swap space is not being used. Which command do you need to execute?

A. swapon

B. swap-en

C. actswap

D. swpact

165. Which option to ioping sets the size of the request?

A. -m

B. -n

C. -f

D. -s

166. Which option to the dumpe2fs command can be used to display blocks that are reserved because of being marked as bad?

A. -v

B. -f

C. -b

D. -m

167. Which command can be used to obtain extended hardware and device information, including information about the motherboard?

   A. mbhw

   B. lsmb

   C. dmidecode

   D. lsallhw

168. You have found that a SATA disk within a RAID array has gone bad. Which option to mdadm removes the disk from the RAID array, placing it into a degraded state?

   A. rm

   B. fail

   C. rem

   D. del

169. Which option to whois suppresses the legal disclaimer information from certain registries?

   A. -L

   B. -q

   C. -H

   D. -s

170. Which option to iftop sets the interface on which iftop will listen?

   A. -m

   B. -i

   C. -l

   D. -a

171. To which file can you echo "- - -" in order to cause a scan of a SCSI host adapter for new disks?

   A. /sys/bus/scsi/hostscan

   B. /sys/class/scsi_host/hostN/scan

   C. /sys/class/<host>/scan

   D. /etc/scsiadm

172. A local user is having password issues. When local authentication is performed, which file provides encrypted password information?

   A. /etc/passwd

   B. /etc/shadow

   C. /etc/encrpass

   D. /etc/passen

173. Which option within a systemd unit file sets the user that a service will run as?

- **A.** RunAs=
- **B.** User=
- **C.** UID=
- **D.** ID=

174. The out-of-memory killer has been killing some processes on the system and you suspect that there are memory leaks. Which columns within ps output are helpful for determining current memory usage for a given process?

- **A.** size and rss
- **B.** mem and swap
- **C.** free and cache
- **D.** phy and vir

175. Which signal number corresponds to SIGKILL?

- **A.** 1
- **B.** 5
- **C.** 9
- **D.** 12

176. Which of the following classes is the default class type queried by the host command?

- **A.** EX
- **B.** HS
- **C.** FO
- **D.** IN

177. Which option to the netstat command displays the current routing table?

- **A.** -r
- **B.** -t
- **C.** -a
- **D.** -l

178. Which option to the du command provides summary output?

- **A.** -o
- **B.** -h
- **C.** -s
- **D.** -u

179. Which of the following commands can be used to find zombie processes?

    A. ps -Z

    B. ps | grep Z

    C. ps | grep zombie

    D. ps -a -z

180. Which command can be used to list all of the detected hardware within a system?

    A. lshw

    B. showhw

    C. lspic

    D. slist

181. Which option to the ioping command sets the number of requests to send?

    A. -r

    B. -c

    C. -n

    D. -a

182. Which process state indicates that the process is currently running?

    A. C

    B. R

    C. T

    D. V

183. A device mismatch is reported by pvs. Which command rescans volume groups after resolving the mismatch?

    A. pv -scanvl

    B. vgscan

    C. rescanvg

    D. vg -scan

184. Which setting disables automatic power state management on an NVMe drive?

    A. ps_max_latency_us

    B. apst_ps_latency

    C. apst_off

    D. ps_apst_enable

185. Which timer expression configures a systemd timer unit file to execute once a week?

    A. OnCalendar=*/7

    B. Time=Week

    C. OnCalendar=weekly

    D. TimedEvent=Sunday

186. Assuming that /var/log/journal exists, which type of storage is used when the Storage= option is set to auto within journald.conf?

A. none

B. journal

C. persistent

D. volatile

187. You need to determine the score at which a process will be killed by the out-of-memory killer. Which file can be examined to determine the current setting for that process?

A. oom_score

B. oom_setting

C. outofmem_num

D. ooe-l

188. Which option can be set for a systemd mount point in order to cause the boot process to continue even if the filesystem cannot be mounted?

A. bootcon

B. nowait

C. nofail

D. skip

189. You need to send a command-line argument into the command started with ExecStart= within a systemd service file. Which character is used to indicate that a command-line argument will be passed?

A. @

B. ^

C. >

D. $

190. Which option to the su command enables the user to log in as a different user?

A. -e

B. -u

C. -l

D. -m

191. Which option to lscpu produces output in JSON format?

A. -J

B. -o

C. --output

D. -s

192. When troubleshooting certificate issues you need to view the entire certificate chain. Which option to `openssl s_client` displays the certificate chain?

   A. `-chain`

   B. `-certchain`

   C. `-showchain`

   D. `-showcerts`

193. You are examining a login issue for a user and you need to determine where their home directory is located. Within which file can you find their home directory?

   A. `/etc/passwd`

   B. `/etc/homedirs`

   C. `/etc/user.conf`

   D. `/etc/defaults/user`

194. Which option is used to configure how to reload a service using a systemd unit file?

   A. `ExecReload=`

   B. `Reload=`

   C. `ConfRel=`

   D. `ExecRes=`

195. Which expression is used to define a timer that should be executed every minute with a systemd timer?

   A. `permin`

   B. `per_min`

   C. `minute`

   D. `minutely`

196. Which option to `chage` is used to set the number of days of inactivity after password expiration until an account is locked?

   A. `-I`

   B. `-X`

   C. `-EX`

   D. `-S`

197. Which option within `/etc/login.defs` is used to configure the maximum number of days until a password change is required?

   A. `MAX_PASS_AGE`

   B. `PASSWORD_AGE`

   C. `PASS_MAX_DAYS`

   D. `DAYS_PASSEXP`

198. You are troubleshooting I/O-related issues and need extended information about disk performance. Which option to `iostat` displays additional information?

A. -u

B. -l

C. -x

D. -e

199. Which option to `tune2fs` displays the current inode size of a filesystem?

A. -n

B. -l

C. -a

D. -f

200. Which `systemctl` command needs to be executed after making a change to a systemd-related configuration file?

A. `systemctl daemon-reload`

B. `systemctl reconfig`

C. `systemctl regen`

D. `systemctl setup`

201. Within the `[Timer]` section of a systemd timer file, which configuration directive is used to specify the process or service to start?

A. `Service=`

B. `Unit=`

C. `Proc=`

D. `Startup=`

202. When managing a service with a `Type=exec` setting in its unit file, what needs to happen in order for systemd to mark it as successfully started?

A. The process needs to return from its `execve()` call.

B. The process needs to return from its `fork()` call.

C. The process needs to send a signal to `systemfork()`.

D. The process needs to send the `running()` signal to `systemctl`.

203. Which configuration option is used within a systemd unit file to configure how to handle an out-of-memory killer?

A. `OOMSetting=`

B. `OOM=`

C. `OOMPolicy=`

D. `OOMSignal=`

204. Which option to `renice` will increase the priority for all processes by the `apache` user?

  A. `renice -1 -A apache`

  B. `renice -1 -u apache`

  C. `renice -1 -UA apache`

  D. `renice apache -a -1`

205. Which option to `repquota` does not resolve UIDs and GIDs to their names?

  A. `-n`

  B. `-b`

  C. `-d`

  D. `-m`

206. Which command is used to change the SELinux type for a file?

  A. `chcon`

  B. `settype`

  C. `typeset`

  D. `setype`

207. While troubleshooting a file access issue, you find that the permissions allow the `accounting` group but that the user is not a member of the group. Which option to the `usermod` command adds a user to a group?

  A. `-ag`

  B. `-groupadd`

  C. `-a -G`

  D. `-addgr`

208. When working with a virtual machine on a hypervisor that handles I/O scheduling, which scheduling mechanism is suggested for virtual machines?

  A. `cfq`

  B. `noop`

  C. `timed`

  D. `vm-opt`

209. When you're using `journalctl` to investigate an issue, which entries are shown first?

  A. Newest entries are shown first.

  B. Oldest entries are shown first.

  C. Failed entries are shown first.

  D. Smallest entries are shown first.

210. While troubleshooting a script that runs via `cron`, you find that the script needs elevated privileges through `sudo` but there will not be a way to enter a password through the script. Which option within `/etc/sudoers` enables the command to be executed without prompting for a password?

    A. PASS=NO

    B. SKIPPASS

    C. NOPASSWD

    D. NOPASS

211. Services are not starting in the correct order. Which configuration option can be used within a systemd service unit file to delay a service from starting until another has started?

    A. Before=

    B. Dep=

    C. Order=

    D. Prior=

212. You are starting a containerized service through systemd but need to ensure that enough memory has been allocated to the container. Which option within a systemd unit file verifies that the specified amount of memory is available?

    A. MinRAM=

    B. VerifyMem=

    C. VerMem=

    D. ConditionMemory=

213. You are looking for systemd-related unit files that have been created locally on the system. Within which directory are administrator-created unit files found?

    A. /etc/systemd/system

    B. /etc/systemd/admin

    C. /etc/systemd/adminunit

    D. /etc/systemd.admin

214. Which systemd target stops the system but does not power it down?

    A. poweroff.target

    B. stop.target

    C. offline.target

    D. halt.target

215. When formatting the `Type=` option in a systemd mount file, you need to examine the man page referred to as `mount(8)`. Which of the following commands ensures that you're viewing the 8th level man page for `mount`?

   A. `man mount 8`

   B. `man mount_8`

   C. `man 8 mount`

   D. `man -n 8 mount`

216. Which of the following commands can be used to determine if an interface link is operational?

   A. `ip link`

   B. `ip state`

   C. `eth state`

   D. `int state`

217. Which target in iptables can be used to log packets that are dropped and can be helpful in determining the cause of packets being lost or blocked?

   A. `INV`

   B. `DEBUG`

   C. `LOG`

   D. `CHAIN`

218. When you're troubleshooting a system that won't boot, which of the following lines can be placed on the kernel command line in order to invoke a debugging shell?

   A. `debug,shell`

   B. `systemd.debug-shell=1`

   C. `shell=debug`

   D. `emerg=debug`

219. When you're rebooting a system for diagnosis of an issue, the system appears to hang. Which option can be sent to the `reboot` command in order to bypass some of the normal shutdown process?

   A. `-b`

   B. `-now`

   C. `-f`

   D. `-f0`

220. Which option to `systemctl` can be used to help find stuck jobs?

   A. `-stuck`

   B. `list-jobs`

   C. `stuck-jobs`

   D. `--hung-jobs`

221. You need to examine which services are started at a given `<target>`. Which command will accomplish this task?

   A. `systemctl show <target>`

   B. `systemctl serdep <target>`

   C. `systemctl <target> list-dep`

   D. `systemctl list-dep <target>`

222. Which systemd-related daemon is responsible for name resolution?

   A. `systemd-dns`

   B. `systemd-resolver`

   C. `systemd-nameservice`

   D. `systemd-resolved`

223. Which option to the dig command follows the DNS lookup recursively starting at the root?

   A. `+trace`

   B. `+fol`

   C. `+x`

   D. `+all`

224. When using `journalctl` to investigate an issue, which option shows the messages related to the specified unit?

   A. `-k`

   B. `-u`

   C. `-p`

   D. `-S`

225. Which command can be used to display all of the timers that are currently active with systemd?

   A. `systemctl timers`

   B. `systemctl show-timers`

   C. `systemctl list-timers`

   D. `systemctl --timers`

226. You are working with an SSD to run `fstrim` and receive the return code 64 when complete. What does 64 mean as a return code?

   A. Trim not supported.

   B. Trim succeeded.

   C. Trim succeeded on some filesystems and failed on others.

   D. Trim failed on all filesystems.

227. Which systemd target can be used to boot into a minimal system that contains a shell and basic services?

   A. `comp.target`

   B. `emergency.target`

   C. `init.target`

   D. `small.target`

228. In order to see more verbose boot messages, which keywords should be removed from the kernel boot line?

   A. `verbose`

   B. `quiet splash`

   C. `silent`

   D. `littleboot`

229. Which of the following addresses is outside of the subnet defined by 192.168.1.0/25?

   A. `192.168.1.56`

   B. `192.168.1.1`

   C. `192.168.1.100`

   D. `192.168.1.200`

230. Which option changes the amount of time that grub waits before booting into the default operating system?

   A. `wait`

   B. `timeout`

   C. `waiter`

   D. `hold`

231. While troubleshooting network congestion, which option to the `ss` command shows the overall number of network connections?

   A. `-s`

   B. `-c`

   C. `-w`

   D. `-h`

232. You are troubleshooting a storage problem, and a Serial ATA (SATA) disk or mount point may be missing. Which of the following identifiers is used by SATA disks?

   A. `/dev/hdX`

   B. `/dev/sataX`

   C. `/dev/sdX`

   D. `/disk/sataX`

233. Which file within `/etc/systemd/resolved.conf.d/` can be used to configure custom DNS servers on a system that uses systemd-resolved for name resolution?

    A. `dns_servers.conf`

    B. `resolverd.conf`

    C. `nss.conf`

    D. `dns.conf`

234. You need to configure additional logging in order to troubleshoot a daemon startup issue. Which of the following is the correct syntax and setting for `/etc/systemd/system.conf` to facilitate additional logging?

    A. `Log=All+Debug`

    B. `LogLevel=Max`

    C. `LogLevel=Debug`

    D. `Logging=all`

235. Which option to `systemctl` can be used to stop one or more jobs that are in progress?

    A. `cancel`

    B. `cancel-jobs`

    C. `--kill-jobs`

    D. `--job-kill`

236. Which command is used to change the state of the interface `eth0` to UP?

    A. `ip link set eth0 up`

    B. `bringup eth0`

    C. `ip up eth0`

    D. `ip ifup eth0`

237. Which character, when prefixed within an `ExecStart=` option, causes a failure exit status to be recorded but otherwise ignored?

    A. `I`

    B. `%`

    C. `#`

    D. `-`

238. Of the following, which is a required section within a systemd service unit file?

    A. `[Service]`

    B. `[Sys]`

    C. `[RunTimeConfig]`

    D. `[Svc]`

239. A user is using `sudo` to run a command and typed their password in wrong. They reported receiving a rude message from the system as a result. Which option has likely been enabled within `/etc/sudoers`?

   A. `fixusers`

   B. `insults`

   C. `failme`

   D. `rude`

240. When you're using `journalctl` to investigate an issue, which option reverses the display of entries so that newest are shown first?

   A. `-a`

   B. `-r`

   C. `-g`

   D. `-t`

241. Due to inode exhaustion, you would like to change the size of inodes on a filesystem. Which option to `tune2fs` can be used for this purpose?

   A. `-I`

   B. `-i`

   C. `-s`

   D. `-v`

242. Another administrator has asked you for help with a machine where user quotas are not working on the root filesystem. While you're troubleshooting the issue, which file should be present to indicate that quotas are enabled?

   A. `/user.quotas`

   B. `/root/aquota.user`

   C. `/etc/userpol.aquota`

   D. `/aquota.user`

243. Systemd is not recognizing that a service is starting correctly even though it is running. Attempts to stop the service through systemd have failed. Which configuration option in the service unit file can be used to set the command to run for this situation?

   A. `ExecStopPost=`

   B. `ExecKill=`

   C. `ExecStopReally=`

   D. `ExecReallyStop=`

244. You are troubleshooting a systemd mounted filesystem that does not appear to be working. The configuration file, `mount-snd.mount`, appears to have the correct configuration for both `What=` and `Where=` and other options. The filesystem should be mounting an NFS filesystem to `/var/snd`. Which of the following is a likely cause of this issue?

    A. The configuration file itself needs to be named in a special way, `var-snd.mount`.

    B. The dependencies are not set up correctly.

    C. The systemd journal is corrupt.

    D. The mount point needs to also be in `/etc/fstab.mount`.

245. When troubleshooting disk-related errors you need to change the behavior of the system so that a kernel panic is not triggered. You will use `tune2fs -e` to change the error behavior. Which of the following are available options for the error behavior?

    A. `resched-io` and `mailadmin`

    B. `offline` and `background`

    C. `continue` and `remount-ro`

    D. `ignore` and `redress`

246. When working with a systemd timer, what is the best possible accuracy setting for the `AccuracySec=` option?

    A. `1m`

    B. `1ms`

    C. `1s`

    D. `1us`

247. Which environment variable contains the primary process ID within a systemd service unit file?

    A. `$DPID`

    B. `$MAINPID`

    C. `$PID`

    D. `$PRIMARY_PID`

248. Which configuration option is used within `/etc/fstab` as the equivalent of the `Requires=` option in a systemd mount file?

    A. `x-systemd.requires`

    B. `requires`

    C. `systemd-requires`

    D. `require-sys`

249. You need to change the startup arguments for a service managed by systemd. Which line within the unit file is used for this purpose?

    A. Command

    B. ExecStart

    C. Startup

    D. StartCmd

250. Which file contains information on currently mounted filesystems, including their mount options?

    A. /etc/mtab

    B. /etc/fstab

    C. /tmp/files

    D. /etc/filesystems

251. Which command and option are used to display the number of times a filesystem has been mounted?

    A. tune2fs

    B. cat /etc/fstab

    C. mount -a

    D. less /etc/fsmnt

252. When you're using `lsblk --discard`, which columns should have nonzero values to indicate that SSD trim support is enabled?

    A. DISC-GRAN and DISC-MAX

    B. TRIM-EN and TRIM-BYTES

    C. FSTRIM and NUMBYTES

    D. TRIM-BYTES and FSTRIM

Chapter 5

Practice Exam

1. Which command enables you to view the current IRQ assignments?
    A. `view /proc/irq`
    B. `cat /proc/interrupts`
    C. `cat /dev/irq`
    D. `less /dev/irq`

2. Configuration of udev devices is done by working with files in which directory?
    A. `/udev/devices`
    B. `/devices/`
    C. `/udev/config`
    D. `/etc/udev`

3. Which command is used to automatically load a module and its dependencies?
    A. `modprobe`
    B. `lsmod`
    C. `insmod`
    D. `rmmod`

4. During boot of a system with GRUB, which key can be pressed to display the GRUB menu?
    A. Shift
    B. E
    C. V
    D. H

5. Which command can be used to view the kernel ring buffer in order to troubleshoot the boot process?
    A. `lsboot`
    B. `boot-log`
    C. `krblog`
    D. `dmesg`

6. Which statement best describes the following, displayed using the `ls -la` command?

    ```
    lrwxrwxrwx. 1 root root 35 Jul 8 2014 .fetchmailrc
    -> .configs/fetchmail/.fetchmailrc
    ```

    A. It is a file called `.fetchmailrc` that is linked using a symbolic link.
    B. It is a file called `.configs/fetchmail/.fetchmailrc` that is owned by lrwxrwxrwx.
    C. It is a directory called `.fetchmailrc` that is owned by user Jul.
    D. It is a local directory called `.configs/fetchmail/.fetchmailrc`.

7. Which command is used with systemd in order to list the available service units?

   A. `systemd list-units`

   B. `systemctl list-units`

   C. `systemd unit-list`

   D. `systemctl show-units`

8. Which option to `lspci` is used to display both numeric codes and device names?

   A. `-numdev`

   B. `-n`

   C. `-nn`

   D. `-devnum`

9. Which command and option can be used to determine whether a given service is currently loaded?

   A. `systemctl --ls`

   B. `telinit`

   C. `systemctl status`

   D. `sysctl -a`

10. When partitioning a disk for a mail server running Postfix, which partition/mounted directory should be the largest in order to allow for mail storage?

   A. `/etc`

   B. `/usr/bin`

   C. `/mail`

   D. `/var`

11. Which YUM option displays the dependencies for the package specified?

   A. `list`

   B. `deplist`

   C. `dependencies`

   D. `listdeps`

12. Which options for an `rpm` command will display verbose output for an installation along with progress of the installation?

   A. `-ivh`

   B. `-wvh`

   C. `--avh`

   D. `--ins-verbose`

13. Which command will search for a package named zsh on a Debian system?
    - **A.** `apt-cache search zsh`
    - **B.** `apt-get search zsh`
    - **C.** `apt-cache locate zsh`
    - **D.** `apt-search zsh`

14. Which `rpm` option can be used to verify that no files have been altered since installation?
    - **A.** `-V`
    - **B.** `-v`
    - **C.** `--verbose`
    - **D.** `--filesum`

15. Which of the following command lines would monitor a single process called nagios in a continuous manner?
    - **A.** `top -n 1`
    - **B.** `top -p 23`
    - **C.** `ps -nagios`
    - **D.** `top -p`pidof nagios``

16. Which option to `xfs_metadump` displays a progress indicator?
    - **A.** `-g`
    - **B.** `-p`
    - **C.** `-f`
    - **D.** `-v`

17. The SAN has crashed again, and one of the filesystems in a Linux server has become significantly corrupt as a result. Which command and option can be used to attempt to examine the contents of the drive without causing more damage?
    - **A.** `fdisk -f`
    - **B.** `mke2fs -c`
    - **C.** `debugfs -c`
    - **D.** `ls -a`

18. Which of the following commands helps you to determine information about a given window within an X session, including information on the window size and its position?
    - **A.** `xkbinfo`
    - **B.** `xdspy`
    - **C.** `xwininfo`
    - **D.** `xver`

19. Which file is used to indicate the local time zone on a Linux server?

   A. `/etc/timez`

   B. `/etc/timezoneconfig`

   C. `/etc/localtime`

   D. `/etc/localtz`

20. Within which directory will you find files related to the time zone for various regions?

   A. `/etc/timezoneinfo`

   B. `/etc/zoneinfo`

   C. `/var/zoneinfo`

   D. `/usr/share/zoneinfo`

21. Within which directory should you place files in order for the files to be copied to a user's home directory when the user is created?

   A. `/etc/skel`

   B. `/etc/homedir`

   C. `/home/usertemplate`

   D. `/etc/template`

22. Which command displays a list of jobs currently scheduled with `at`?

   A. `atlist`

   B. `atq`

   C. `atl`

   D. `at --jobs`

23. Which of the following encodings provides a multibyte representation of characters?

   A. ISO-8859

   B. UTF-8

   C. ISO-L

   D. UFTMulti

24. On which port does LDAP over SSL operate?

   A. Port 53

   B. Port 389

   C. Port 636

   D. Port 443

25. Which of the following commands will set an account to expire based on the number of days elapsed since January 1, 1970?

    A. `passwd -e`

    B. `chage -E`

    C. `usermod -l`

    D. `chguser`

26. Which option to SSH enables the use of a key for authentication?

    A. `-i`

    B. `-k`

    C. `-f`

    D. `--key`

27. In a scripting scenario, you need to prevent `sudo` from prompting for credentials or for any other reason. Which option to `sudo` is used to indicate this?

    A. `-n`

    B. `--noprompt`

    C. `-i`

    D. `-q`

28. Which runlevel is typically used for single user mode, as indicated in `/etc/inittab`?

    A. 1

    B. 2

    C. 5

    D. 6

29. Which of the following commands provides an overview of the current memory usage along with swap space and its current utilization?

    A. `mem`

    B. `free`

    C. `pstat`

    D. `swap`

30. Which of the following commands can be used to display the current disk utilization, including free space?

    A. `df`

    B. `du`

    C. `diskutil`

    D. `diskuse`

31. Which of the following commands displays CPU-related performance information a total of 10 times gathered every 2 seconds?

    A. `sar -u 2 10`

    B. `sar -u 10 2`

    C. `sar -u 2`

    D. `uptime -t`

32. Which option to `iostat` causes the display to output in megabytes?

    A. `-k`

    B. `-l`

    C. `-m`

    D. `-o m`

33. You are working with a legacy CentOS 5 system and need to re-create the initial RAM disk. Which of the following commands is used for this purpose?

    A. `mkinitrd`

    B. `mkramdisk`

    C. `mkdisk --init`

    D. `mkfs.init`

34. Which compression method is used for creation of a bzImage?

    A. zip

    B. bzip3

    C. gzip

    D. Cannot be determined

35. Which options to the `fsck` command will find errors and automatically assume that it should repair them?

    A. `-ry`

    B. `-vy`

    C. `-my`

    D. `-xy`

36. What is the name of the unit to which a `systemd` system is booted in order to start other levels?

    A. `default.target`

    B. `init.target`

    C. `initial.target`

    D. `load.target`

37. Which command is used to format a swap partition?

   A. `mkfs -swap`

   B. `mkswap`

   C. `format -swap`

   D. `mksw`

38. You see the word `defaults` within `/etc/fstab`. Which options are encompassed within the defaults?

   A. `ro, exec, auto`

   B. `rw, suid, dev, exec, auto, nouser, async`

   C. `rw, exec, auto, nouser, async`

   D. `rw, exec, nouser, async, noauto, suid`

39. Which command is used to remove unused filesystem blocks from thinly provisioned storage?

   A. `thintrim`

   B. `thtrim`

   C. `fstrim`

   D. `fsclean`

40. Which option to `mdadm` is used to create a new array?

   A. `--create`

   B. `--start`

   C. `--begin`

   D. `--construct`

41. Which of the following commands creates a logical volume with LVM?

   A. `lvc`

   B. `lvcreate`

   C. `lvlist`

   D. `lvmake`

42. Which of the following commands shows network sockets and their allocated memory?

   A. `ss -m`

   B. `mpas`

   C. `mem`

   D. `free`

43. When troubleshooting a potential hardware problem, you need to determine which physical interface is being used for a certain address. One way to accomplish this is with the ping command in order to monitor the activity lights on the device. Which of the following options to ping will flood the interface with ECHO_REQUEST packets?

    A. -e

    B. -a

    C. -c

    D. -f

44. Which of the following dd commands reads and writes bytes one megabyte at a time?

    A. dd bsl=1024M

    B. dd size=1M

    C. dd bs=1M

    D. dd rw=1M

45. Which option to the rsync command examines only the file size as a means of determining whether the file should be synchronized?

    A. --filesize

    B. --size-only

    C. --list-size

    D. --file-size

46. When creating MX records for a zone, which of the following is the highest-priority mail exchanger?

    A. 0

    B. 10

    C. 20

    D. 100

47. On which protocol and port are zone transfer requests sent?

    A. UDP/53

    B. ICMP/53

    C. TCP/143

    D. TCP/53

48. Which type can be used with the dig command to test a zone transfer?

    A. xfr

    B. transfer

    C. zxfr

    D. axfr

49. Which of the following files is used to define the filesystems shared by NFS?

   A. `/etc/nfs.cfg`

   B. `/etc/nfs.conf`

   C. `/etc/export.nfs`

   D. `/etc/exports`

50. Which option in `dhcpd.conf` specifies the maximum amount of time that a client is allowed to have a DHCP lease?

   A. `max-time`

   B. `max-lease-time`

   C. `lease-max`

   D. `maximum-lease-duration`

51. You are troubleshooting an authentication issue for a user. You believe the system uses local files and LDAP for authentication. Which of the following lines in `/etc/nsswitch.conf` shows those authentication mechanisms?

   A. `passwd: files ldap`

   B. `passwd [files ldap]`

   C. `auth: local ldap`

   D. `auth: localfiles ldap`

52. Which of the following commands can be used to generate a private and public key pair for authentication with SSH?

   A. `ssh-createkey`

   B. `sshkey`

   C. `ssh-key`

   D. `ssh-keygen`

53. Which file contains a list of keys that will be accepted for authentication for a given user?

   A. `~/ssh/keys`

   B. `~/.ssh/pubkeys`

   C. `~/.ssh/keyauth`

   D. `~/.ssh/authorized_keys`

54. A newly added SATA disk is not showing up during the boot process. Where can you check to begin troubleshooting this issue?

   A. Using system logging

   B. Using `debugfs`

   C. Within the `fdisk` utility

   D. Within the computer BIOS or firmware

55. Which of the following commands will set the environment variable JAVA_PATH equal to /home/user/java2 when using the Bash shell?

A. invoke JAVA_PATH=/home/user/java2

B. export JAVA_PATH=/home/user/java2

C. envvar JAVA_PATH=/home/user/java2

D. echo JAVA_PATH=/home/user/java2

56. Which option in .bashrc sets the number of commands to keep in the .bash_history file?

A. HISTLIMIT

B. HISTORYFILE

C. HISTFILESIZE

D. HISTNUM

57. You are creating a Bash script of user information. Which of the following commands prints the username and real name of all users in /etc/passwd in a tab-separated format?

A. cut -d: -f 1,6 /etc/passwd

B. sed 's/://' /etc/passwd

C. awk -F: '{print $1,$5}' OFS="\t" /etc/passwd

D. cat -o "\t" /etc/passwd

58. Which git clone command will clone a repository called portalutils into a directory called utils?

A. git clone ssh://sourcehost/portalutils -d utils

B. git clone ssh://sourcehost:portalutils utils

C. git clone ssh://sourcehost/:portalutils utils

D. git clone ssh://sourcehost::portalutils -d utils

59. Which of the following commands is necessary for making a variable defined in your current shell available to child processes?

A. export

B. source

C. let

D. def

60. You are watching another administrator perform some work on a server. As part of that work, the admin uses the following command:

. variables.sh

Which of the following is the equivalent of . variables.sh?

A. let variables.sh

B. set variables.sh

C. source variables.sh

D. var variables.sh

61. Which of the following shows a valid Bash function called sayHello?

    A. `function sayHello() { echo "hello"; }`

    B. `function sayHello{}`

    C. `function sayHello() { echo Hello }`

    D. `function sayHello() { echo Hello } ;`

62. Which option to useradd sets the number of days between password expiration and when the account is disabled?

    A. -n

    B. -f

    C. -e

    D. -g

63. Which command option can be used to remove all cron jobs for a given user using the crontab command?

    A. -d

    B. -e

    C. -r

    D. -l

64. Which command is used to parse log-file entries on a systemd-based system?

    A. logger

    B. journalentry

    C. jrnctl

    D. journalctl

65. Which of the following syslog facilities captures messages from the lp printing facility?

    A. auth

    B. messages

    C. lpr

    D. root

66. Which port needs to be allowed through the firewall for standard LDAP traffic to be received by the server?

    A. TCP port 25

    B. TCP port 443

    C. TCP port 143

    D. TCP port 389

67. Which of the following is the correct syntax to connect to `host.example.com` using SSH on port 2200?

   A. `ssh -l 2200 host.example.com`

   B. `ssh host;example.com`

   C. `ssh host.example.com:2200`

   D. `ssh host:2200 -d example.com`

68. Which option to the `tar` command preserves permissions?

   A. `-x`

   B. `-v`

   C. `-z`

   D. `-p`

69. When working with a patch file, which option can be used to have the patching process ignore white space?

   A. `-w`

   B. `-i`

   C. `-e`

   D. `-p`

70. When using the `dm-crypt` command, which type of encryption is used by default?

   A. plain

   B. SHA-256

   C. LUKS

   D. loop

71. Which option to `journalctl` displays the output in reverse, with newest entries first?

   A. `-n`

   B. `-r`

   C. `-f`

   D. `-b`

72. Which `systemd` target can be used as an alternative to rescue mode when recovery is not possible in rescue mode?

   A. `emerg`

   B. `recover`

   C. `control-recover`

   D. `emergency`

73. When performing an `rsync` across devices, you receive errors that file ownership cannot be preserved, likely due to missing users or groups on the destination system. Which option should be removed from the `rsync` options in order to not preserve user and group ownership?

   A. -go

   B. -o

   C. -no-ownership

   D. -remove-owners

74. Which option to `ping` enables the bypass of the routing tables?

   A. -q

   B. -r

   C. -b

   D. -A

75. Which option to the `patch` command makes a backup of files?

   A. -d

   B. -b

   C. -s

   D. -c

76. A piece of software on client machines that listens for connections and executes commands on behalf of the server in an orchestration is commonly known as which of the following?

   A. Executor

   B. Runner

   C. Agent

   D. Host

77. Which escape characters represent a carriage return and newline in Bash?

   A. \enter

   B. \r\n

   C. \n

   D. \c\n

78. Which file test within a Bash script checks to see if the file exists?

   A. -f

   B. -o

   C. -l

   D. -p

79. Which of the following will execute a Bash script called `test.sh` even if the execute bit is not set?

A. `./test.sh`

B. `test.sh --execute`

C. `bash test.sh`

D. `run test.sh`

80. When testing an exclude pattern for a `.gitignore` file, which `git` command and option can be used to see the results of what will be ignored?

A. `git ls-files -i --exclude-standard`

B. `git ls-files --ignored`

C. `git show-ignored`

D. `git -ls ignored`

81. Which of the following characters is used to redirect `STDIN`, sending the contents of a file called `file.txt` into a script called `script.sh`?

A. `script.sh < file.txt`

B. `script.sh | file.txt`

C. `file.txt | script.sh`

D. `./script.sh > file.txt`

82. Which option to the `tune2fs` command sets the maximum mount count before the system will automatically run `fsck` on the partition on boot?

A. `-b`

B. `-c`

C. `-C`

D. `-a`

83. Which option to the `mount` command can be used to simulate the mount process without actually mounting the filesystem?

A. `-q`

B. `-v`

C. `-l`

D. `-f`

84. Which of the following commands shows the current default route without performing DNS lookups on the IP address(es) involved?

A. `netstat -rn`

B. `netstat -n`

C. `netstat -r`

D. `netstat -f`

85. Which tool can be used to measure the memory usage of individual processes in order to aid in capacity planning?

   A. ps

   B. iotop

   C. iostat

   D. ifconfig

86. When you're viewing statistics with `vmstat`, which statistic represents the time that the CPU spent waiting for I/O?

   A. sy

   B. us

   C. wa

   D. io

87. What time intervals are represented by the three numbers in the load-average output obtained with the `uptime` command?

   A. 1, 5, and 15 minutes

   B. 5, 10, and 15 minutes

   C. 10, 30, and 60 seconds

   D. 1, 3, and 5 minutes

88. Which option to `sysctl` displays all values and their current settings?

   A. -a

   B. -b

   C. -d

   D. -c

89. When you're using `systemctl` to kill a process, what is the default signal sent to a process?

   A. SIGKILL

   B. SIGTERM

   C. SIGINT

   D. SIGCALL

90. You are having difficulty with shared libraries on the system. Which of the following commands will print the current directories and libraries in the cache?

   A. ldconfig -C

   B. ldd -f

   C. ldconfig -p

   D. ldd -b

91. Which flag should be found within `/proc/cpuinfo` in order to determine if a host can be configured with hypervisor support?

    A. rob

    B. vmx

    C. run

    D. dmc

92. When using `ss` to determine listening sockets, you need to turn off name resolution. Which option should be passed to `ss` in order to disable name resolution?

    A. -n

    B. -x

    C. -a

    D. -r

93. Which option to `systemctl` shows the current target to which the system will boot?

    A. show

    B. get-default

    C. show-target

    D. get-target

94. If you suspect there is an active memory leak on the system, which option to the `free` command displays the output every N seconds apart?

    A. -b

    B. -v

    C. -d

    D. -s

95. Which `docker` command displays detailed information about a container?

    A. mine

    B. inspect

    C. show

    D. list

96. You are working with an image created by `dracut`. Which command can be used to display the contents of the image?

    A. dsl

    B. dracutls

    C. lsinitrd

    D. drat

97. Which of the following commands verifies the current status of a chronyd implementation?

   A. `chronyd info`

   B. `chronyc tracking`

   C. `chrony --info`

   D. `chrony --detail`

98. You are troubleshooting network issues and notice a potential attack originating from a single IP address. Which command can be used to determine the owner of that IP address?

   A. `whoip`

   B. `ip-owner`

   C. `ip info`

   D. `whois`

99. When you're working with the `nftables` command to build a web front end, which option to `nftables` prints output in JSON format?

   A. `-j`

   B. `-i`

   C. `-m`

   D. `-s`

100. Which of the following commands displays only IPv6-related connections?

   A. `ss -o 6`

   B. `ss 6-ip`

   C. `ss ipv6`

   D. `ss -6`

101. Within which directory will you find configuration files for the Postfix mail server on a Debian-based Linux server?

   A. `/etc/postfixd`

   B. `/var/postfix`

   C. `/etc/postfix`

   D. `/var/postfixd`

102. A developer is reporting that their webpage called index.html cannot be viewed on the web. While re-creating the issue, you receive the error "Forbidden" in a web browser and you notice that the file's permissions appear as `-rw-------` on the server. Using this information, which of the following describes the problem and its solution and, if applicable, the command to correct this issue?

   A. The developer did not load the file into the correct location. Move the file with the command `mv /var/web/`

   B. The file's permissions do not allow the file to be read and the `chmod 644` command will correct the issue.

   C. The file does not exist. Have the developer upload the file to the server.

   D. The file has the wrong extension. Rename the file with `ren index.html index.htm`

Appendix

Answers to the
Review Questions

Chapter 1: System Management (Domain 1.0)

1. A. The `modprobe` command loads the module and its dependencies, if applicable. The `lsmod` command is used to list currently loaded modules, making option B incorrect. The `insmod` command will load a given module but not its dependencies. Option D, `rmmod`, is used to remove a module from memory.

2. C. The keyword `single` given on the Linux kernel command line will boot the system into single-user mode. The other options are not valid.

3. D. The `systemctl get-default` command will show the default target. The other commands and options are not valid.

4. B. The `lsusb` command is used to obtain a basic list of USB devices on a system. This can be helpful when preparing a USB device with a boot image, such as when you need to boot the system from USB. The other commands are not valid. In the case of option D, the `ls` command is valid, but there is no `--usb` option.

5. D. The `lsmod` command is used to list currently loaded kernel modules, thereby making option D correct for this question. The `insmod` command (option A) is used to load modules. Option C is a valid command but not a valid option for that command, and option B does not exist.

6. D. The ESP is typically mounted at `/boot/efi`.

7. A. The `mount` command is used to mount drives in Linux. The source and destination mount point are expected as arguments. Drive partitions begin at number 1, making the first partition number 1.

8. D. If a working device does not appear in `lsmod`, it typically means the kernel has a driver already loaded by virtue of being compiled into the kernel itself rather than loaded through a module. The use of `systemd` (option A) or an `initrd.img` (option B) would have no effect.

9. C. The `-w` option causes the module to wait until it's no longer needed prior to unloading. The other options are not valid for `rmmod`.

10. A. The `update-grub` is an alias or shortcut for the `grub-mkconfig -o /boot/grub/grub.cfg` command. On some variants of Linux, the `update-grub` command is known as `grub2-update`. The other options are not valid for this purpose. Options C and D are not valid commands, while option B contains invalid options and an invalid location for the destination file.

11. B. MBR-based disks can be partitioned with up to four primary partitions, one of which can be further partitioned or extended into logical partitions.

12. B. 0x82 is Linux swap, while 0x83 is Linux. NTFS is 0x07, and FAT is 0.0c.

13. A. The `/etc/default/grub` file can be used for this purpose. You may also edit `/boot/grub/grub.cfg`, but this was not an option given for this question.

14. C. The `-o` option can be used to specify a destination file to which output will be sent instead of to `STDOUT`. The other options listed in this question do not exist.

15. A. The recommended `/boot` partition size has increased and it is now recommended to be at least 1 GB. The used space within `/boot` will increase as more kernels are added, such as during an upgrade process. The size should not be set too small because upgrade processes can fail if the partition becomes full.

16. B. The `pvcreate` command initializes a physical partition for future use as a logical volume with LVM. The `pvs` command displays information about physical volumes but is not used to initialize the physical disk partition. The `vgextend` command is valid but not for the scenario provided. The `lvmcreate` command does not exist.

17. D. The `grub2-install` command is used to install GRUB onto a disk. The second SATA disk would be `/dev/sdb`, therefore making option D the correct answer.

18. C. The `lvcreate` command is used to create logical volumes with LVM. The `pvcreate` command initializes physical volumes prior to creating logical volumes. The commands in the other two options for this question do not exist.

19. A. Physical volumes are initialized first, followed by volume group creation, and then logical volume creation.

20. B. The `grub-mkconfig` command should be run after making a change to the `/etc/default/grub` file so that a new configuration file can be created with the changed option(s).

21. C. The `lvchange` command configures details about a logical volume, including whether that volume appears to be available.

22. D. GRUB Legacy begins counting at 0 and separates the disk letter and partition with a comma, therefore making `0,0` the first partition on the first disk. Options A and C are not the first disk on the system, and option B contains a nonexistent partition.

23. B. The command to install GRUB is `grub-install`, and the first SATA drive is `/dev/sda`. A device listed as `hda` is typically a PATA drive, thereby making those options incorrect.

24. C. The `yum install` command will install a given package. The `update` option will update a package. The other options listed do not exist.

25. D. The first step is to use `fdisk` to create one or more partitions. Then format the partitions, and then mount the partitions for use. Various filesystem types can be created with `mkfs` and its subcommands. These filesystem types include `ext3`, `ext4`, `xfs`, and `ntfs`.

26. A. `rpm2cpio` sends its output to `STDOUT` by default, and therefore that output needs to be redirected to a file in most cases.

27. B. The addition of journaling in `ext3` increased filesystem reliability and performance.

28. D. The /opt hierarchy is used for add-on application software packages. The /etc hierarchy is configuration information, while /var is also data files but variable files such as mail files. The /tmp directory is for temporary files. Because each path begins with a /, it is considered an absolute path.

29. C. The -a option mounts all filesystems in /etc/fstab that are currently available. Of the other options listed, only the -f option is available, and it is a shortcut to the "fake" option, which does not do anything except perform a dry run of the mount.

30. A. The enable option configures the service to start on boot. The start option, option D, is used to start a service immediately. The other options are not valid for this command.

31. A. The -g option displays progress of the dump. The other options listed do not exist.

32. A. The du command will report on disk usage for the specified directory in a recursive manner, unlike the other commands shown here.

33. C. The /etc/fstab file is used to store information about the filesystems to mount within the system. The systemd.mount option refers to the configuration files used by systemd related to filesystems.

34. D. The /media mount point is used for removable media. See https://refspecs.linuxfoundation.org/FHS_3.0/fhs/index.html for more information on the FHS.

35. A. SCSI supports 7 to 15 devices per bus, depending on the type of SCSI. The lsscsi command displays device information.

36. B. The -r option causes umount to attempt to remount in read-only mode. The -v option is verbose mode, and the -f option forces the operation. The -o option does not exist.

37. D. The proper order is the device (UUID or partition) followed by the directory to mount that device, followed by its type and options, and then the dump and fsck settings.

38. A. The blkid command will show partition UUIDs. You can also get this information with the lsblk -no +UUID <partition> command. The partprobe command is used to update the partition table at the kernel level. The other commands shown in this question do not accomplish the required task.

39. D. The xfs_info command is equivalent to xfs_growfs -n.

40. B. The mkfs.btrfs command is used to create btrfs filesystems on block storage and does not require the drive to be partitioned.

41. C. Out of the options given, the systemctl status command and option are the most appropriate. The telinit and sysctl commands are not used for this purpose. Likewise, the --ls option is not valid for systemctl.

42. B. The parted command can be used to resize partitions in such a way. The mkfs command is not used for this purpose, and the other two options do not exist.

43. C. The VFAT filesystem is known as vfat to the mount command, and the other elements of the mount command are standard.

44. D. The c option in `gdisk` is used to change the partition name. The n option creates a new partition, the v option verifies the disk, and the b option creates a backup of GUID Partition Table (GPT) data to a file.

45. B. The `isolate` option is used to move the system into the target specified, thereby making option B the correct one. The `stop` option stops a service. The other options do not exist.

46. B. The −A option checks all filesystems in `/etc/fstab`, while the −R option excludes the root filesystem.

47. C. The `fsck` option, which is represented as a number in the `/etc/fstab` file, sets the order in which the device is checked at boot time.

48. C. The file `/etc/timezone` is used to indicate the local time zone. The other files listed as options do not exist.

49. D. Within the `/usr/share/zoneinfo` hierarchy, you will find information on the various regions and time zones available. The files within this hierarchy can be symlinked to `/etc/localtime`.

50. A. The listing shows a symbolic linked file created with the `ln` command located in the current directory, linked to `.configs/fetchmail/.fetchmailrc`. The file is owned by the root user and root group and was created on July 8, 2014.

51. C. The `LC_TIME` environment variable is used to control the display and behavior of the date and time and can be changed to a different locale in order to achieve the desired display and behavior of date and time formatting. The other options shown for this question do not exist.

52. B. UTF-8 provides multibyte character encoding and is generally accepted as the standard for encoding moving forward. ISO-8859 is single-byte encoded. The other answers are not valid.

53. C. The `timedatectl` command includes a `list-timezones` subcommand to show known time zones. The `tzsel` command does not exist, but there is a similar command called `tzselect` that will, by default, display a step-by-step menu to select a time zone. The eventual output will include a region/time-zone line, such as America/Chicago, as output.

54. C. The −nn option displays both numbers and device names, thus making option C correct. The −n option (option B) displays only numbers. The other two options do not exist.

55. C. Setting LANG=C is an alias for POSIX compatibility and will cause programs to bypass locale translations. The other options shown for LANG are not valid.

56. C. The `LC_ALL` variable can be used to set environment variables such as the locale and will override others. This can be used when there is a need for a temporary change. The other variables listed here are not used for this purpose and are not created by default.

57. A. The `ln` command is used for this purpose, and the −s option creates a symbolic or soft link, while −f forces or overwrites the destination. The other options and order of commands are not valid.

58. C. The `LC_MONETARY` variable is used by certain programs to determine the localization for currency.

59. D. The `hwclock` command is used to both query and set the hardware clock, such as the one maintained by the system firmware or Basic Input/Output System (BIOS). The `ntpdate` command is used to set the local system time but is not related to the hardware clock. The other commands are not valid.

60. D. The `-s` option sets the date and time as specified within the command. If there is another means to automatically set the date, it may override the change. For example, if `ntpd` or `chrony` is running, one of those processes may alter the date even after it has been set with `date -s`.

61. A. The `-w` option sets the hardware clock to the current system time. The `-s` option does the opposite, setting the system time to the hardware clock. There is no `-a` or `-m` function for `hwclock`.

62. A. `--systohc` will set the hardware clock according to the current system time. The use of `--utc` is required in order to ensure that the time is set to UTC. If `--utc` is omitted, the time will default to whatever was used last time the command was run, which could be UTC but might be local time instead. Therefore, the best option is A.

63. A. The `netstat` command can be used for this purpose, and the `-r` option displays the current routes. The addition of `-n` prevents DNS lookups, which can help with performance.

64. C. SATA disks are addressed as `/dev/sdX`, just like a SCSI disk. `/dev/hdX` is a traditional ATA disk. The other options do not exist.

65. C. The `route` command is used for this purpose, and adding a route is done with the `add` option. The default gateway is added using the `default gw` keywords followed by the IP address of the gateway and the adapter.

66. A. The `host` command enables changing of the query type with the `-t` option. Using `ns` as the type will query for the name servers for a given domain. There is no `all` type, and the other options are also invalid.

67. B. The `-I` option enables the choice of interface. A lowercase `-i` option sets the interval, while `-a` indicates an audible ping. Finally, `-t` enables a TTL-based ping only.

68. A. The `host` or `dig` command can be used for this purpose by setting the type to `mx`. The `mx` type will query for the mail exchanger for the given domain. There is no `smtp` type.

69. B. The localhost address for IPv6 can be written as `::1`. Addresses shown like 127 represent the IPv4 localhost range but are not written properly for IPv4 or IPv6.

70. A. The `ip` command with the `monitor` option/subcommand will display netlink messages as they arrive. There is no `netlink` subcommand for `ip`, and the `route` command will not work for this purpose.

71. A. The syntax is `database: <databasename>` with additional database names separated by spaces, as shown in the correct option for this question.

72. A. The @ symbol is used to indicate a server to which the query will be sent directly. This can be quite useful for troubleshooting resolution problems by sending the query directly to an authoritative name server for the domain. Of the other options, -t sets the type, and the other options are not valid.

73. A. The getent command is used for working with NSS databases, and getent hosts will display the available hosts using the databases configured in /etc/nsswitch.conf.

74. C. The configuration option is nameserver, and the value for the option is the IP address of the desired name server. Several options affect how name resolution is performed, such as the number of attempts and timeout. See resolv.conf(5) for more information.

75. A. The route command can be used for this purpose, and the syntax includes the network range, denoted with the -net option, followed by the word netmask and the masked bits, followed by the letters gw and the IP address of the gateway. The other options shown are invalid for a variety of reasons, including missing keywords and options and order.

76. A. The netstat command is used for this purpose, and the -a option displays all sockets, listening and non-listening. Note that it's frequently helpful to add the -n option, or combine options as in netstat -an, in order to prevent name lookup. Doing so can significantly improve performance of the command.

77. D. The partition containing /var should be the largest for a mail server because mail spools are stored within this hierarchy. The /etc/ hierarchy is usually small, as is /usr/bin. The /mail directory does not exist by default.

78. B. The ip route command can be used for this purpose, and its syntax uses a change command and the via keyword. The same operation could be completed with the route command but would require deleting the existing gateway first and then re-adding a new default gateway.

79. A. The soa type is used to query for Start of Authority records for a domain. Note that in many cases, dig will attempt to look up the domain within a given command and may not appear to have had an error. For example, when running option D (dig -t auth example.com), you will receive information about example.com, and there will be a line in the output saying that dig has ignored the invalid type of auth.

80. A. The search option is used for this purpose and can be provided with multiple domain names, each separated by a space or tab. The domain option is valid within /etc/resolv.conf but does not allow for multiple domain names.

81. A. The route command can be used for this purpose, and in the scenario described, a reject destination is used for the route. The other options shown are invalid because they use invalid options to the route command.

82. D. The -c option provides the count of the number of pings to send. The -n option specifies numeric output only, while -p specifies the pattern to use for the packet content. Finally, the -t option sets the TTL.

83. D. The best option for this question is to add an entry for the host in `/etc/hosts`. Doing so will always cause DNS queries to resolve to 127.0.0.1. The other options are not as robust because they rely on `www.example.com` always having the same IP address, or the solutions require additional maintenance to constantly add new IP addresses if `www.example.com`'s IP address changes.

84. A. The `ip route flush cache` command should be executed after changing the routes. The other commands shown for this question are not valid.

85. A. SPF records are stored in the `txt` record type in DNS, thereby making `-t txt` the correct option for this. Of the other answers, only `-t mx` is valid; it returns the mail exchangers for the given domain.

86. C. The G signifies a gateway within the route table.

87. A. The `axfr` type is a zone transfer, and the @ symbol signifies the server to which the query will be sent. There is no `xfer` type, and option B is just a normal query for the domain sent to the specified server.

88. B. The `deplist` option displays the dependencies for the given package. The `list` option displays information about a specific package, while the other two options are not valid.

89. A. The `df` command displays information on disk usage and can help with planning disk utilization over time. For example, if you note that disk utilization is increasing significantly, preparations can be made to bring more disks online or even to change the log rotation schedule such that logs are rotated faster, thereby freeing up space.

90. A. The `mkinitrd` command is used on older systems to create the initial RAM disk. The initial RAM disk is used to load (some might say preload) essential modules for things like disks and other vital components needed for booting.

91. B. The `lsmod` command is used to display currently loaded modules. This is useful for scenarios where you are migrating from the stock or distribution-provided kernel to a custom kernel and need to know which modules to compile into the new kernel. Of the other commands, the `tree` command is valid but not for the scenario provided.

92. B. The `depmod` command is used to create a list of modules. The list is kept in a file called `modules.dep`, the location of which is dependent on the distribution of Linux in use.

93. A. The `-a` option displays all values and their current settings for `sysctl`. The `-b` option is binary and displays values without any newlines. The `-d` option is an alias for `-h`, which is help display. There is no `-c` option. The `sysctl` options can also be found in `/etc/sysctl.conf`.

94. B. The `modprobe` command examines dependencies for a given module and loads both the dependencies and the requested module.

95. A. The `modinfo` command provides information on a given kernel module. You can use `modinfo` to find out the parameters needed for a given module and the modules on which it depends, among other information. The `modprobe` command is used to load a module. There is no `tracemod` or `modlist` command.

96. C. The `insmod` command inserts a module into the running kernel. It does not, however, attempt to resolve dependencies but rather outputs an error if there are dependent modules or kernel symbols that are not available.

97. B. The `-r` option removes the named kernel modules and attempts to remove any modules on which the named module depends, where possible. The `-d` option sets the root directory for modules, while `-v` is verbose and `-f` forces the module to load.

98. B. The `/etc/modprobe.d` directory is used for storing configuration information related to modules such as that used for blacklisting purposes and also for other configuration information such as `udev` and module options.

99. B. The `dracut` command is used to create the initial RAM disk for newer systems and has replaced the legacy `mkinitrd` command used for the same purpose.

100. B. Variables and values placed in `/etc/sysctl.conf` will take effect on boot. The other files listed are not valid.

101. B. The `--show-depends` option displays the dependencies for a given module. The other options are not valid for the `modprobe` command.

102. A. The `-ivh` options will install a file using `rpm`, displaying both verbose output and hash marks for progress. The other options presented do not exist or do not accomplish the specified task.

103. D. The `-n` option changes the boot order for the next boot only and boots from the specified partition. The `-b` along with `-B` modifies and then deletes the option. The `-o` option sets the boot order. The `-c` option creates a boot number.

104. A. ISOLINUX provides a means by which CD-ROMs formatted as ISO 9660 can be booted. It's very common to have live CDs or rescue/recovery CDs that use ISOLINUX for boot. The other bootloaders are not valid for this purpose or don't exist.

105. B. Due to the decidedly insecure decisions made with the design of Microsoft's UEFI, a shim is often needed to enable Linux to boot on a system with UEFI. The file `shim.efi` can be used as an initial bootloader for this purpose.

106. B. The `bcfg` command within the UEFI shell is used to configure bootloaders on a UEFI-based system. The command can accept various parameters to configure how the bootloader and kernel will load on boot. Of the other commands shown, `grub-install` is valid but not within the UEFI shell.

107. B. The master boot record, or MBR, is the first sector on a disk and contains information about the structure of the disk. If the MBR becomes corrupt, all data on the disk may be lost. The other options shown for this question are not valid.

108. D. The file `pxelinux.0` must exist within `/tftpboot` on the TFTP server in order for a system to use PXELINUX for booting. The other files are not valid or necessary for PXELINUX. Once booted, PXE boot can boot using an NFS-mounted filesystem where the filesystem is physically hosted on a different computer.

109. D. The `--boot-directory` option enables you to specify an alternate location for GRUB images rather than the default `/boot`. The other options shown for this question are not valid.

110. C. The `shim.efi` bootloader loads another bootloader, which is `grubx64.efi` by default. The other options are not valid filenames for the purpose described.

111. C. The `-t` option sets the filesystem type as ext2, ext3, or ext4. The mke2fs command is typically symlinked from `/sbin/mkfs.ext2`, `/sbin/mkfs.ext3`, and `/sbin/mkfs.ext4`. The `-f` option forces `mke2fs` to create a filesystem. The `-a` and `-e` options do not exist.

112. B. The `/etc/crypttab` file contains the filesystems and devices that are encrypted such as those with Linux Unified Key Setup (LUKS). The other file locations do not exist by default and are not related to this question.

113. A. The `apt-cache` command is used to work with the package cache, and the `search` option is used to search the cache for the supplied argument, in this case `zsh`. The `apt-get` command is used to work with packages themselves, while the `apt-search` command does not exist. The `apt.conf` file, found either in `/etc/apt/` or `/etc/`, contains several options for how `apt` behaves.

114. D. Configuration files related to the repositories for yum are located in `/etc/yum.repos.d`. Of the other options, `/etc/yum.conf` is a file and not a directory, and the other directories do not exist.

115. A. The block size for import or restore must match the block size used on export or dump. Block size is specified with the `-b` option, thus making option A correct. The other options are not valid for `xfsrestore`.

116. B. A filesystem with the word `defaults` for its mount options will be mounted read-write (`rw`), `suid`, with the ability to have executables (`exec`). The filesystem will be auto-mounted (`auto`), but users will not be able to mount it (`nouser`). Character and block special devices will be interpreted (`dev`), and operations on the disk will be performed in an asynchronous manner (`async`).

117. C. The `-z` option sets the maximum size for files to be included in the dump. The `-b` option sets the block size but is not related to what is being asked for in this scenario. The `-s` option sets the path for inclusion in the dump, and `-p` sets the interval for progress indicators.

118. D. A partition type of 0xFD is used for software RAID arrays. This can be set or viewed using a tool such as `fdisk`. The other options shown are not valid partition types.

119. C. The `/dev/disk/by-id` directory contains symbolic links to `/dev/sd`, such as `/dev/sda`. Because WWIDs can be used to identify a device across systems, they are often used within the context of SANs. The other directories listed as options do not exist.

120. C. The `pvdisplay` command shows information about a given physical volume. You can use `pvdisplay` to view the device on which the PV is built along with the extent size of the PV. The other commands shown are not valid.

121. B. Logical unit numbers (LUNs) that contain the characters fc are those found through Fibre Channel. Therein lies the difference between options B and C, where option C contains the letters scsi, which would usually represent a local disk. The other options are not valid.

122. C. The multipath command is used for administration of devices such as LUNs and can be used for finding the path to LUNs for a server, such as in a SAN configuration. Related, the multipathd daemon checks for paths that have failed. The other commands are not valid, with the exception of ls: it is valid, but the option shown is not related to LUNs but rather is a combination of various flags to the ls command.

123. C. The fstrim command is used to remove blocks that are not in use. The fstrim command is frequently used in a SAN configuration to give back unused storage to the SAN. The fstrim command can also be used with solid-state drives for the same purpose. The other commands shown are not valid.

124. B. The -E option signals that an extended option follows, such as stripe_width. The -f option forces an operation but should not be necessary for this solution, and the -e option sets the behavior on error. There is no -extend option.

125. A. The --create option enables creation of a RAID array that will use md. The typical argument is the /dev/mdN device along with the level. The other options listed are not valid for mdadm.

126. C. The /dev/mapper directory contains information about multipath devices such as logical volumes. The other directories are not valid.

127. C. The --monitor option is used to actively watch an array for issues such as disk failure. The monitoring can be done as a daemon and run in the background, thereby alerting when there is an issue.

128. B. The MAILADDR option sets the destination address for mail about RAID events that are noted by mdadm when in monitor mode.

129. C. The ip command defaults to the inet family if not otherwise specified with the -f option. The command will attempt to guess the correct family and fall back to inet. The other families listed as options for this command are not valid for use with the ip command.

130. B. The iwconfig command, which is similar to the ifconfig command, works with an individual wireless interface to set and display parameters. Of the other commands, the ifconfig command is valid but not used for wireless, and ifcfg is intended as a replacement for ifconfig. The other commands are not valid.

131. A. The ss command provides many of the same functions as netstat but can show some extended information, such as memory allocation for a given socket. The free command shows memory usage but not by socket, and the other two commands do not exist.

132. C. The -p option shows the process IDs associated with a given socket within the ss output. The -a option is all sockets, while -l is listening sockets. The -f option is used to specify the protocol family.

133. D. The /etc/network directory contains information on network interfaces and contains directories that then further contain scripts to be executed when interfaces are brought up or down. The other directories listed do not exist.

134. B. Only alphanumerics, minus sign or dash, and dot are valid for hosts in /etc/hosts.

135. B. Options within /etc/resolv.conf are preceded with the options keyword followed by one or more options such as debug.

136. C. The -f option will force the umount to occur. The --fake option is essentially a dry run in that it won't actually unmount a filesystem. The other two options do not exist.

137. A. The --output option configures the location for output of the command instead of STDOUT.

138. A. The file lpxelinux.0 contains the necessary code to support booting from HTTP and FTP.

139. B. The file /etc/grub2.cfg is usually a symbolic link to /boot/grub2/grub.cfg.

140. C. The vmlinuz file has been compressed and therefore consumes less disk space than vmlinux. Both contain the Linux kernel in binary format.

141. C. Modules are stored in /usr/lib/modules/{kernel-version}.

142. A. The -V or, --verify, option will check the files in a given package against versions (or checksums) in the package database. If no files have been altered, then no output is produced. Note that output may be produced for files that are changed during installation or for other reasons. Note also the use of an uppercase V for this option, as opposed to the lowercase v for *verbose*.

143. B. The /etc/lib directory is not typically associated with library files and does not typically exist on a Linux system unless manually created. The other options either contain system libraries or can be used for that purpose.

144. C. The apt-get update command will cause the package cache to be updated by retrieving the latest package list from the package sources. There is no cache-update option or update option to apt-cache. The upgrade option is used to update the system's packages, not the cache.

145. C. The /etc/apt/sources.list.d/ directory contains repositories for Debian packages. The other file and directory locations do not exist by default.

146. C. The localectl command is used to view and configure settings such as the keyboard layout for a given locale. The other commands listed do not exist.

147. D. The directory /etc/sysconfig/network-scripts contains files related to network configuration. It is not preferable to edit these files directly any longer but rather to use commands such as nmcli and nmtui through the Network Manager. The other paths do not exist by default.

148. A. The e2label command changes the filesystem label. The other commands do not exist.

149. A. The dpkg-reconfigure program will cause an already-installed package to be reconfigured or changed. The -r option for dpkg removes a package, thus making option B incorrect. There is no reconf option for dpkg or reinstall option for apt-get.

150. D. The search option performs a search of various fields such as the package name and description.

151. B. The file /etc/modprobe.conf, which is a legacy file and may be removed in a later version of Linux, contains information on the configuration of modules on the system. The other files do not exist.

152. B. The rpm -q kernel command will show the kernel version. You can also use uname -r for the same purpose.

153. D. The kernel-install command uses the files found in the /usr/lib/kernel directory to install a kernel and related files into /boot. The other commands listed here are not valid.

154. A. The exclude option can be used to exclude certain packages. The argument accepts wildcards, and therefore excluding all kernel* updates will create the desired behavior.

155. C. A raw device is one that has not been partitioned. Raw devices are sometimes used for virtualization and also database scenarios, where the higher-layer software manages the disk. The other options shown are not relevant to this answer. Highly available would only typically refer to a redundant disk or network scenario.

156. B. The -s option to dpkg searches for the given package and provides information about its current status on the system. The apt-cache command is not used for this purpose, and the -i option for dpkg installs a package. The apt-info command does not exist.

157. A. The -i option to dpkg will install a previously downloaded .deb Debian package. The other commands don't exist, and the -U option for dpkg does not exist.

158. C. The info option displays information about a given package on a system that uses the zypper tool.

159. D. Blob, or Binary Large Object, is a storage format frequently associated with cloud environments. Blob storage enables a single object to be stored as an individual object. The other formats are valid, but none of the other options is the most appropriate mechanism for this scenario. File storage refers to the hierarchy of folders and files that you would see when using a command like ls.

160. A. The search option looks for packages by the name given on the command line. The path that is searched can be controlled by the configuration file at /etc/dnf/dnf.conf. The other options are not valid for the dnf command.

161. C. The ext2, ext3, and ext4 filesystems can be resized using resize2fs. Both NFS and CIFS are network filesystems and therefore are not relevant to this question.

162. D. The `connect` subcommand connects to the hypervisor. The other options are not valid subcommands for `virsh`.

163. C. The `--list` option shows the available character sets on the system. Character sets such as ASCII, UTF-8, and UNICODE are displayed if they are supported on the system. The other options given for this question do not exist.

164. A. The `/dev/` filesystem is used to store information about connected devices, including block and character devices. The `/dev/` filesystem also contains special character devices such as `/dev/null`, `/dev/zero`, and `/dev/urandom`. The `/etc/` filesystem is used for configuration files, and there are no proscribed directories for development or kernel device lists.

165. B. The `/proc/mounts` file shows the currently mounted filesystems. The file `/etc/fstab` is used for mounting filesystems but is not kept up-to-date with filesystem mounts as they change. The other files listed do not exist.

166. B. CIFS is the Common Internet File System and is now considered a legacy filesystem, having been superseded by SMB3. CIFS is an implementation of SMB typically used by older versions of Microsoft Windows.

167. A. The g option, also known as `global` or `greedy`, will apply the matched operation to the entire line rather than just the first instance of the match. The other options apply as they would for a Perl Compatible Regular Expression.

168. C. The -g option clears the cache to remove devices that do not exist. The -p option bypasses the cache. There are no -a or -m options for `blkid`.

169. D. The `/dev/disk/by-uuid` file shows the UUID of the disks on a system. The other locations do not exist.

170. C. The `/etc/sysconfig/network` file is created by default but is no longer populated on systems like RHEL7. It can be used in place of Network Manager for environments that rely on this location. The other options given for this question do not exist.

171. B. The -rf options to `rm` will recursively remove contents of a directory, including other directories. The -f option alone will not work in this case because of the additional directories. The options given for `rmdir` do not exist.

172. A. The cat command will display the contents of the file `/etc/passwd` and then pipe that output to the awk command. The awk command then parses its input, splitting along the specified separator for `/etc/passwd`, which is a colon (`:`). The output is then printed and piped to the sort command. The sort command in option B will not work because the cut command requires an argument. Likewise, the echo command in option C will only echo `/etc/passwd` to STDOUT.

173. A. The timestamp of the file will change when `touch` is run on a file that already exists.

174. D. The -i option will cause both cp and mv to be interactive, that is, prompt before overwriting. The -f option will force the command to run, while -r is recursive.

175. D. The `/proc/partitions` file contains a list of partitions on the system along with their major and minor numbers and the number of blocks. The `/dev/disk/` option is a directory and not a file and so is not correct for this question. The other options shown do not exist.

176. C. The file `/sys/block/sda/stat` contains information about the `sda` device. The `/sys/block` hierarchy contains information about block devices on the system.

177. A. The `-p` option will cause `mkdir` to create additional levels of directories without error. Running `mkdir` without options will not work in this case. The `-r` and `-f` options to `mkdir` do not exist.

178. D. The `fg` command will bring a command to the foreground if it has been backgrounded with either & or the `bg` command.

179. A. You need to write the changes to the file, so you'll need `:w`. The addition of q will also quit. Note that you could use `ZZ` to write and quit as well. The `dd` command in Vi deletes a line, while x deletes a single character.

180. B. The WWID, or Worldwide Identifier, is globally unique. UUID and GUID are not valid acronyms for multipath devices. UUID is typically found for plain block devices, and GUID is a term sometimes used in applications. There is no DISKID name relevant as a potential answer for this question.

181. C. The `-9` option invokes `SIGKILL`, which will force the process to end. The `15` signal is the default. The `-f` and `-stop` options do not exist.

182. C. The `o` command opens a new line below the current cursor location. The `a` command begins an insert-mode session at the character after the cursor, not the line. The `i` command begins an insert-mode session at the current cursor location.

183. B. The `-D` option tells `dmesg` to stop displaying messages to the console. The `-F` option is valid but is used to read from a file, so it is not relevant for this question. There are no `-o` or `-Q` options.

184. A. The `-f` option forces unload of the module. The other options are not valid for `rmmod`.

185. A. The `-A` option examines `modules.dep` for newer modules rather than regenerating the file automatically if there are no changes. The `-C` option changes the configuration file location. The other options are not valid for `depmod`.

186. B. The `lsblk` command shows device information in a tree-like structure and shows the other information specified along with major and minor information and whether the partition is read-only. Of the other options given, `fsck` is the only command, and it is not used for the purpose described.

187. C. The `-m` option displays output in a machine-readable format. The `-v` option prints the version of `parted`. There is no `-p` or `-S` option.

188. B. The `brctl` command is used to create ethernet bridges and is also used to manage bridges once they are created. The other options shown are not valid.

189. A. Sending -HUP as part of the `kill` command will restart a process. Of the other options, -9 will kill the process completely. The other two options do not exist as valid means to kill a process.

190. C. The `mv` command is used to move files, and `*.txt` will look for all files with a `.txt` extension. Note the fully qualified destination with a / preceding the name `tmp`.

191. B. The `server` command changes the destination for queries sent from `nslookup` during the session in which it's used. The other options shown are not valid.

192. C. The file is almost certainly a hard link to the original script. While `ls` won't show this information, the `stat` command will show that it is a link and also show the inode to which the file is linked.

193. B. The `-s` option to `ln` creates a symbolic link, or symlink.

194. B. The l within the listing indicates a symlink. There is no way to tell if a file or directory is temporary. A directory will display a d instead of an l.

195. D. Scripts are stored in `/etc/init.d` on a system using SysVinit. You may sometimes find these linked from `/etc/rc.d/init.d` as well. The other options are not valid for this question.

196. B. The `-R` option will copy directories recursively. Note that if the `-i` option is not enabled, the recursive copy will overwrite files in the destination. The `-v` option adds verbosity but does not cause any recursion, while the `-Z` option does not exist.

197. A. The `-h` option displays output in human-readable format, meaning that the output will be displayed as megabytes, gigabytes, terabytes, and so on. The other options are not valid.

198. A. The `netcat` tool used with the `nc` command can create a network connection, and the format is `nc <host> <port>`, thus making options other than that incorrect.

199. B. The `-z` option causes `file` to look inside compressed files. The `-b` option specifies brief output, and the other options don't exist.

200. B. The `-b` option enables binary and executable editing with Vim. The `-c` option is related to commands, while the `-d` option starts Vim in diff mode. There is no `-a` option.

201. B. The `-p` option removes the hierarchy of directories. The other options do not exist.

202. C. The `/dev/zero` special file is used as input to the `dd` command to write zeros or clear a block device. The other options either do not exist or are not used for this purpose.

203. B. The `-f` option freshens the files within the archive. The `-d` option deletes from the archive. The other options do not exist.

204. B. The format for `cron` is [`minute hour day-of-month month-of-year day-of-week`], thereby making option B the correct option for this question.

205. B. The `/etc/cron.allow` file is a list of users who have permission to create and remove their own `cron` jobs. The `/etc/crontab` file is used to store `cron` jobs. The other files do not exist.

206. B. The `at` command is used to run a series of commands that you enter. Unlike with `cron`, you can schedule commands from the command line to be executed in the same order entered rather than having to create a specific script for the commands. The syntax shown in option B sets the time to be one hour from now.

207. C. The `/proc` filesystem contains information about currently running processes and additional information about the kernel and current boot of the system.

208. B. The `-l` option lists partitions available on a given device. The `-s` option prints the size in 512-byte block sectors. The other options do not exist.

209. A. The `/var/spool/cron/crontabs` directory contains a file for each user that currently has one or more `cron` jobs or entries. Note that the other files listed here are not valid for this purpose.

210. C. The `atrm` command removes jobs given their ID. The ID can be obtained with the `atq` command. The `atq` and `at -l` commands shown will list jobs but not delete them. The `rmat` command is not valid.

211. C. The `/etc/crontab` file is a plain-text file that is treated as a system-wide `cron` file. As such, the file is generally not associated with any single user, and it's not necessary to run a special command after editing this file.

212. A. The `/etc/cron.daily` directory contains files such as scripts that are executed daily. There are corresponding `cron.hourly`, `cron.weekly`, and `cron.monthly` directories that run on their respective schedules as indicated by the name of each directory.

213. A. The `ls` command from within the `grub >` prompt will show the available partitions in a format such as (`hd0,1`).

214. A. With cable select, ATA drives will be detected in the order in which they are plugged in on the cable from the motherboard. It's likely that the drives need to be swapped physically on the cable.

215. A. The format when adding a username places the username between the schedule and the command to run, thereby making option A correct. The other options shown for this question are invalid. In the case of option B, there is no schedule. In the case of options C and D, the schedule is incorrectly formatted.

216. B. The `upgrade` option for `apt-get` will upgrade the system to the latest version of software for packages already installed. The `apt-update` command does not exist, nor does the `-U` option to dpkg. The `apt-cache` command is used to work with the package cache.

217. B. While the `ps auwx` command combined with `grep` will provide information on the running Apache instances, it will provide much more information than is required or useful for this problem. The `pgrep` command provides only the process IDs and therefore meets the criteria presented in the question.

218. B. The `nice` command, when run without arguments, will output the priority for the currently logged-in user, which is normally 0. The `renice` command can be used to change the priority of running processes. The other two commands shown as options for this question do not exist.

219. A. The −i option to df produces information on inodes across all filesystems. The ls −i option will produce inode listings but only for the current directory. The −i option is invalid for du, and dm does not exist as a command.

220. A. The crontab command can be used for this purpose, and the −l option is used to list the crontab entries. The −u option is needed to specify a user other than the current user.

221. A. The ifconfig command will be used for this purpose and requires the addition of the −a option because the adapter is currently down. The ifup command can be used to bring up an interface but does not display information by default. The netstat command displays information about the network but not with the −n option.

222. A. The −T option causes traceroute to use TCP packets. This option, which requires root privileges, can be helpful for situations where a firewall may be blocking traceroute traffic. The −i option chooses the interface, while −s chooses the source address. A lowercase −t option sets the Type of Service (ToS) flag.

223. C. Secure Shell, or SSH, operates on TCP port 22 by default. TCP/23 is used for Telnet, TCP/25 is SMTP, and TCP/2200 is not associated with a well-known service.

224. B. The nc command is used to start netcat, and the −l option causes it to listen. The −p option is used to specify the port on which netcat will listen. The −s option specifies the local source address and is not used for this scenario.

225. A. The soa type is used to query for Start of Authority records for a domain. Note that in many cases, dig will attempt to look up the domain within a given command and may not appear to have had an error. For example, when running option D (dig −t auth example.com), you will receive information about example.com, and there will be a line in the output that dig has ignored the invalid type auth.

226. A. Setting your address to 127.0.0.1 will use the localhost interface. Other local NTP clients would contact this server by its normal IP address.

227. C. The application could theoretically use any of the logging facilities, depending on the type of application being developed. However, the requirement to log to a custom log file means the logs will have a different name and possibly a different location than the standard logs. Therefore, logging to any of the standard or system-level facilities is not appropriate for this scenario, so one of the local (local0 through local7) facilities is appropriate.

228. B. NXDOMAIN is the status for a nonexistent domain or host: basically, the host for which the query was sent does not exist. A normal status when there has not been an error is "NOERROR."

229. A. The systemctl command is used for controlling services. In this case, restart should be sent to the CUPS service as denoted by the name cups.service.

230. A. If /etc/nologin exists, users will be prevented from logging in to the system. The root user can still log in, assuming that root logins are enabled within the SSH configuration.

231. A. The correct format is YYYY-MM-DD for the usermod command.

232. A. The systemctl command will be used for this purpose, and the subcommand is disable. There is a stop subcommand, but it will only stop the given service rather than prevent it from starting on boot. The other options are invalid for various reasons, including that they use systemd as the command name rather than systemctl.

233. B. The find command will be used for this purpose, and the permission can be described as 4000 to indicate the presence of the setuid bit. The -type option can be used for changing the type of object to be returned but is not relevant for the scenario described.

234. B. The make oldconfig command will integrate the existing configuration file into the new configuration for the kernel. Care still needs to be taken for items that have moved or changed within the new kernel, to ensure that the configuration is correct.

235. C. The systemctl command will be used for this purpose, with the daemon-reload subcommand. The reboot option would work to reload the systemd configuration but is not correct because it requires the entire server to reboot, which is not what was asked for in this question.

236. B. The file /etc/auto.master contains the configuration for autofs. The other files listed as options are not valid for this scenario.

237. B. The directory /sys/class/fc_host contains other directories based on the Fibre Channel connections available. Within those host directories will be found the WWN (World Wide Name) in a file called port_name. The fcstat command can be used to obtain statistics related to a given device. The other directory hierarchies are not valid.

238. C. The -a option provides archive mode, which is a substitute for several other options. The -r option is recursive, the -o option indicates that ownership should be preserved, and the -f option enables a filter.

239. A. According to the man(1) page for the make command, the name Makefile, with an uppercase M, is the recommended name for the file. The name makefile is valid as a default but is not the recommended option. The other options are not valid as default names.

240. B. The gunzip command is used to uncompress files that have been compressed using gzip compression.

241. D. The install target installs the final compiled files in their appropriate location and makes them executable, if applicable. Of the other options, distclean is sometimes included as a target to return source files to their pristine state. The other targets listed are not valid.

242. D. The baseurl option is used to set the URL and must be fully qualified, meaning it must include the protocol, such as http:// or file://.

243. A. The /boot partition almost certainly exists but has not been partitioned into its own space. The /boot partition would not be hidden from lsblk if it was indeed a separate partition.

244. The `lsof` command can be used for this purpose; with the `-i` option, it will display the network ports along with their process. The `netstat` command will display network ports but not the process with the `-a` option. The `ps` command is used for processes but not network ports. Finally, there is no `netlist` command.

245. B. The `-o` option logs output to the file specified. The `-k` option converts links, and the `-r` option indicates recursive. There is no `-b` option.

246. D. The `service status` command is equivalent to `systemctl status` on systemd-enabled computers. The other commands do not exist with the specified option.

247. B. The `-1`, or `-HUP`, signal reloads the given process. The `-15` signal, also known as SIGTERM, is the default terminate signal, while `-2` is an interrupt signal. The `-9` signal is `kill` and is considered bad practice except in emergencies when the process doesn't respond to normal signals.

248. C. The Ctrl+C key combination terminates, or kills, a process in a scenario such as the one described here. The Ctrl+D option is a valid key combination but is used to delete the character underneath the cursor.

249. B. The `stop` command, when used with the `service` command, causes a given service to shut down. The service can be started again with the `service start` command. The other options shown are not valid commands to use with the `service` command.

250. D. The `chassis` subcommand configures the type of machine on which the `hostnamectl` command is running. This can be useful for certain types of applications. Of the other options, the `hostname` command can be used to set the hostname. The other commands shown are not valid.

251. B. The `-o` option sets the local filename. The `-O` option preserves the remote filename. The `-f` option causes `curl` to fail silently, and the `-l` option is used with FTP to cause a name-only listing.

252. D. The `find` command will be used for this purpose, and the `-perm` option is needed, specifically as the 2000 permission to indicate `setgid`. Note the use of / to indicate that the entire server will be searched. The `grep` command shown cannot be used for this purpose because it looks for the presence of the string `setgid` within files located in the current directory only.

253. B. The `/dev/null` location will accept input and not consume additional disk space when output is redirected to it. The `/dev/random` device exists but is not valid for this scenario. Likewise, redirecting to a network interface or regular file does not meet the criteria for this scenario.

254. D. The `reload` target or command, used as part of a `service` command, causes the daemon to reload or reread its configuration files.

255. C. The Ctrl+Z key combination will suspend a process. The other options are not valid for this purpose. The Ctrl+C key combination kills the process.

256. B. The Nano editor is appropriate for this scenario. While Vi is indeed a text editor, beginners typically struggle with it. The `nc` command is not used for text editing, and there is no ShellRedirect text editor.

257. C. The `mask` command links the unit file to /dev/null, thereby ensuring that the service cannot run. The `disable` command deletes the symlink between /etc/systemd and /lib/systemd, but the service could still run. The other options shown are not valid.

258. A. The `printf` command can be used to add special formatting to strings for printing. The `echo` command can be used somewhat for this purpose but is not as powerful at special-formatting capabilities as the `printf` command is. The other commands are not valid for this purpose.

259. A. The `scp` command copies or transfers a file over SSH. The `ncftp` command cannot be used for this purpose. The other commands are not valid.

260. B. Pressing Shift+F within `top` enables you to choose which columns display as well as the sort order for the columns. In the scenario described, you can view the processes using the highest amount of memory.

261. A. The `-f` option forces `fsck` to run on an otherwise clean filesystem. This can be helpful for times when you suspect there is an error on the filesystem and need to verify as part of the troubleshooting process. This can also be helpful to prepare the filesystem for conversion, such as might be the case with a tool like `btrfs-convert`.

262. D. SFTP would be the preferred option because it provides additional security over legacy FTP. In general terms, FTP usually should be disabled because credentials and other traffic are not encrypted. Among the other options, email (SMTP) offers no encryption, and SSL by itself does not transfer files. Because the scenario did not include details of whether the transfer was over a long distance, it is difficult to tell whether USB would be appropriate. However, the use of a USB device is frequently discouraged on servers because it can be another attack vector.

263. C. The `cpio` utility can work with various archive formats, one of which is HPUX-created archives. The `gzip` or `bzip2` command likely would not be able to open or extract from the file; those are typically used for compression and not archival purposes.

264. A. Making a bit-level image of the partition with `dd` is a good idea in order to preserve any evidence of the break-in. Creating a backup using `tar` is a less preferred option. Examining the partition with `fdisk` would not reveal any relevant information, and reformatting the partition usually should not be done until the extent of the attack is understood.

265. C. The `-r` option tells the `zip` command to traverse directories when creating the archive. The other options are not valid for this purpose.

266. A. The `ps` command, when given with arguments such as `auwx`, will show all processes and the owner of those processes. Combining with the `grep` command reveals the processes with the word *apache* in them. On other systems, this might be called `httpd` instead of `apache`, but the question specified a Debian system.

267. B. The `./configure` pattern is typically used to invoke a configure script. Option A might work, but the `build` directory is typically not in the path.

268. B. The `lvresize` command changes the size of a logical volume. The other commands shown are valid Logical Volume Manager commands but do not solve the problem presented.

269. A. The file `/proc/mdstat` displays information regarding the RAID arrays found a system.

270. A. Parity and striping are configured using `--layout` or `-p`. The `-x` option specifies spare devices while `-R` starts the array. The `--level` option can be used to set the type of RAID, such as mirroring (RAID1) or striping (RAID5).

271. D. The `dmidecode` command displays information related to the DMI, or Desktop Management Interface.

272. D. SSHFS, or Secure Shell Filesystem, is an implementation of FUSE (Filesystem in User-space) because it allows non-privileged users to mount a remote filesystem without needing elevated privileges.

273. D. The `.rpmnew` and `.rpmsave` files are used to store configurations for packages that are installed, whether a new configuration file or an existing configuration file.

274. A. The `renice` command can be used to set the priority of a running process. The `nice` command can be used to set the priority, but because the `nc` command was already running, `renice` must be used. The `nc` command can be used to transfer files, so killing the process isn't a great option. The `ps` and `top` commands do not change priorities.

275. A. The `flatpak-builder` command is used to create the application for Flatpak. The other commands do not exist.

276. D. The `snapd` process runs in the background and maintains the list of snap packages available.

277. A. The `appimagetool` command is used to create an AppImage package. The other commands are not valid.

278. C. The `mtr` command combines elements of both ping and traceroute. Among the other commands, `nmcli` is the NetworkManagement manage tool for network. Both tcpdump and wireshark/tshark are used for monitoring the network.

279. C. The `-p` option specifies the protocol with the `resolvectl` package. The other options are not valid.

280. A. The `jobs` command shows background processes related to the current shell. The `htop` command shows running processes but beyond just the current shell. The `pidof` command displays the process id of a specific process. The other options are not valid.

281. A. The `arp` command, part of the `net-tools` package, displays the known MAC addresses and IP addresses on a given machine.

282. B. The `cd ~` command changes the current directory to the home directory, which is `/root` when you are the root user. The `/home` directory is used to as the default home directory location for normal users. The `/bin` and `/sbin` directories are used for binary programs.

283. A. The `file` command examines and reports the type of file based on its contents. The `xz` command is used for file compression. The `lsof` command lists open files but not types. The `pgrep` command is related to processes.

284. D. A process in Zombie state will have a state of Z in the output for `ps`. The other states shown are valid process states but not with Z in the output for `ps`.

285. A. The `pkill` command is used to terminate a process by name. The other commands shown are not valid.

286. D. Using `cd` with `..` changes up one level. Using `cd` with `.` does not change directory. Using `cd` with `~` changes to the home directory, and the `mv ~` command is incomplete and does not work for the scenario provided.

Chapter 2: System Operations and Maintenance (Domain 2.0)

1. B. The `userdel` command is used for this purpose, and the `-r` option (lowercase) deletes both the home directory and mail spool files. The `-R` (uppercase) option informs the `userdel` command to use a `chroot` directory.

2. A. The best option among these choices is to change the group to `www-data` and change the permissions such that the group can write into the directory. Option B should never be used because it enables world-writing to the directory. The other options will not allow the web server group to write into the directory.

3. D. The `chage` command is used for this purpose. The `-d` option sets the days since the last password change and is measured in days since January 1, 1970. The `-W` option is the days of warning for changing a password, and the `-l` option displays a list of the various settings related to the account. There is no `-f` option.

4. B. User-based configuration files are located in the order `.bash_profile`, `.bash_login`, and `.profile`. Only the first file found is executed; the others are ignored. The file `/etc/profile` is a system-wide bash profile.

5. C. The `/etc/skel` directory contains files to be copied to the user's home directory. The other directories listed for this question do not exist by default.

6. C. The `--norc` option causes bash to execute without reading the `/etc/bash.bashrc` (Debian derivatives) or `/etc/bashrc` (Red Hat derivatives) file or the local `~/.bashrc` file. The other options listed do not exist as options for bash, which is the default shell on most popular Linux distributions.

7. A. The `.bash_profile` file, if it exists in your home directory, will be executed on login. Note that placing the function in `/etc/profile` would technically work, but then the function would be available to all users, which is not what the question asked for.

8.   A. The DISPLAY variable can be used to remotely send the windows of an X session to another computer when using protocols like SSH. There is no XTERMINAL or XDISP environment variable, and XTERM is typically a terminal window and not an environment variable.

9.   B. The X11Forwarding option must be enabled in order for X connections or windows generated from the X server to be sent over an SSH connection.

10.   C. The /etc/passwd file contains various information about users on a system such as username and real name, along with user ID (UID) and login shell. The file is world-readable. The /etc/shadow file contains encrypted passwords but is not readable by all users. The other two files shown as options do not exist by default.

11.   A. The groupmod command is used for this purpose, and the −n option is used to change the group name. The other commands listed do not exist.

12.   B. The −m option causes the user's home directory to be created. By default, if this option isn't specified and CREATE_HOME has not been set, the home directory won't be created. The −h option displays help text, and the other options shown are not valid.

13.   A. The usermod −L command locks an account by placing an ! in the encrypted password. If the user has another means to log in, such as with an SSH key, using usermod −L will not prevent their login. Among the other answers, userdel −r deletes a user and useradd −h displays help related to adding a user to the system. There is no userlock command.

14.   C. The passwd command will be used for this purpose. The −a option displays all users but requires the use of −S to indicate status. The −S option alone will not produce a report for all users, and the −−all option is an alias for −a.

15.   B. The /etc/shadow file contains usernames, UIDs, and encrypted passwords and is not readable by any non-root user on the system due to the sensitive nature of the encrypted passwords. The /etc/passwd file contains usernames and UIDs but not encrypted passwords. The other two files listed for this question do not exist.

16.   A. The usermod command is used for this purpose. The −d option changes the home directory from its normal location at /home. The −m option moves the contents. The other commands shown for this question are not valid.

17.   D. The −G option is a list of supplemental groups to which the user will be added. A lowercase −g option provides the primary GID. The −l option causes the user to not be added to the lastlog and faillog databases. There is no −x option.

18.   A. The −r option creates a system user, which will typically entail no expiration, no home directory, and a UID below 1000. The −s option defines the shell and is not typically used for this purpose. The −a and −S options do not exist.

19.   B. The /etc/gshadow file contains secure information such as an encrypted password for groups, where applicable. The /etc/group file contains general information on groups. The other two files listed as options do not exist.

20. B. The `groupdel` command cannot delete groups unless there are no users who have the given group as their primary GID. Therefore, option B best fits the scenario. There is no `-f` or `-r` option, making options A and D incorrect.

21. A. The `id` command shows the username, UID, primary group, and GID along with supplemental groups. The `passwd` and `chage` commands are not used for this purpose. There is no `getid` command.

22. D. The `-c` option changes the comment field in `/etc/passwd`. The comment field is typically associated with the real name of the account. The `-R` option indicates a `chroot` directory, while `-d` indicates a change of home directory. There is no `-n` option.

23. B. The `usermod` command with the `-aG` option is used to append a group onto the user's list of groups. In this case, the user needs to be a member of the `lpadmin` group.

24. D. The `w` command shows currently logged-in users along with information such as uptime and load average and is similar to the `who` command. The `fuser` command is used to show open files, and the `-u` option to `ls` controls the display for file listings. There is no `listuser` command.

25. C. The date of the last password change, as measured in days since January 1, 1970, is contained in the third field of a `shadow` entry. The expiration date would be the eighth field, as separated by colons.

26. B. The `who` command displays who is currently logged in and the date and time they logged in. The `whois` command displays information about domains. The other commands are not valid.

27. A. The `groupadd` command is used to add a group to the system. The other options shown are not valid.

28. C. The sticky bit is set using `+t`. For this question, the user permission is being affected, thus the `u` as an argument to `chmod`. Among the other answers, the `chown` command is valid but changes ownership, not permissions, and thus isn't used for the purpose described in the question.

29. C. The 022 umask will translate into 644 permissions on a new non-executable file.

30. D. There is no direct relationship between the UIDs and GIDs on a system. UIDs represent users, while GIDs represent group IDs. On some systems, the UID and GID numbers will match for regular users, but this is not a requirement and is more of a coincidence.

31. D. SNMP traffic takes place on ports 161 and 162. Although the traffic is usually on UDP, the TCP ports are also reserved for SNMP. Ports 110 and 143 are used for POP3 and IMAP, respectively, while 23 and 25 are Telnet and SMTP. Finally, ports 80 and 443 are HTTP and HTTPS.

32. D. Loading of alternate files is accomplished using the `-f` option. Doing so facilitates exactly the scenario described: being able to examine logins from old log files. The `-a` option controls the location of the display for the host, while `-t` controls the display to show the logins as of the specified date and time. There is no `-e` option.

33. A. The `openssl` command will be used for this purpose, with the `genrsa` option. An output file is specified with `-out`. The other commands containing `openssl` all contain an invalid option. The final command is `openssh` and is not used for this scenario.

34. A. The `PermitRootLogin` directive, set to `yes` or `no`, determines whether the root user can log in directly. This option is set within the server configuration file at `/etc/ssh/sshd_config`. In general, server-wide configuration files for SSH are stored in `/etc/ssh` while user-specific configuration files are stored in each user's home directory. The other options shown are not valid.

35. B. The `-R` option creates a port forward and enables remote clients to connect. The `-L` option also creates a port forward but does not allow remote clients to connect. The `-P` and `-E` options are not valid for this scenario.

36. A. The `req` option begins the CSR generation process, typically also requiring `-new` as an additional option. The other subcommands are not valid.

37. D. The `/etc/profile.d` directory can be used to store files and scripts that are then executed on login. Of the other answers, `/etc/profile` does exist, but it is a file and not a directory. The other answers are not valid directories.

38. B. The `NAME` parameter sets the name for the device. The other options shown are not valid udev parameters.

39. D. Port 3306 is the default port for MySQL. Of the other options, 25 is SMTP, and 389 is typically used with LDAP.

40. C. The `SSLCertificateKeyFile` directive points to the location of the private key for an SSL configuration. The other options shown are not valid directives.

41. A. The `chgrp` command can be used to change group ownership of a file. The order is `chgrp <groupname> <target>`.

42. C. The `-S` option displays output in a format such as `u=rwx,g=rx,o=rx`. The other options listed do not exist.

43. B. The `-R` option will perform the change ownership in a recursive manner.

44. C. The `-R` option sets the recursive option, which means `chgrp` will traverse the given directory and perform the group ownership change operation throughout the specified hierarchy.

45. D. You minimally need to be able to read the file being sourced; therefore, `chmod 400` will correctly set the permissions. Any `chmod` that gives additional permissions is not necessary. When permissions are granted using octal notation, the number 4 is read, 2 is write, and 1 is execute. There are three permissions: user (owner), group, and other or world. Therefore, `chmod 400` grants "read" privileges to the owner and no permissions to group and other/world.

46. B. The `chage` command will be used for this purpose, specifically with the `-E` option. When provided with a date, `chage` will expire the account on that date. When provided with `-1`, the expiration will be removed, thus removing the user lockout. The use of `sudo` in the options for this question notes the need for elevated privileges in order to run the command successfully.

47. B. The getent command is used to display entries based on the /etc/nsswitch.conf file. One use case for getent is when integrating with Microsoft Active Directory or another LDAP service, to check whether the connection can be made to the LDAP server. The usermod command is valid but is not used for this purpose, and the other commands shown for this question are not valid.

48. A. The suid bit enables the program to run as the user who owns the file, regardless of who executes the program. Using SUID typically is not recommended for security reasons. The other permissions allow read (r) and write (w) for the owner of the file. The group and "other" permissions include read (r) and execute (x) but not write.

49. C. The kern facility receives messages from the kernel for logging purposes. Of the other options, syslog is used for logging messages about syslog itself. The other two options shown are not valid syslog facilities. Kernel messages are sometimes placed in a separate log called /var/log/kern.log.

50. A. The service used for logging on a computer managed by systemd is called systemd-journald. You use journalctl to view logged entries rather than the standard Linux toolset.

51. A. The mail command will send the log to the specified email address on completion of the logrotate process. The other options shown do not exist as options in /etc/logrotate.conf.

52. B. SMTP operates on TCP port 25, and if other servers are contacting your SMTP server, you'll need to listen on this port and allow traffic to it as well. Port 23 is used for Telnet, port 110 is POP3, and port 143 is IMAP, none of which are necessary for SMTP traffic.

53. B. Traditionally, udp/53 is used for DNS queries, but with a primary and secondary server, it is assumed that zone transfers may occur. DNS zone transfers typically take place over tcp/53.

54. D. The /etc/services file contains standard port-to-protocol information based on the well-known and assigned ports from IANA. If you'd like to provide a custom name for the service, you can do so by editing this file. There is no /etc/ports or /etc/p2p file by default, and /etc/ppp is usually a directory for the point-to-point protocol daemon and related services.

55. D. ICMP is a layer 3 protocol, meaning it does not use ports for communication. TCP/43 is used for whois, while port 111 is used for sunrpc. UDP/69 is used for the TFTP protocol.

56. D. The chage command is used for working with account aging information such as expiration date, password change, days between password changes, and so on. The -l command lists information for the given account. The usermod command is used to make changes to an account, and the other two commands are not valid.

57. B. The ssh-keygen command is used to create a key pair for use with SSH instead of a password. Of the other options, the ssh command does exist, but the -k option is used to disable GSSAPI credential forwarding and not for the purpose described.

58. A. The file authorized_keys, stored in the .ssh directory in your home directory, contains public keys that are authorized to log in to the server using their corresponding private key.

59. A. The -u option is correct for this purpose. An uppercase -U option sets the user context for listing privileges. The -s option sets the shell, and the -H option sets the home directory.

60. B. The NOPASSWD option causes sudo to not prompt for a password for a given sudo command. This is useful for scripted scenarios where a password prompt would cause problems.

61. C. The ulimit command shows such limits, and the -a option shows all limits for the currently logged-in user. The other commands are not valid.

62. C. The syntax to block access to every service uses the ALL keyword followed by the address or network to which the policy will apply. This is important because you may notice attacks coming from certain IP blocks, and blocking with TCP wrappers provides a fast method for effective blocking.

63. A. The file is named id_rsa by default, and the public key is named id_rsa.pub. For DSA keys, the names are id_dsa and id_dsa.pub.

64. C. The -c option executes a single command but does so without an interactive session. The -s option specifies the shell to be used. There is no -u or -e option for the su command.

65. C. The send-key option followed by the name of the key sends the key to the key server specified by the keyserver option. This is a typical scenario for sending a locally generated public key to a public server for others to use. The other options shown as potential answers do not exist.

66. C. While any text editor can be used, it is highly recommended to use the visudo command to edit /etc/sudoers. Using visudo enables syntax checking, which will help prevent issues with an invalid configuration causing problems for those who rely on sudo.

67. B. The file ssh_known_hosts, usually kept in either /etc/ or /etc/ssh/, is used for the purpose described. Note that on some systems, this file and other SSH-related configurations may be found in /etc/sshd/. The answers that indicated ~ or within /root are incorrect because the question specified a server-wide list. A known_hosts file found within ~/.ssh would indicate the user's home directory.

68. A. The option PasswordAuthentication configures whether users will be allowed to authenticate using a password rather than key-based or another form of authentication. The other options shown are not valid. Note that on some distributions, the configuration files are found in /etc/sshd/, while on other distributions, the configuration files are found in /etc/ssh/.

69. A. The --gen-key subcommand is used for the purpose described and will generate a self-signed private and public key pair in a PKI scenario. The other options shown do not exist.

70. B. The file pubring.gpg, found in ~/.gnupg, contains the public keyring.

71. C. The - option is the typical option passed to su for login. There is no -u or -U option, and the -login option does not exist. There is a --login option with two dashes, but that is not what's shown.

72. C. The SSLEngine option needs to be set to On for SSL to be enabled for a given site or server. The other options are not valid. Enabling SSL is important in order to provide a level of security such that the actual data within an HTTP transaction cannot be viewed.

73. B. The -k option enables Kerberos authentication for the net command. The -a option indicates that non-interactive mode should be used, and -l sets the log directory. There is no -b option.

74. C. The directory /etc/pam.d stores configuration files for individual PAM-aware services. Each service typically has its own file, which is managed for that service according to its usage of PAM. Of the other options, none of the directories are the default directories used for PAM.

75. A. The standard port for LDAP is 389, and that is the port on which slapd listens for connections. Port 3389 is RDP, while 3306 is MySQL. Finally, 110 is POP3.

76. C. The pam_nologin.so module facilitates a scenario whereby non-root logins are prevented when /etc/nologin exists. This module must be specified within a configuration file for a given service. For example, within the sshd PAM configuration file, the following line creates this configuration for SSH: account required pam_nologin.so.

77. C. The pam_unix.so module is used for standard login. The manpage for pam_unix.so indicates that it is for "traditional password authentication." The other modules listed are not standard PAM modules, although there is a similar pam_auth or squid_pam_auth module for Squid.

78. B. The pam_cracklib.so module enforces password strength options. The other files listed are not valid PAM modules.

79. B. PEM format is used for public and private keys with a Postfix TLS configuration. The other methods listed are valid cryptographic algorithms or systems but not for the scenario described. As with Sendmail, system administrators should take steps to secure mail servers so that the servers are not used for sending unsolicited email. For many scenarios, a full mail server like Postfix or Sendmail is not required in order to simply relay mail from a server.

80. B. The PREROUTING chain, part of the nat table, contains rules that are applied as packets arrive. A common use for this chain is to apply redirect rules. Among the other answers, REDIRECT may appear valid but is in fact a target and not a chain. The other options shown are not valid.

81. C. The iptables-save command sends the current iptables rules to STDOUT. The output can be saved to a file and then applied the next time the server is restarted. The other commands shown are not valid.

82. D. The iptables -n option causes iptables to not resolve host names or port names. The -L option lists current rules. There is no -a option and the other options are not valid.

83. D. The /etc/fail2ban directory contains configuration files related to fail2ban. The other directories shown are not valid. The use of fail2ban is helpful for SSH when compared with other methods like the recently deprecated pam_tally2 and faillock, both of which would not prevent key-based authentication for SSH.

84. B. The PermitEmptyPasswords directive specifies whether empty passwords can be used for authentication. Enabling empty passwords would be a specialized use case and generally is not recommended. The other options shown are not valid.

85. C. The -P option sets the policy for a given chain in iptables. In this case, the chain is INPUT and the policy necessary is DROP.

86. B. OpenVPN listens on UDP port 1194 by default. The other combinations are not the valid OpenVPN configuration.

87. B. The DROP target silently discards packets that match the rule. An ICMP unreachable message is sent back for REJECT. In general, DROP is preferred in order to reduce the chances of denial of service (DoS) or other information-gathering issues.

88. B. The -m match limit, along with the configuration options shown including the LOG target, creates the scenario described. There will be three log entries per minute. This can be useful to prevent denial of service caused by filling up log files or overwhelming the server I/O while another attack is under way.

89. A. The INPUT chain will be used. When used with the -A option, it will append a rule to the chain. The -p option specifies the protocol, ICMP in this case; the -j option specifies the target, ACCEPT in this case. The -P option specifies a policy and will not be used for this scenario.

90. B. The INPUT chain will be used, and a rule needs to be appended with -A. The ALL option, when specifying a protocol, means all protocols will be included in the rule. The -s option specifies the source, which in this case is a single IP address. Finally, the DROP target silently discards packets. There is no BLOCK or DISCARD target, and the ACCEPT target will not block but will accept all traffic.

91. B. A rule will be appended to the INPUT chain with -A. In this case, the protocol should be specified with -p TCP and a destination port of 2222. The source address indicated, 0/0, applies the rule to all hosts. The ACCEPT target will be used.

92. B. Echoing a 1 to the /proc/sys/net/ipv4/ip_forward file enables forwarding of IP packets. This is necessary in order to utilize NAT and for other uses. There is a similar file for IPv6 at /proc/sys/net/ipv6/ip_forward. There is no /proc/sys/net/ipv4/nat file.

93. A. The logpath directive determines the log file that will be monitored for failures by fail2ban. This file is used as part of a larger configuration for a given jail. The other directives are not valid for fail2ban.

94. D. The ssh-copy-id command sends an identity to a remote server that can then be used for key-based authentication. The other commands shown are not valid.

95. B. The `mailto` configuration option sets the destination for emails related to `sudo`. The other options listed are not valid for `sudo`.

96. C. Port 123 is used for NTP communication by default. Port 161 is SNMP, while 139 is NetBIOS, and 194 is IRC.

97. C. Files related to SSL are typically stored in either `/etc/ssl` (or a subdirectory therein) or in the `/etc/pki` hierarchy. There is no `/etc/private` or `/usr/share/ssl` directory. The other directories shown as options do not exist.

98. A. The `AllowUsers` directive is used to specify users who will be allowed to log in to the server. The other options shown are not valid.

99. A. The `--log-prefix` option specifies the string that will be prepended when a log entry is created by `iptables`. The other options shown are not valid for use with `iptables`.

100. B. The `SELINUXTYPE` option can be set to targeted or strict. With targeted, only specific network daemons are protected.

101. A. When `Permissive` is returned, SELinux is not enforcing rules but is using DAC rules. Other return outputs are `Enforcing` and `Disabled`.

102. B. The `sshd.conf` file is used for server configuration. On some distributions, this file is called `sshd_config`. The `ssh.conf` file is used for client configuration at the system level.

103. D. When a required module returns a failure, other modules continue to process, but the authentication ultimately fails. This is done so that logging will occur and other modules have had a chance to handle the authentication attempt. If a failure should be immediate without processing other modules, then the `requisite` option should be used instead of `required`.

104. B. The root account has UID 0 on a Linux system. Typically, service accounts have UIDs below 1000, many times below 100. Normal user accounts usually begin at UID 1000.

105. B. Although a hardware token may be available, the default option is software based. Note also that OTP solutions to generate a one-time passcode are similar in functionality to provide multifactor authentication.

106. B. The directory `/usr/lib/firewalld/zones/` contains predefined zones for use with `firewalld`. The files are copied to `/etc/firewalld/zones/` when modified.

107. D. The `password` configuration option is set in `/boot/grub/grub.conf`. The other options shown for this question are not valid for the scenario.

108. B. The `setenforce` command is used for this purpose and can be given an argument of the number 1 or the word `Enforcing` to enable `Enforcing` mode. This can be verified with the `sestatus` command.

109. C. The `ssh-add` command is used for this purpose. The other commands shown do not exist.

110. A. The getfacl command is used to display access control list information for a file. The setfacl command is used to set this information. The other commands shown are not valid Linux commands.

111. C. The file ~/.ssh/config is the appropriate location for this type of configuration information. Of the other answers, only ~/.ssh/known_hosts exists and contains public key information for hosts to which you have connected.

112. A. The -R option is used to indicate recursive behavior. Of the other options, only -v is valid and provides verbose output.

113. B. The -P option makes the values persistent across reboots for SELinux system booleans. The other options are not valid with setsebool.

114. B. The directory /etc/apparmor.d/ is the location in which profiles and application permissions are located.

115. D. The klist command shows the current tickets when using Kerberos authentication. Of the other answers, the kinit command is used to retrieve the initial ticket-granting ticket. The remaining answers are not valid commands.

116. B. The -l option provides a long or detailed listing of files and directories, including ownership and permissions. The -m, -b, and -f options are not related to the scenario described.

117. A. The -a option returns all booleans. The other options are not valid with getsebool.

118. C. The aa-unconfined command displays processes that are offering network ports but do not have an AppArmor profile. The other commands are not valid.

119. C. The wheel group can be used to restrict access to the su command to those accounts that are members of the group. The other groups do not exist by default.

120. C. The chcon command is used to change the security context.

121. A. An SSL VPN can sometimes work around firewalls that otherwise block VPN traffic. SSL-based VPNs are not typically the default in Linux.

122. A. When RSA is chosen as the key type, SHA256withRSA is available along with SHA512withRSA. The other answers shown are not valid hashing algorithms with RSA.

123. B. A password set in the BIOS can be used to prevent the system from booting or handing off the boot process to a bootloader. Neither GRUB nor a root password will help with this scenario because physical access is available.

124. A. The -n option to restorecon shows current contexts without changing them. Of the other options that are valid, -r changes recursively, and -p shows progress.

125. D. The ps command shows processes. When the command is given the -Z option, SELinux contexts are shown.

126. B. The `pam_tally2` module keeps track of failed logins and can be used to lock out an account after a certain number of failed attempts. Note that `pam_faillock` provides similar functionality now that `pam_tally2` has been deprecated.

127. A. The command `aa-complain` is used to place profiles into complain mode. Profiles are located in `/etc/apparmor.d/`, and thus the command shown places all profiles into complain mode.

128. B. The `Match User` option is used to change the configuration for a specific user. The other options shown are not valid.

129. C. The `--runtime-to-permanent` option sets the current runtime configuration to become permanent and available on next boot.

130. A. The `ufw allow` command is used to add rules, and SSH operates on TCP port 22.

131. A. The software used to create firewalls found on most systems is `iptables`. Notably, later versions are called `nftables`, but `iptables` is still found on many systems in use today.

132. B. The `scp` utility uses SSH as transport and therefore requires TCP port 22. TCP ports 20 and 21 are used for legacy FTP, while UDP/53 is used for DNS queries.

133. A. The `-a` option shows files and directories that begin with a dot. The other options shown are not related to this scenario.

134. B. The `-i` option is used to specify a private key to use for authentication with SSH. Of the other options, `-a` is used to disable forwarding of the authentication agent, `-k` disables GSSAPI credentials, and `-m` specifies message authentication code (MAC) algorithms.

135. A. The `chown` command changes ownership of a file or directory, and the `www-data` user was specified in the question, thus making option A the only correct option for this scenario.

136. C. Noninteractive mode for `sudo` is triggered with the `-n` option. The other options are not valid for this scenario.

137. A. The `aa-disable` command is used to turn off profiles used with AppArmor. The other commands shown are not valid.

138. C. The `-Z` option to `ls` is used to view the SELinux security context. The `file` command is a valid command but does not have a `-Z` option.

139. B. GnuPG can be used to provide digital signatures through its `gpg` command. The other answers shown are not valid.

140. D. The directory `/etc/apparmor.d/tunables` contains parameters and configurations that are commonly changed.

141. C. The directory `/etc/ufw` typically contains configuration information for UFW. On many systems, `/etc/default/ufw` will also contain commonly changed default configuration items.

142. B. The ipset project and software facilitates more effective rule management by helping to create sets of IP addresses to which common rules can be applied.

143. A. The public key should be copied to the remote host. When it is copied and the contents placed into ~/.ssh/authorized_keys, authentication will be allowed from anyone presenting the corresponding private key.

144. C. When octal notation is used, the number 4 is read, 2 is write, and 1 is execute. User, group, and other permissions appear in that order with octal notation. Therefore, 7 grants the user read+write+execute, and 5 grants read+execute for group and other.

145. B. The -v option shows contexts of files listed in /etc/sestatus.conf. The other options are not valid for use with sestatus.

146. C. The -M option sets the maximum days for password validity, while -m sets the minimum days between password changes. The other options are not relevant to this scenario.

147. B. KerberosAuthentication is the option within the SSH server configuration that controls whether users can authenticate using Kerberos.

148. A. The -t option, along with the table name, limits output to just the specified table rather than all. The other options are not valid for use with iptables-save.

149. C. Sometimes called privileged ports, well-known ports are considered to be those ports under 1024. These ports are usually made available by system daemons and system-level services and can be disabled if not in use.

150. D. The pam_limits.so module is responsible for enforcement of limits such as those mentioned in the question as well as several others like the maximum size of files, memory usage, and so on. The other modules listed are not valid.

151. D. There are multiple ways to specify log levels and debugging for slapd, including by keyword, by integer, or, as shown in the question, by hex. All the values shown are valid for loglevel. No debugging is 0, trace is 1, stats logging is 256 or 512 depending on type, and packets sent and received is integer 16 or hex 0x10.

152. C. LDAP over SSL uses port 636 by default. Of the other options, port 389 is LDAP but without SSL, port 443 is used for HTTPS communication, and 3128 is used for Squid proxy.

153. B. The pam_listfiles.so module is used to create scenarios whereby you can create files that control authentication and authorization through the PAM system. The other files are not valid for the scenario described.

154. B. The -t option sets the key type for ssh-keygen. The other options do not set the key type but may be valid for other purposes.

155. C. The apt-get remove command is used to remove packages from a Debian system. There is no remove-update option or remove option to apt-cache. Likewise, there is no delete option for apt-get.

156. B. The format is username (or other specifier) followed by `hard` or `soft`, depending on the limit type, and then the keyword followed by the value for that given keyword.

157. D. The `sysctl` command can be used for changing parameters within the running kernel. The changes are not saved between reboots, though, and need to be reapplied if the system is restarted. The other commands shown are not valid.

158. B. The `account` module interface is where access verification occurs. Among the other options, the `auth` and `password` interfaces are used for different purposes, and there is no `policy` interface.

159. C. The `chattr` command is used to change file attributes, including making them immutable. The other commands are not valid.

160. A. UIDs less than 1,000, not including 0, are typically used by service accounts. This is not required but is done by convention.

161. A. Looking for access vector cache (AVC) messages within the `ausearch` command can reveal information about policy violations. It's typical to also include USER_AVC within the query. The other options shown are not valid.

162. B. The `lsattr` command can be used to show extended attribute information about a file, such as whether the file is immutable. The other options shown are not valid.

163. C. Self-signed certificates are not automatically trusted by clients when connecting, whereas a list of trusted certificate authorities enables certificates issued by those authorities to be automatically trusted. Both self-signed certificates and those issued by third parties can be valid for any length of time, making option A incorrect.

164. D. The Chkrootkit software package can be used for security scanning such as examining a host for signs of tampering often associated with a rootkit. The other commands shown as options do not exist.

165. A. The file `/etc/profile` is where the umask is typically set for most Linux distributions. The other files shown do not exist.

166. C. The file `/var/log/kern.log` contains kernel messages and can be used to troubleshoot a kernel panic.

167. C. The `journalctl` command is used to work with the `systemd` journal. On `systemd`-based systems, `journalctl` is a central command for debugging and troubleshooting.

168. B. The `$UDPServerRun` option is used for the purpose described. The port on which the server should listen is then provided as the value for this option. The other options shown are not valid configuration items for `rsyslogd`.

169. A. The `SystemMaxFileSize` option controls the size of the journal log file to ensure that a log does not cause problems related to disk usage. The `SystemMaxUse` option controls overall size of journal files, and the default for `SystemMaxFileSize` is one-eighth of the `SystemMaxUse` setting to allow for rotation of files.

170. D. The `nocompress` option is used to prevent the log file from being compressed or zipped as part of the rotation process. This might be needed on systems where compression negatively affects performance or where additional processing is necessary.

171. C. The `/etc/issue` file is used to provide a message to users, such as a login banner, prior to local login. The other files shown are not valid for the purpose described.

172. C. The contents of the file `motd`, an abbreviation for Message of the Day, are displayed when a user logs in successfully. Among the other options, the contents of `/etc/issue` are displayed prior to local login. The other filenames are not valid for this purpose.

173. C. The `realm` command is used to join a computer to an Active Directory domain. The other commands shown do not exist.

174. A. A wildcard certificate is appropriate for this use case. The wildcard certificate is then valid for all hosts in the same domain. While a self-signed certificate could be used, the scenario specified public-facing hosts, which means that a trusted certificate authority will need to be used in order for public end users to automatically trust the certificate. The other two options are not valid.

175. C. The file `/etc/login.defs` is where options related to shadow-based authentication are set. The other options shown are not valid.

176. A. The new connection state indicates a communication path or session that has not yet been established between source and destination. The new connection state was also available in `iptables`. None of the other options shown are valid connection states in nftables.

177. C. The file `/etc/ssh/ssh_config` contains default values for client behavior that can be overridden by `~/.ssh/config` values on a per-user basis. Of the other files, `/etc/ssh/sshd_config` is valid but defines server-related configuration.

178. D. A Socks proxy is used when dynamic port forwarding is configured with SSH. Of the other answers, Squid can be used as a proxy server but is not associated with dynamic port forwarding for SSH. The other options shown are not valid.

179. A. Rules are added with a call to the `addRule()` function in polkit, which is the executable associated with PolicyKit and is used to create rules. The other options shown for this question are not valid functions.

180. B. Using the `touch` command to touch the file `/.autorelabel` will trigger a relabel for SELinux. The other commands shown are not valid.

181. C. The `audit2allow` command is used to create a new set of rules based on a logfile that contains actions that have been denied. Care should be taken when doing so in order to prevent allowing processes and permissions that should not be allowed. The other commands shown in this scenario are not valid.

182. C. The `semanage` command can be used to make changes such as ports, booleans, and contexts in order to keep a policy in Enforcing mode but still make changes. The other commands shown are not valid for this purpose.

183. D. The `system-config-selinux` command is used to change policies on a Fedora system. The other commands shown are not valid.

184. B. The `g-s` syntax removes the SGID bit from a directory. The other syntax is incorrect and invalid for `chmod`.

185. C. The `--user` option specifies the user under which the program will be executed. The other options are not valid for this purpose.

186. B. Local forwarding is accomplished with `-L`. The first port is the local port, which is then followed by the destination hostname and port. The other answers do not use the correct syntax for this scenario.

187. D. A stateless firewall examines only the source and destination and does not inspect elements inside packets. Stateless firewalls are not typically associated with particular zones such as internal, external, or DMZ, thus making option A incorrect. Linux has firewalls that can be configured as stateful, thus making option B incorrect.

188. A. The UID_MIN configuration option defines the lowest value that will be used when creating users. The other configuration options shown are not valid.

189. A. The presence of an asterisk within the name `*.example.com` indicates that this is a wildcard certificate. While the certificate may be self-signed, there is not enough detail within the given information to determine the chain of trust. An asterisk is not a valid hostname for DNS but is valid to indicate a wildcard certificate.

Chapter 3: Scripting, Containers, and Automation (Domain 3.0)

1. A. The `echo` command is used to send output from a Bash script. The other options are not valid commands.

2. A. Ansible is agentless, using SSH and Python for orchestration. Puppet does have an agentless mode but typically uses agents for orchestration. The others are not valid orchestration packages.

3. B. The `env` command executes a command and enables a custom environment for that command execution. The `set` command changes environment variables but does not change variables for the single command execution, as specified in the scenario. The other options are not valid commands.

4. B. The `pull` command in git fetches the changes and incorporates them into the current working copy. The `fetch` command retrieves but does not incorporate the changes. The other options are not valid `git` subcommands.

5. B. Infrastructure as code typically means managing infrastructure components using some of the same tools that developers would use, such as source code management along with programs or scripts and automation for deployments and configuration changes. These practices help to facilitate continuous integration/continuous deployment (CI/CD) scenarios by automating many processes.

6. A. The chmod command will be used for this solution. The option granting 700 enables execute privileges for the owner. The other options have incorrect syntax, an incorrect path, or inappropriate permissions for the scenario described. It is important to differentiate between relative and absolute paths, noting that ~/ is an alias for your home directory.

7. A. The source command adds functions found in the file argument to the current shell. The source command is frequently used for software installs to ensure that the environment is set up properly prior to execution of the install scripts.

8. D. The character sequence #!/bin/bash invokes the commands that follow as a Bash script.

9. C. The greater-than sign is used to redirect output to a file and will overwrite the file if it already exists. The pipe character can be used to chain output but is not considered redirection of output. The less-than sign will redirect input and the ampersand will send a process into the background.

10. A. Creating a git repository requires creating the directory, changing the current working directory to the new directory, and then running git init --bare. The other commands will not create an empty git repository.

11. B. The term *inventory* is most often used in orchestration to refer to the collection of devices under management.

12. D. A backslash is used to escape characters such as a single quote in a Bash script. The other characters will not achieve the desired result.

13. A. An exit code of 0 indicates that the script did not encounter an error. This exit code is generally associated with a successful execution of a program in Linux.

14. A. Shell expansion, or more accurately, brace expansion, can be used to create the output shown. The other options will not produce output as shown.

15. C. The pound sign (#) is used to indicate that what follows is a comment and will not be executed for the remainder of the line. The other options are valid comment styles in other languages but not for a Bash script.

16. D. No special extension is necessary for a Bash script to be executed. The extension .sh shown as an option is a common extension that you will see for shell scripts of any variety, but the extension isn't required.

17. C. The merge command incorporates changes to a previously cloned git repository. The push command is valid but is used to send code to a remote repository or origin. The other commands are not valid.

18. A. An agent is software that runs on clients and listens for commands from the server in an orchestration architecture.

19. C. *Infrastructure automation* is the term most closely associated with adding (and removing) servers in response to load and demand and is frequently associated with continuous integration/continuous deployment (CI/CD) concepts.

20. C. When executed as part of a function, the `local` command can be used to create a local variable in a Bash script.

21. A. The `clone` command retrieves a copy of the repository for local use. The `checkout` and `co` commands are used with Subversion and not with git.

22. D. The `$0` parameter contains the name of the script being called. The other answers do not fulfill the requirements of this scenario.

23. B. The `printenv` command can be used to print the contents of the current shell environment such as environment variables. Within the output you'll find things like the `$SHELL` variable, which specifies the current shell. The other options shown are not valid commands.

24. B. A single equal sign is used for string comparison in a Bash script. Of the other answers, `-ne` is valid but is used when comparing integers. The string *eq* would be an operator if preceded by a single dash, as in `-eq`. In that case, `-eq` is used for integer comparison.

25. B. A `while` loop that evaluates boolean `true` will accomplish the task described. The other options given are syntactically incorrect in various ways.

26. B. The `git checkout` command switches the working copy to the specified branch and points the HEAD toward that branch. The other commands shown as options are not valid with git.

27. C. The `export` command adds a variable to the current environment and is frequently used for the scenario described. The other options are not valid commands.

28. B. The current contents of the PATH variable, or any other shell environment variable, can be displayed using the `echo` command. Variables in Bash use a `$` as part of the identifier. Therefore, any option without the `$` would not work.

29. A. The `$()` sequence executes a command within a subshell, which is helpful for ensuring that global variables in a Bash script cannot be modified. The other sequences shown are not valid for the scenario described.

30. B. Managing configuration with orchestration is described in this scenario, so option B is the closest response.

31. B. The `-u` option or `--unset` will remove a variable from the environment. The other options are not valid with the `env` command.

32. C. The double-ampersand metacharacter executes the right-hand command only if the first command exits with a successful exit code. A single ampersand sends the command into the background, thus making option B incorrect. A pipe character executes the second command but does so regardless of the success or failure of the first command, thus making option D incorrect.

33. B. Two greater-than signs append output to the specified destination. Option A includes only one greater-than sign, which overwrites rather than appends output. The pipe character in option C does not send output to a file, and option D does not work for the purpose described.

34. D. File globbing is the process of expansion of special characters, which is required for this scenario. In this case, the negation character is the caret, thus making option D correct. Option C is missing the crucial globbing pattern needed for this scenario.

35. B. The .gitignore file is used to store files that will not be versioned.

36. C. The for loop should be used for this purpose because it iterates through a list. An until loop would require additional code, thus making it a less-preferable construct for the purpose described. There is no do loop or foreach loop in Bash, thus making those options incorrect.

37. C. Command substitution can be accomplished using backquotes or $(). These two methods are substantially but not completely equivalent.

38. C. The git log command is used to show a commit history. The other commands shown are not valid with git.

39. A. The -m option enables a message to be included in the commit, thereby alleviating the need to go into an editor to create the commit message. The other options shown do not accomplish the required task.

40. B. Build automation is the most appropriate name for kicking off the compilation of software on commit and is frequently found in organizations that use continuous integration/continuous deployment (CI/CD).

41. A. In this scenario, STDIN redirection is accomplished with a less-than sign to take the contents of customers.sql and send those contents into the mysql command. It's also likely that the mysql command would have things like -u for the username and -p to prompt for the password, but those were not relevant to the scenario and are not required in all circumstances. The other options shown are not valid for the purpose described. Options B and C take output from the mysql command, while option D is an invalid character sequence.

42. C. More than likely you have not executed git push to send the code to the server. Of the other options, you do not need to send commit IDs to teammates and there is nothing to indicate that you have been having problems committing the code itself.

43. B. The -R option performs a recursive change to the targets identified by the chmod command. The other options do not perform recursive changes for chmod.

44. D. The closing parenthesis is used to denote a case; when preceded by an asterisk, the default case is indicated.

45. B. The character sequence fi, which is the if statement backward, indicates the end of an if conditional within a Bash script. The other sequences shown as options may be used in other languages.

46. B. The main branch is the branch created by default within a git repository. The other names shown can be used but are not the default.

47. B. The pipe character sends, or pipes, the output from one command into another and is commonly used in a Linux environment for creating complex command sequences, whether through scripting or directly on the command line. The other options shown are not used for the purpose described in the scenario.

48. B. The git status command is used to show the current state of the working copy, displaying things like untracked files, files staged for commit, and so on. The other options shown are not valid for the scenario.

49. B. The –n option suppresses the trailing newline character from the echo command and is quite useful in scripting scenarios. The other options are not valid for the command.

50. A. The inventory of an infrastructure contains things like the version of software installed on clients.

51. C. Redirecting STDERR is accomplished with the character sequence 2>. The plain greater-than sign redirects STDOUT. The other character sequences shown as options are not valid for the purpose described.

52. A. The git config command will be used for this purpose, and the parameter is user.email.

53. B. The readonly command displays the list of read-only variables that have been declared in the current session. The other commands listed for this question do not exist.

54. D. The set command can be used for a variety of purposes to change how the shell environment works. One such option is –C, which prevents output redirection such as that done with > from overwriting a file if the file already exists.

55. C. The file command can be used to determine which type of file is being used. This can be particularly helpful for files without extensions, where you are unsure if you should view the contents of the file. Option A, grep, is used to look within files but would not be helpful in this case. The telnet and export commands are not used for this purpose.

56. B. The history command will display your command history, including commands from the current session. You can specify how many lines of history to display, as shown in the answer for this question. Note that .bash_history will not show the current session's history.

57. A. Preceding the command with a ! will search history and execute the specified command. For example, !vi will start your last Vi session.

58. A. The type built-in command returns the location that the shell will use in order to run the given command. The find command cannot be used for this purpose, and the other commands do not exist.

59. C. The source command is used to execute commands from a file. A typical use case is to create functions or variables that are then available for use within the current session. The other commands listed do not exist.

60. B. While it's true that every user has a `.bash_logout`, the file exists in their home directory and therefore can be edited by the user. Therefore, to ensure that the required command is executed at logout, the file `/etc/bash.bash_logout` must be used.

61. B. The `env -u` command will unset an environment variable for the current session. The `unset` command can also be used for this purpose.

62. A. The `env` command, when used as `#!/usr/bin/env bash`, will determine the location of the Bash interpreter automatically. This makes the resulting script more portable for systems where Bash may not be located in `/bin/`.

63. B. The `PS1` variable usually has its default set in `/etc/profile` and is used as the shell prompt. Users can customize the prompt to include hostname, working directory, and other elements.

64. C. The `$1` variable is automatically available within Bash scripts and represents the first command-line argument. The `$0` variable is the script itself. The other variables listed in this question do not exist by default.

65. B. The `seq` command is used to print a sequence of numbers in a variety of formats. The answer for this question provides a starting point (0), an increment (1), and the final number (5), thus resulting in six numbers being displayed as output.

66. D. The `exec` command executes the command given as its argument and will then exit the shell. The `source` command does not exit the shell.

67. C. The `read` command awaits user input and places that input into the specified variable. The `exec` command is used to execute commands, and the other options are not valid for the purpose described.

68. A. Parentheses are used to denote a function, such as `myFunction()`. The parentheses are optional but are then followed by curly braces containing the commands to be executed when the function is called.

69. C. The sequence `esac`, which is `case` spelled backward, is used to indicate that a `case` statement has ended. Of the other options, the `done` statement is used for termination of certain loops in Bash.

70. C. The `-p` option displays `declare` statements in a way that the commands are fully qualified and could then be used as input for another command, through either piping or redirection to a script.

71. C. Square brackets are used to denote the beginning and end of the test portion of a `while` loop in a shell script. Other languages generally use parentheses for this purpose.

72. B. The `test` built-in will return true and can be used to test for the value existence of a variable not being null. Note that the behavior of the `test` built-in differs depending on the number of arguments.

73. C. The HOME environment variable, set automatically to the user's home directory, is consulted when the command `cd ~` is entered. The other paths beginning with HOME do not exist by default, and the `MAILPATH` environment variable shown contains a list of locations where mail is checked when the shell is used interactively.

74. B. The `git log` command will be used for this purpose, with an option of `--follow` and the filename/path to follow through history.

75. A. Parameters and other facts about the clients are also called *attributes* in an orchestration.

76. C. The integer comparison `-eq` is used for comparing integers within Bash scripts. The other answers are not valid for Bash script comparison.

77. C. The semicolon metacharacter chains multiple commands together but does not use the output from one command as input to the next. If the output needs to be sent into the next command, the pipe character (option D) is used. A single ampersand places a task in the background, thus making option A incorrect; a greater-than sign redirects standard output, making option B incorrect as well.

78. A. The `\a` escape sequence, when used with the `echo` command, sounds an alert or bell. The `\b` option is a backspace. The `\c` option indicates that `echo` should not produce any additional output. There is no `\d` option for `echo`.

79. D. It is important to note that there cannot be any spaces between the variable name and the equal sign. Likewise, there cannot be any spaces between the equal sign and the contents of the variable. This makes option D the only correct answer.

80. A. The provided answer performs command substitution and places the value from the resulting command into a variable. Note the use of `+%s` formatting on the date, which then formats the output as seconds since the epoch, as specified in the question. Option C will provide the date within the `DATE` variable but will not format it as specified.

81. B. In shell scripts, the commands to execute begin at the `do` keyword and end at the `done` keyword. Other languages generally use either curly braces or tabs.

82. A. The `-r` option to `declare` will create or mark the variable as read-only. The `-p` option prints output in a format that can be reused. The `-x` option declares the variable for export.

83. C. The `LC_TIME` environment variable is used to control the display and behavior of the date and time and can be changed to a different locale in order to achieve the desired display and behavior of date and time formatting. The other options shown for this question do not exist.

84. A. The `-i` option shows interface information in a table-like format. This option is used to see information such as transmit and receive bytes as well as the MTU for the interface and other information. The `-r` option shows routes, while `-l` shows listening sockets. There is no `-t` option.

85. C. The Ctr\l+C key combination kills a shell script that you are running interactively. The other key combinations may have an effect but not within this context or for the desired behavior.

86. C. Shell scripting syntax uses the format shown, with square brackets around the condition to be tested and double equal signs for a string test. Variables are preceded by a dollar sign as shown.

87. A. The syntax for setting the PATH separates the new path with a colon, as shown in the correct option. A primary difference between the correct and incorrect options for this question is in how the actual specified path is shown.

88. B. The --abort option attempts to roll back a problematic merge. The other options shown do not exist as options to the git merge command.

89. A. The GIT_DIR environment variable can be used to change the default location away from the ./.git directory in which a new repository would normally be created. The other options are not used by git as environment variables.

90. B. The \t escape sequence adds a horizontal tab. The other characters may have different meaning and so are not valid for this question. For example, \a is alert or bell.

91. C. The double-asterisk sequence has special meaning and indicates that the file will be ignored in all directories.

92. A. The scenario requires alternation. Therefore, square brackets will be used to indicate the beginning of the sequence. After the brackets, a single asterisk indicates a wildcard. The other options will not work for the scenario described.

93. B. The git remote command will be used for this purpose, and when the command is given the show option and the remote name (origin, in this case), additional information about that remote will be displayed. The command is useful for displaying information about the destination for pushed code.

94. D. The $# character sequence contains the number of command-line arguments that were passed to a shell script. The other options shown are not predefined by Bash.

95. B. The TMOUT variable can be set in a given user's shell, and they will be logged out after the value given (in seconds) of inactivity. The other environment variables listed here do not exist.

96. C. The line will output the contents of the NUM variable. The comment occurs after the command on the line, and only code after the # appears is ignored.

97. A. Using the --origin or -o option enables the name to be changed from the default of origin. The other choices are not options with git clone.

98. D. The steal column shows the percentage of time that was spent waiting due to the hypervisor stealing cycles for another virtual processor and can be used with infrastructure automation to indicate that additional CPU resources need to be deployed.

99. C. The LC_ALL variable can be used to set environment variables for the locale and will override others. This can be used when there is a need for a temporary change. The other variables listed here are not used for this purpose and are not created by default.

100. A. A procedure is one or more commands that are executed on a client node as part of infrastructure automation.

101. C. Double semicolons are used to indicate the end of an individual clause within a Bash script. The other sequences shown do not accomplish the task described.

102. C. The `unalias` command is used to remove a previously defined alias. The `rm` command will remove regular files but not aliases. The other commands do not exist.

103. B. The `-e` option checks to ensure that a file exists and is typically used in the context of a conditional within a shell script. The other options may work within shell scripts but are not tests for file existence.

104. C. Setting `LANG=C` as an alias for POSIX compatibility will cause programs to bypass locale translations. The other options shown for `LANG` are not valid.

105. A. The `--list` option shows the current configuration parameters for git. The other options do not exist as options for the `git config` command.

106. B. The number 2 indicates `STDERR` redirection, and double greater-than signs indicate that the output will be appended rather than overwriting.

107. A. A file with a `.yml` extension usually contains YAML. The question also gave a hint of infrastructure as code, where many tools use YAML for configuration and procedures.

108. A. The passwd file will be sent to `STDOUT`, where it will be captured and sent into the `cut` command. The `cut` command will separate the contents of the file line-by-line using a colon as a delimiter. The first field will be sent to `STDOUT` and placed into a file called `users.txt`.

109. C. The `shift` command moves positional parameters down by one. This can be helpful for complex scenarios with several command-line arguments, each containing an option.

110. D. The `--no-commit` option should be added to `git pull` to prevent the merge from being automatically committed.

111. A. As with the `for` loop, the commands within an `until` loop are delineated with `do` and `done`.

112. B. An exit code of 1 indicates a general error. The exit code of 0 indicates success, and 256 is out of range. There is no -1 exit code for Bash.

113. B. The `<<` operator is used for this purpose and will read from `STDIN` until the specified character or characters are encountered. This is sometimes called a Here Document or HEREDOC. Among the other options for this, only `>` is valid and causes `STDOUT` to be redirected.

114. A. The `-a` option, when added to `git commit`, automatically commits previously known files. The `-c` option invokes the editor for the commit, and the other options do not exist.

115. C. The `LC_MONETARY` variable is used by certain programs to determine the localization for currency.

116. D. The `TZ` environment variable is used for this purpose, and the general format is as shown, thus making option D the correct answer.

117. A. Array creation in a shell script involves parentheses when used in this manner. You can also use square brackets to define individual elements, as in `ARRAY[0] = "val1"`.

118. C. The −lt operator is used to test for "less than" conditions within a script. The other operators are not valid for use in a shell script.

119. C. The for loop construct in this case will require the variable name LIST to be preceded with a dollar sign ($), thus making option C correct. The other options will not work for the purpose described.

120. C. The elif keyword is used to create an alternative execution path within a shell script. The other constructs, such as else if and elsif, are used in other languages.

121. C. The .git directory is used for storage of metadata for the repository.

122. B. The character sequence shown in option B is the correct sequence to redirect both STDERR and STDOUT. Of the other options shown, option A will redirect only STDERR. The other options shown are not valid.

123. D. The double-pipe metacharacter executes the right-hand command only if the first command fails. A single ampersand sends the command into the background, thus making option B incorrect. The double-ampersand metacharacter executes the second command, but only if the first command succeeds, thus making option C incorrect.

124. C. The git checkout command switches the location to which HEAD is pointing. By adding the −b option, the branch is also created.

125. D. Both while and until loops execute until a condition changes. The while loop stops when the condition is no longer true, and an until loop executes until the condition is true.

126. A. Comparing integers is typically accomplished using the binary comparison operators like −gt, −eq, and so on. Option B is incorrect because the > operator is used in square brackets. There is no −gta operator or gt operator, making both option C and option D incorrect.

127. C. SSH is typically used for communication between nodes in an agentless orchestration. Less common would be a protocol such as HTTPS. The other protocols shown as options would not be used for agentless orchestration.

128. C. Variable or parameter expansion is accomplished using ${ } wrapped around the parameter name.

129. C. Normal Terraform syntax files use a .tf extension, while those that use JSON should have a .tf.json extension.

130. D. The kubectl get pod command displays status of a given pod within a cluster. The other answers shown are not valid.

131. B. Pods can contain multiple containers in Kubernetes and this facilitates a shared resource use case, where containers can share resources within a pod. When two containers work together within a pod, it is sometimes referred to as a sidecar configuration or a sidecar container.

132. B. A dual-homed networking configuration is one that has two network interfaces. Bridged networking refers to using the host adapter in a virtualization scenario. An overlay network is one that is built on top of another network. Forwarding is not related to this solution.

133. D. A persistent volume, sometimes called persistent storage, keeps data between deployments of the virtualized environment. A container image is used for the original boot.

134. A. Network Address Translation (NAT) effectively hides the virtual machine behind the host IP address. Bridging enables the virtual machine to get its own IP and thus have external clients access it as well.

135. B. The YAML format is used for configuration files that will be used with `cloud-init`. XML and the other formats listed are not used for `cloud-init`.

136. C. A relative path begins with something other than a / whereas an absolute path always begins with a /, indicating the root of the filesystem. The other options, virtual and symbolic, are not valid names used to describe paths.

137. A. The first number, 14, is the line count. The second number is word count and the third number is byte count.

138. A. The `json-file` logging driver is the default logging mechanism for Docker. The other options shown are not valid for Docker logging.

139. D. The `rmi` command removes an image from a host but notably does not remove the image from the registry. The other commands shown are not valid for use with `docker`.

140. B. An overlay network describes virtual networking typically created for and used within the context of virtualization or containerized applications. With Kubernetes, an overlay network facilitates communication within a pod.

141. A. Linkerd, Consul Connect, and Istio are examples of service mesh frameworks or management systems for Kubernetes. A service mesh is used to provide abstraction and management of microservices and networking.

142. C. The `tee` command will send output to both STDOUT and the specified file, thus making option C correct. Option A will redirect output to the correct file but not to STDOUT simultaneously. The other answers will not work for this question.

143. B. The `cut` command uses Tab as its default delimiter. This can be changed with the -d option.

144. D. The -n option changes the number of lines of output for both `head` and `tail` to the number specified. The other options listed in this question are not valid for `head`, and the -f option follows a file with `tail` as the file grows.

145. D. Within a regular expression, * represents 0 or more characters, and in this case the problem doesn't care whether a person is using /bin/bash or /usr/bin/zsh. Likewise, . matches a single character. But in the case of Bash and zsh, you need to look at the first and optionally a second character: thus the ?, which makes the second . optional. Finally, $ anchors the pattern at the end of the string and is key for this regular expression.

146. B. The `find` command beginning with the path and then the `-name` argument will locate all files called `.bash_history`. The output from the `find` command should be piped to `xargs`, which can then build further commands from standard input. Note that this question and solution assume that all users use the Bash shell and are keeping history.

147. D. The `tr` command can be used for the purpose described. The `tr` command is quite powerful for text conversion and search and replace scenarios. The other commands shown do not exist.

148. A. The g option, also known as `global` or `greedy`, will apply the matched operation to the entire line rather than just the first instance of the match. The other options apply as they would for a Perl-Compatible Regular Expression.

149. D. The exit status of the most recently executed pipeline is found with the `$?` environment variable. The other environment variables shown do not exist by default.

150. D. A git pull request is created with the `request-pull` subcommand. Of the other options shown, there is a `pull` subcommand but that is used to fetch and merge code. The other options shown do not exist.

151. C. The `<<<` character combination reads input from `STDIN`, or Standard Input, and uses it as the body of the message for the `mail` command.

152. D. The `-type` option causes `find` to limit its search to directories only, while the `-name` option limits the names of returned elements. Note the use of the wildcard due to the phrasing of the question. Also note the use of `./` to denote beginning the search in the current directory.

153. B. When performing a rebase with Git, the latest common point between the two branches is used and then changes from one branch are reapplied, thus making option B the most accurate. Rebasing does not use soft links, making option D incorrect. Option A is incorrect because the application of changes may or may not come from the origin master branch and may not come from the first commit.

154. A. YAML is used for SaltStack configuration files. Other configuration management software also uses YAML, while others, like Chef, use JSON. None of the configuration management tools use DOC as a type of file for configuration.

155. D. The `-l` option to `git tag` searches the repository for the specified tag. The other options shown as potential answers are not valid for this purpose.

156. C. Host networking typically means that communication will flow through the host network stack in virtualization or containerized applications. You may sometimes see host networking mean that containers can only communicate with the host itself. While option B was similar to that, the option referred to communication exclusively through inter-process communication, thus making it incorrect.

157. D. Performing a `docker pull` will download and prepare an image for use. From the other options, `build` is a valid docker command but is used to create an image from a Dockerfile and other related context files. The other options shown are not valid with Docker.

158. A. The `more` command provides simple paging capabilities. Unlike the `less` command, which needs to be installed on many systems, `more` is usually available even on base installs. The `grep` command is not a pager, and the other commands are not valid.

159. B. The `container ls` command to docker displays the current list of containers. None of the other commands are valid.

160. B. OVF files, which are used for certain virtualization scenarios, are formatted in XML. There is a file extension frequently seen as YML that typically contains YAML-formatted data, but that is not related to this question. HTML is a valid document standard but not for OVF files. There is no OVFMeta document standard.

161. A. The `grep` command will be used for this purpose. Note the difference between `grep -r` and `grep -ri`. The question did not ask for case insensitivity, and therefore the use of `-i` in option B makes it incorrect.

162. A. The `run` command creates a container and starts a Docker image. When you're working with containers, the `start` command is used to start a container and the `stop` command subsequently stops the container from running.

163. C. The `push` command sends an image to be shared at the configured location. None of the other commands shown are valid for use with Docker.

164. B. The `EXPOSE` configuration option indicates ports and protocols to be opened. These options can also be given on the command line at runtime by using the `-p` option. The ports to be exposed can also be found when running the `inspect` command and are listed as `ExposedPorts` within the output.

165. D. The `docker attach` command can be used to connect to a running container. None of the other commands shown are valid for this purpose.

166. A. The `cat` command will display the contents of the file `/etc/passwd` and then pipe that output to the `awk` command. The `awk` command then parses its input, splitting along the specified separator for `/etc/passwd`, which is a colon (`:`). The output is then printed and piped to the `sort` command. The `sort` command in option B will not work because the `cut` command requires an argument. Likewise, the `echo` command in option C will only `echo /etc/passwd` to `STDOUT`.

167. C. The `-l` option provides the number of lines given as input. For example, `wc -l /etc/passwd` would print the number of lines in the `/etc/passwd` file. The other options given in this question are not valid for the `wc` command.

168. C. Both `head` and `tail` print 10 lines of output by default.

169. B. YAML is the format used for creating an application with `compose`. The other formats are valid but not for the purpose described.

170. B. JSON-formatted files are JavaScript Object Notation. These files, along with YAML files, are frequently used to provide templates and configuration information because both formats are lightweight and descriptive. When working with a VM template or automation, you may encounter these formats.

171. B. An Ambassador container is a container that acts as a proxy to connect to and provide a single point of connection through which other containers in the pod communicate. Among the other answers, *sideload* refers to a means to install an application onto a device outside of the normal app store process.

Chapter 4: Troubleshooting (Domain 4.0)

1. A. The -l option displays listening ports and the -t option limits the ports to TCP only, thus making -lt correct. The -m option shows socket memory usage and -f is used to define the family to return. There is no -c option, thus making option B incorrect.

2. B. The lsusb command is used to obtain a basic list of USB devices on a system. The other commands are not valid. In the case of option D, the ls command is valid, but there is no --usb option.

3. C. The keyword single given on the Linux kernel command line will boot the system into single user mode. The other options are not valid.

4. B. Checking to ensure that the disk is detected in the BIOS is a good first step in troubleshooting. Option A, unplugging the disk, won't help it to be detected. Restarting the web server won't help detect the disk, and the disk-detect command does not exist.

5. A. The tune2fs command is used for this purpose, and the -c option sets the mount count for the specified partition. The dumpe2fs command is used to print the superblock and block group information.

6. C. The -R option skips the root filesystem when the -A option is used. The -M option does not check mounted filesystems. There is no -S option.

7. D. Of the options presented, running dmesg is a common way to find out the location to which the kernel has assigned the drive. Rebooting the system is not a good option, although it would work. There is no such thing as /var/log/usb.log, and the location of the drive may change regardless of port, depending on how the drive may be detected in the system.

8. A. SCSI supports 7 to 15 devices per bus, depending on the type of SCSI.

9. C. Unit configuration files are stored in /lib/systemd/system. The other directory options for this question are not relevant or do not exist by default.

10. B. The network-online.target is used to signify that the network is online and operational for services that depend on the network. Of the other options, network.target is a legitimate target but is typically used to help with an orderly shutdown to ensure that services are stopped prior to the network. The other options shown are not valid.

11. D. Creating a symbolic link to /dev/null effectively disables the unit file so that the service cannot be started. The other options shown are not valid files.

12. B. The `ExecStop` configuration option specifies the command that should be executed to stop the service. The other options shown are not valid for this purpose.

13. D. Using `Wants=` creates a weak dependency between two services, while using `Requires=` creates a stronger dependency. The other options shown are not valid unit dependency directives.

14. A. Using the `-s` option displays statistics including a count of collisions that have occurred for the interface. Of the other options, `-c` changes output colors, `-o` prints all information on one line, and `-f` changes the family.

15. B. Swap space is used when there is insufficient RAM memory on a system.

16. C. Steal is the metric used to measure the number of cycles being used by other virtual instances in either a cloud or virtualization scenario. The steal metric is abbreviated as `st` in the output of `top`. The other options are not valid for this scenario.

17. C. The `lscpu` command shows statistics about the CPU that include architecture, cache, speed, and other information. Among the other options, `cpuinfo` is not a command but rather the file `/proc/cpuinfo` contains the same information as `lscpu`. The other options are not valid commands.

18. D. The `ls -Z` command shows information regarding the SELinux security context applied to a file and can help determine if the issue is policy/non-policy related. There is no `-P` option and the other commands shown are not valid.

19. A. The `strace` command is vital to debugging system-call-related application crashes, especially when the daemon or service does not log any error but silently crashes. The other commands are not valid.

20. C. The `Storage=` option controls whether journal logs are written to disk, kept in memory, or not kept at all. The other options shown are not valid for journald.conf.

21. D. A space is used to separate services within a systemd unit file on the `Before=` and `After=` configuration lines. The other delimiters shown as options are not valid for this purpose.

22. D. The `-s` option summarizes the output by directory, while the `-h` option presents the output in a more human-friendly manner.

23. A. The `-f` option forces the specified operation to complete and can sometimes be necessary if there is no other option to fix the issue. However, data loss can occur with this option so care must be taken when using it. The other options shown are not valid.

24. B. NVMe-capable drives are named as `/dev/nvme*`. No special drivers are needed other than those found in the native kernel on a modern system. The other answers do not exist as paths by default.

25. C. The format for the `mount` command is `[partition] [target]`, thereby making option C correct. The other options are not valid because the arguments are in the wrong order.

26. A. Each processor core can run a job, meaning that there are four available run queues on the system described in this scenario. Four of the six processes are therefore running while two are waiting in the run queue. Presence of high run queues can mean that additional processors are needed or that applications should be changed to utilize existing resources more efficiently.

27. C. The lvmdiskscan command looks for physical volumes that have been initialized for use with LVM.

28. A. The OnBootSec option defines the time to wait, in seconds, until launching the command specified within the unit file. It is notable that OnBootSec is an alias for OnStartupSec. The other options shown are not valid.

29. B. The env command will print the current environment variables from Bash. The printenv command will also perform the same operation. The other commands listed in this question do not exist.

30. A. The nice command displays the scheduling priority and can also be used to set the scheduling priority for a command to be executed. The other options shown are not valid.

31. D. The free command displays overall memory usage for both RAM and swap and can be used to determine when additional memory might be needed.

32. A. The uptime command shows basic information such as that described along with the number of users logged into the system and the current time. The bash command is a shell environment, and the ls command will not display the required information.

33. D. The screen command starts a new terminal that can be disconnected and reconnected as needed. Processes running from within the screen session do not know that they are running in a screen session and therefore meet the criteria needed to satisfy this question. The fg and bg commands will not meet the criteria, and the kill command will stop a process.

34. D. The ForceUnmount= option is equivalent to passing the -f option to umount and forces the filesystem to be unmounted. The Options= directive is valid but not for this purpose. The other options shown are not valid.

35. C. The jobs built-in command shows the list of jobs running in the background. Its output includes both a job number and the status of the job.

36. C. The killall command is used to terminate processes using their name.

37. D. The id output represents CPU idle time and therefore is telling for this scenario insofar as further investigation will be needed to determine the cause of reported slowdowns on the system. The id output is not associated with a process or user ID, and user processes are represented by us in the output of top.

38. C. The -y option will attempt to repair automatically, essentially answering y or yes instead of prompting. Of the other options, only -V is valid and will produce verbose output.

39. B. The tune2fs command can be used for this purpose but should be used with care because it can result in data corruption.

40. B. The `mkswap` command formats a swap partition. The `fdisk` command is used to create the partition but not format it. The other two options do not exist.

41. A. The du command will report on disk usage in a recursive manner, unlike the other commands shown here.

42. C. The `usrquota` option will enable user-level quotas on the given mount point. This is typically set within `/etc/fstab`.

43. D. The `-c` option creates the files for the first time. The `-f` option is used for force checking, `-u` is used for user quotas, and `-m` is used to not attempt remounting read-only.

44. D. The `-r` test determines whether a given file exists and can be read by the current user. The `-e` test only checks to see if the file exists, while `-s` determines if the file exists and has a size greater than zero. There is no `-a` file test.

45. C. The default type is `simple` if no other `Type=` or `BusName=` specification is found within the unit file. Of the other options, both `exec` and `oneshot` are valid but not for the scenario described.

46. C. The `sudo` command can be used to execute a process as root. The other commands shown are not valid.

47. D. Setting a user's shell to `/bin/false` will prevent them from logging in interactively to the system, such as with SSH. The other options shown for this question are all valid shells and would allow an interactive login.

48. C. The `journalctl` command is used for this purpose, and the `--disk-usage` option displays the disk space used by journal log files, which are typically stored in `/var/log/journal`.

49. A. The command `timedatectl status` shows the current time zone along with other information about time and date on the device. The other commands shown are not valid for this purpose.

50. D. Private IP addresses are found within the 10.0.0.0/8, 172.16.0.0/12, and 192.168.0.0/16 ranges, thus making an address in the 143 range a public IP.

51. C. The `route` command is used for this purpose, and adding a route is done with the `add` option. The default gateway is added using the `default gw` keywords followed by the IP of the gateway and the adapter.

52. A. The `host` command enables changing of the query type with the `-t` option. Using `ns` as the type will query for the nameservers for a given domain. There is no `all` type, and the other options are also invalid.

53. B. The `-I` option enables the choice of interface. A lowercase `-i` option sets the interval, while `-a` indicates an audible ping. Finally, `-t` enables a TTL-based `ping` only.

54. A. The `host` or `dig` command can be used for this purpose by setting the type to mx. The mx type will query for the mail exchanger for the given domain. There is no `smtp` type.

55. D. The openssl s_client -connect www.example.com:443 command accomplishes the task described. The other commands shown are not valid.

56. A. The ip command with the monitor option/subcommand will display netlink messages as they arrive. There is no netlink subcommand for ip, and the route command will not work for this purpose.

57. A. The @ symbol is used to indicate a server to which the query will be sent directly. This can be quite useful for troubleshooting resolution problems by sending the query directly to an authoritative name server for the domain. Of the other options, -t sets the type, and the remaining options are not valid.

58. A. The getent command is used for working with NSS databases, and getent hosts will display the available hosts using the databases configured in /etc/nsswitch.conf.

59. C. The configuration option is called nameserver, and the value for the option is the IP address of the desired nameserver. There are several options that affect how name resolution is performed, such as the number of attempts and timeout. See resolv.conf(5) for more information.

60. A. The route command can be used for this purpose; the syntax includes the network range, denoted with the -net option, followed by the word netmask and the masked bits, followed by the word gw and the IP of the gateway. The other options shown are invalid for a variety of reasons, including missing keywords and options and order.

61. A. The netstat command is used for this purpose, and the -a option displays all sockets, listening and non-listening. Note that it's frequently helpful to add the -n option, or combine them as in netstat -an, in order to prevent name lookup. Doing so can significantly improve performance of the command.

62. A. The correct format is IP address followed by canonical hostname and any aliases for the host. You can use entries in /etc/hosts to override DNS lookups, which can be useful to prevent those names from resolving or to provide a different resolution.

63. A. The time command includes timing information such as sys time, user time, and real time. The other commands are not valid.

64. B. The ip route command can be used for this purpose, and its syntax uses a change command and the via keyword. The same operation could be completed with the route command but would require deleting the existing gateway first and then re-adding a new default gateway.

65. C. Bad blocks are shown with the -b option. The -f option forces dumpe2fs to perform the requested operation, and the other command options do not exist.

66. C. The -f option specifies that xfs_check should check the contents of the named file for consistency. The -v option sets verbosity, and there are no -d and -a options.

67. D. The What= option specifies the filesystem to be mounted. The Where= option defines the destination to which the filesystem will be mounted. The other options shown are not valid.

68. A. The `search` option is used for this purpose and can be provided with multiple domain names, each separated by a space or tab. The `domain` option is valid within `/etc/resolv.conf` but does not allow for multiple domain names.

69. A. The `route` command can be used for this purpose, and in the scenario described, a `reject` destination is used for the route. The other options shown are invalid because they use invalid options to the `route` command.

70. B. The `tracepath` command provides the Maximum Transmission Unit (MTU) of the hops, where possible. Both `traceroute` and `tracepath` can be used internally or externally, and both provide IPv6 capabilities. Certain options with the `traceroute` command can require root privileges, but not enough information was given in the question for that to have been the correct answer.

71. D. The `-c` option provides the count of the number of pings to send. The `-n` option specifies numeric output only, while `-p` specifies the pattern to use for the packet content. Finally, the `-t` option sets the TTL.

72. C. The `-f` follows the log much like `tail -f`. There is no `--tail` option for `journalctl`. Of the other options, `--du` dumps the catalog, and `-m` merges all available journals.

73. A. The `ip route flush cache` command should be executed after changing the routes. The other commands shown for this question are not valid.

74. A. SPF records are stored in the `txt` record type in DNS, thereby making `-t txt` the correct option for this. Of the other answers, only `-t mx` is valid and returns the mail exchangers for the given domain.

75. C. The only viable possibility of those listed is that ICMP traffic is blocked. TCP traffic is obviously passing because of the ability to get there using HTTP, and DNS must also be working.

76. C. The G signifies a gateway within the route table.

77. A. The `axfr` type is a zone transfer, and the @ symbol signifies the server to which the query will be sent. There is no `xfer` type. Option B is just a normal query for the domain sent to the specified server.

78. B. The `SystemMaxUse=` option controls the amount of space that the journal can use. The other options shown are not valid.

79. A. A `Type=dbus` for a service file has implicit dependencies of `Requires=` and `After=` on `dbus.socket`. The other options are not valid.

80. A. The `nmap` command is used to scan for open ports. It will scan for open TCP ports to the address or addresses specified. The other commands shown do not scan for open ports to external (off-host) IP addresses.

81. B. The `Type=` option is used to specify the type of filesystem that will be mounted. It is similar to the types used with the `mount` command itself. The other options shown are not valid.

82. D. The `.timer` file extension is used with systemd timer files that provide an alternative to `cron`. The other options are not valid.

83. A. Setting `-P0` will cause no ping requests to precede the scan and is useful for the scenario described. There is a `-s` option, but it is not used for this purpose. The other options are not valid.

84. C. The `maxlogins` parameter is used to control the number of simultaneous logins for a given account.

85. A. The `-s` option sets the type of scan and, when followed by an uppercase S, sets the option to SYN. The T option is a `Connect()` scan. There is no Y option or `-type` option for `nmap`.

86. B. The `-J` option enables specification of various settings for the journal such as its location. The other options shown are not valid.

87. D. The `-p` option to `iostat` displays information on devices and partitions. The `-c` option shows CPU utilization, and `-d` shows device utilization and can be used to display Input/Output Per Second (IOPS) information. There is no `-a` option.

88. D. The `vmstat` command is used to display extended information about performance, including blocks in and out. The `iptraf` command is used to provide network-level monitoring, and the other two commands listed are not valid.

89. B. The `w` command shows various useful information that includes load average, logged-in users, and other uptime information. The `uptime` command does not show who is currently logged in. There is no `swap` or `sysinfo` command.

90. C. The `lsmem` command shows statistics about the memory in the system, including block size. Among the other options, `free` shows in-use memory information but not block size. The other options are not valid commands.

91. C. Cacti is a graphing tool that uses scripts for gathering performance data as well as SNMP. The graphs can help to visualize performance of networks and systems alike. The `pstree` command is used to show a tree-like structure of processes.

92. B. The `-e` option causes `swapon` to skip those partitions that do not exist. The other options are not valid for this scenario.

93. C. The `sy` abbreviation in the output of `top` represents the percentage of CPU time used by the system. Of the other options, `us` represents user CPU time. Options A and D are not valid for this scenario.

94. A. The `swapoff` command deactivates swap space, thereby making it unavailable as virtual memory on the system. The other commands shown as options are not valid.

95. C. The `--show` option displays information about the swap spaces on the computer, including how much swap is currently being used. The `-a` option activates all swap spaces. There is no `--list` option, and `-h` displays help.

96. C. The `pvdisplay` command shows information about a given physical volume. You can use `pvdisplay` to view the device on which the PV is built along with the extent size of the PV. The other commands shown are not valid.

97. A. The vgscan command looks for both physical volumes and volume groups related to an LVM configuration. The vgscan command is run at system startup but can also be run manually. The other commands are not valid.

98. C. The pvscan command displays a list of physical volumes on a given server. The PVs displayed are those that have been initialized with pvcreate for use with LVM.

99. C. The ip command defaults to the inet family if not otherwise specified with the -f option. The command will attempt to guess the correct family and fall back to inet. The other families listed as options for this command are not valid for use with the ip command.

100. D. The -n option causes route to use numeric values only, performing no name resolution. This option is useful for the scenario described. The -e option causes the output to be in netstat format. There is no -d or -f option for the route command.

101. A. Because you're working with MAC addresses, the arp command will be used. The -d option removes or deletes an ARP entry, which would be appropriate here so that the MAC address resolution occurs again. The netstat command will not be used for this purpose. The hostname and dig commands work with name resolution but not for MAC addresses or the ARP table.

102. B. The -o option removes newlines from the output, thereby making the output more suitable for the grep command. The -l option specifies the number of loops for the ip addr flush command. The -f option specifies the protocol family. There is no -n option.

103. A. The -s option creates an ARP table entry. The -d option removes an entry. The -c and --add options do not exist.

104. C. The -D option lists the interfaces on a given computer. The -d option dumps compiled matching code, and -i selects an interface. There is no -a option.

105. B. The -R option requires that an attempt at name resolution be performed. The -n option does the opposite: it disables name resolution. There is no -b or -a option.

106. B. The mtr command provides a unique way to view real-time information about each hop in a route between hosts. Both the traceroute and route commands are valid, but the options shown for each are not. There is no liveroute command.

107. A. The --delay option sets the interval between checks of array health. The argument value is in seconds. The other options shown are not valid.

108. C. The !H sequence indicates host unreachable. Network unreachable is !N.

109. A. The -m option specifies how the packet should be marked or tagged. The -a option is an audible ping, and -p enables specification of custom padding. There is no -k option.

110. B. The -r option displays a report that includes CPU time and exit status about the just-completed fsck operation. The -f option forces whatever operation is being requested, -s serializes fsck operations, and -l creates an exclusive flock.

111. D. The file /proc/meminfo provides a wealth of information about memory usage and utilization. Much of this information is displayed by various commands, but the canonical source for those commands is usually found in this file. Of the other options, only /proc/cpuinfo is valid, and that file provides information on the CPU(s) for the computer.

112. D. An Xmas scan is available using the -sX mode of nmap. The -sT mode is a TCP connect, and -sS is TCP SYN. There is no -sP option.

113. A. The -s option sets the snapshot length, or snaplen, of the capture instead of its default of 65,535 bytes. The -l option provides line buffering, -c stops after the indicated count of packets are received, and -d dumps compiled packet-matching code into a format that is readable.

114. D. There is no port for ICMP. The protocol does not use ports.

115. B. The -B option changes the format, and T sets the scale to terabytes. The other options do not exist.

116. C. The -c option checks for bad blocks. The -b option sets the block size. There is no -a or -d option.

117. C. The -U option shows latency. Of the other options, -d is used for debugging, -L suppresses multicast loopback packets, and -i sets the interval between packets.

118. B. The iperf command can be used to measure throughput and can be used for troubleshooting latency issues. The other options are not valid commands.

119. C. The itop command displays information about interrupt usage in real time, with a display that is somewhat like the top command. The other options shown for this question are not valid commands.

120. B. The ibstat command shows information about InfiniBand devices. The other commands are not valid.

121. A. The renice command is used to change priorities. The lower the number, the higher the priority. The correct syntax is shown in option A. Option B will set the priority lower. Options C and D are invalid syntax.

122. D. The -n option is used with netstat to prevent hostname lookups, which can slow the output. The other options do not perform the required task.

123. B. The pidof command shows all of the processes associated with the given argument. In this case, option B shows the correct syntax. The ps command shown in other options is a valid command but not with the syntax shown.

124. A. The number 1, or SIGHUP, is the signal that sends a hangup to the process. The other options shown are valid signals but not for the purpose described.

125. A. The command ls -l /etc/systemd/system/default.target shows the current target to which the system will boot. The other commands are not valid.

126. C. The −i option sets the byte-to-inode ratio. The −b option sets the block size, −r sets the filesystem revision, and there is no −u option for mke2fs.

127. C. The /sys/class/fc_host directory contains information on HBA adapter ports on the system. The other options are not valid directories.

128. B. The account module interface is where access verification occurs. Among the other options, the auth and password interfaces are used for different purposes, and there is no policy interface.

129. A. The default policy should be deny. A deny-by-default policy discards packets. It's notable that a reject policy might also be used, which would send a reject back to the sender. The other options are not appropriate for the task described.

130. C. The −l option displays ownership information, including user and group owners of a file or directory. The −o option only shows the user but does not display the group. The other options shown are not valid for this purpose.

131. B. The program should be created to use local sockets for communication. Socket-based programs do not need to incorporate network or protocol information, thus making them preferred over a network-based program for the purpose described. If the program needed network connectivity, then option A would be appropriate. The other options are not appropriate for this scenario.

132. C. The buffers column shows the amount of RAM allocated to kernel buffers. Cache indicates page cache usage, and shared usually indicates tmpfs usage.

133. C. The nmcli command provides a command-line interface into Network Manager. The other options shown are not valid commands.

134. A. The iftop command is used to display real-time network usage through an interface that is reminiscent of the top command. The other options given are not valid commands.

135. C. The iptraf command shows cumulative network usage in real time for a given interface. The other options shown are not valid.

136. C. The cfq scheduler is the default for Linux systems. Of the other options shown, deadline and noop are valid but are not the default. There is no iqueue IO scheduler.

137. D. The ipset command can be used for the purpose described. It's worth noting that you could create a separate iptables rule for each IP address and rule, but doing so would be less efficient than using an ipset group and having a single rule applied to that group.

138. A. The tcptraceroute command should be used for this purpose. This command attempts to connect to the destination on the TCP port specified. This method is preferred over a simple ping because ICMP may be filtered, thus giving an inaccurate diagnosis. The other commands would not be used for this purpose.

139. C. The tshark command enables capture of network traffic into a file. The other commands shown are not valid.

140. C. The whois command is used for lookups of domains and IP addresses, among other things, and would be used for this purpose. The other commands are not valid for this purpose.

141. D. The ioping command sends requests to a given disk and records the time taken for the request. Of the other commands, fdisk is valid but would not be used to determine performance-related issues. The other commands are not valid.

142. C. The partprobe command causes a partition update for the kernel. The other options are not valid commands.

143. A. The sar command can be used to display a wide variety of performance-related information, including that captured over time. The other commands are not valid.

144. A. The -a option shows all available parameters. The other options shown are not valid with sysctl.

145. C. A state of D means uninterruptible sleep. There is no state for debug or dead processes, and interruptible sleep has a state of S.

146. B. The multiuser target is below (before) the graphical target and therefore could be used for further troubleshooting. The rescue target, not listed as an option, could also be used. The poweroff and reboot targets are valid systemd targets but will not help with troubleshooting. There is no SafeMode target.

147. C. The default port is 631. The other ports listed for options are not used for CUPS.

148. A. The .mount extension is required for systemd mount files. Systemd frequently requires specific filenaming conventions in order to work correctly, and knowing the filenames, extensions, and special locations will be helpful for the exam.

149. D. The ausearch command can be used to find recent violations of an SELinux policy. The other commands are not valid.

150. C. The dmesg command shows the kernel ring buffer and is a primary tool to determine whether the system has detected a new piece of hardware. The other options are not valid.

151. A. The signal number or symbolic name can be used and is prefaced with a single dash (-) as shown in option A. The other options are not valid for the purpose required in the question.

152. A. Execute permissions for directories must be present, so the top-level directory must not allow the "other" permission to execute, which is needed for a directory listing within a subdirectory.

153. B. The default size for ioping is 4 KB.

154. A. The IO scheduler in use is found in /sys/block/<device>/queue/scheduler. The other options are not valid locations for this scenario.

155. D. The -n option prevents hostname lookups from occurring with iftop. This is helpful for reducing the amount of noise or unnecessary information displayed within the iftop output. The other options do not accomplish the task required.

156. B. The server command, when run within the nslookup interface, will set the server to which the query will be sent. The other options shown are not valid for this purpose.

157. D. A user would need write and execute permissions in order to write into a directory for which they are not the owner and do not have group ownership.

158. C. LDAP can be used for external authentication scenarios with Linux and is frequently used to provide authentication in an integrated environment with Microsoft Windows and Active Directory. Of the other options, neither SSL nor SSH provides the external authentication, although SSH may be able to integrate with other authentication means. AD is frequently used as an abbreviation for Active Directory. While Active Directory has LDAP capabilities, it is different and separate from LDAP.

159. B. The ulimit command shows the various limits that apply to a given user, including file size limitations. The other options are not valid.

160. A. The permissions should be 755 in order for a user to execute the script. The other options won't work for the purpose described or are too permissive.

161. A. The OnCalendar= configuration option is used to set the time when an event will run when using systemd timer unit files. The other options shown are not valid for use with systemd timer files.

162. C. The wa abbreviation in the output of top represents the percentage of time spent waiting for I/O operations such as disk or network. The other options are not valid for this scenario.

163. B. The groups command is used to retrieve a list of groups. The other commands are not valid.

164. A. The swapon command activates the swap space for use. The other commands are not valid.

165. D. The size of the request can be set using the -s option for ioping. The other options shown are not valid with ioping.

166. C. The -b option prints known bad blocks. The -f option is used to force the display of information, and the other options don't exist.

167. C. The dmidecode command shows extended information about hardware and devices within a Linux system. The other options shown are not valid commands.

168. B. The fail option to mdadm indicates that the disk has failed. The other options shown are not valid.

169. C. The -H option suppresses the legal disclaimer when possible. The other options do not complete the task described in this scenario.

170. B. The −i option sets the interface for iftop. The other options shown are not valid for the required task.

171. B. The file /sys/class/scsi_host/hostN/scan is used for this purpose, where N is the adapter number. The other paths are not valid for the purpose described in this scenario.

172. B. The /etc/shadow file stores encrypted passwords. The /etc/passwd file does not store encrypted passwords, and the other options are not valid.

173. B. The User= option sets the process to run as the given user. The other options are not valid.

174. A. The size and rss columns within ps output are helpful for determining memory usage for a given process. The other options are not valid for process-level troubleshooting.

175. C. SIGKILL corresponds with signal number 9. The other numbers shown are valid signal numbers but are not SIGKILL.

176. D. The IN class, or Internet class, is the default type of class queried with the host command. This can be changed by using the −c option for the host command.

177. A. The routing table is displayed with the −r option. The other options do not display the routing table.

178. C. The −s option displays summary output for the arguments given. The other options shown do not accomplish the required task.

179. B. The ps command lists processes, and using grep for the state of Z will show zombie processes. Of the other options, there is a −Z option for ps but it is not used for the purpose described.

180. A. The lshw command shows all hardware within a system, giving detailed information about many aspects of that hardware. The other commands shown are not valid.

181. B. The −c option sets the number of requests to send with ioping. The other options given are not valid for use with ioping.

182. B. The R state indicates a process is running. The other options do not indicate a running state.

183. B. The vgscan command can be used to resolve mismatch issues between volume groups with LVM. The other commands shown are not valid.

184. A. The ps_max_latency_us setting, typically set as part of the GRUB configuration within nvme_core, can be used to disable power save functions on an NVMe drive. The other options shown are not valid configuration options.

185. C. The OnCalendar=weekly expression will cause the event to run weekly. The other options shown are not valid for this scenario. It is notable that Option A contains OnCalendar, and asterisks or wildcards are valid when configuring event timing with systemd timers. However, that option is not correct because the syntax of the wildcard is wrong.

186. C. The `persistent` option is the default when `auto` is configured and `/var/log/journal` exists. Of the other options, `none` is valid and will not log but will forward to other targets and `volatile` will use memory. There is no journal setting for the `Storage=` option in journald.conf.

187. A. The `oom_score` file, found in `/proc/<pid>/`, contains the number at which the process will be considered within the out-of-memory killer process. A higher number means that there is an increased chance of the process being killed.

188. C. The `nofail` option is used to indicate that the boot process should continue even if the mount point is not available. The other options are not valid.

189. A. The `@` character prefixed to the command indicates that the first argument after the command will be sent as `argv[0]`. The other options are not valid.

190. C. The `-l` option enables login as a different user. The other options are not valid.

191. A. The `-J` option produces output in JSON format. Of the other options, `-s` is used to change the sysroot directory. The other options are not valid.

192. D. The `-showcerts` option displays the certificate chain for the connection. The other options are not valid.

193. A. The `/etc/passwd` file contains user information, including their home directory. The other options are not valid.

194. A. The `ExecReload=` option is used to configure the command that will be executed when the service is reloaded. The other options are not valid.

195. D. The `minutely` expression is used to signify a job that should run once per minute. The other options are not valid.

196. A. The `-I` option sets the number of days after password expiration until the account is locked. The other options are not valid.

197. C. The `PASS_MAX_DAYS` option sets the number of days that a password is valid until it needs to be changed. The other options are not valid.

198. C. The `-x` option shows additional statistics. The other options are not valid.

199. B. The `-l` option shows several properties of the filesystem, including the inode size. The `-f` option causes `tune2fs` to force completion of the specified operation. The other options are not valid.

200. A. The `systemctl daemon-reload` command executes the generators that re-create links and other systemd-related items. Even after running `daemon-reload`, you still typically need to restart the service too. The other options are not valid.

201. B. The `Unit=` directive specifies the command that will be run when the timer is used. The other options are not valid.

202. A. The process needs to return from `execve()`, meaning that the actual daemon has started successfully. This is a primary difference from the `Type=simple` configuration where only the `fork()` needs to happen (option B). The other options are not valid.

203. C. Out-of-memory configuration is controlled by `OOMPolicy` within a service file or can be set to a default value in a systemd configuration file. The other options are not valid.

204. B. The `-u` option to `renice` completes the task successfully. The other options are not valid.

205. A. The `-n` option will not resolve UIDs and GIDs to their names and can be used to speed up the report. The other options are not valid.

206. A. The `chcon` command is used to change the SELinux type of a file and can be helpful when troubleshooting file access issues. The other options are not valid.

207. C. Using `-a -G` appends the group onto the user's list of groups. The other options are not valid to accomplish the necessary task.

208. B. The `noop` scheduling algorithm is recommended for virtual machines on a hypervisor host that performs the I/O scheduling. Of the other options shown, `cfq` is the default scheduling algorithm. The other two options are not valid.

209. B. The oldest entries are shown first when running `journalctl`, thus making the other options incorrect.

210. C. Using the `NOPASSWD` option causes `sudo` to not prompt for the password. The other options shown are not valid with `sudo`.

211. A. Using `Before=` and `After=` ensures ordering of services, thus making option A correct. The other options are not valid for ordering of systemd unit files.

212. D. Using `ConditionMemory=` defines the amount of memory that needs to be available. Mathematical operators such as greater-than, equal, less-than, and others are available. The other options are not valid for specifying the amount of memory within a systemd unit file.

213. A. Administrator-created unit files are stored in `/etc/systemd/system`. The other locations specified are not valid.

214. D. Using `halt.target` stops the system but does not power it down. Of the other options, `poweroff.target` exists and stops the system and also powers it down. The other options are not valid targets.

215. C. Using `man 8 mount` ensures that the 8th level man page is viewed. The other options are not valid for this purpose.

216. A. Looking for the `state` field within the output of the `ip link` command shows whether an interface is considered up or down. The other commands shown are not valid.

217. C. The `LOG` target is used to log packets within iptables. The other targets presented as options are not valid in iptables.

218. B. Using `systemd.debug-shell=1` on the kernel command line results in a debug shell being made available early in the boot process. The other options are not valid for this purpose.

219. C. Using `-f` forces the reboot, although the shutdown process is still noted as clean. The other options shown are not valid for this purpose.

220. B. Using `list-jobs` shows the state of jobs in progress. The other options shown are not valid for this purpose.

221. A. The `systemctl show` command is used for this purpose. The output can be further refined through the use of the `-p` option. The other options shown are not valid for this purpose.

222. D. The `systemd-resolved` service is responsible for name resolution on systemd-enabled systems. Troubleshooting for `systemd-resolved` name resolution follows the same pattern as that of troubleshooting other systemd services. The other options shown are not valid.

223. A. Using `+trace` causes dig to follow recursively through the lookup process. The other options shown are not valid for this purpose.

224. B. Using the `-u` option shows entries related to the unit file specified. The `-k` option displays kernel messages. The `-p` option is used to specify priority and the `-S` option displays messages since the specified time.

225. C. The `systemctl list-timers` command shows the timers that are active on the system. The other options are not valid.

226. C. A return code of 64 indicates that trim succeeded on some filesystems and failed on some filesystems, so further investigation will be required. Trim succeeded is return code 0 and all failed is return code 32. The `fstrim` command won't run on an unsupported filesystem, making option A incorrect.

227. B. The `emergency.target` provides minimal boot with the service manager and facilitates starting individual unit files for further troubleshooting. The other targets shown are not valid.

228. B. Removing the combination of `quiet splash` results in additional verbosity being displayed on the console, which is needed for many troubleshooting scenarios. The other targets shown are not valid.

229. D. The address `192.168.1.200` falls outside the 192.168.1.0/25 address range, which ends at 192.168.1.127. The other options shown fall within the range.

230. B. The `timeout` setting is used to configure the length of the pause before grub boots into the default operating system. The other answers are not valid for this purpose.

231. A. The `-s` option displays summary numbers of connections. The `-h` option displays help and `-w` displays raw sockets. There is no `-c` option.

232. C. SATA disks are addressed as /dev/sdX, just like a SCSI disk. /dev/hdX is a traditional ATA disk. The other options do not exist.

233. A. The dns_servers.conf file configures the DNS servers that will be used. The other options shown are not valid files.

234. C. Setting LogLevel=Debug configures the maximum logging level for daemon processes started by systemd. The other options shown are not valid for this purpose.

235. A. The cancel option stops jobs in progress using their job ID as an argument. If no argument is given, then all jobs will be canceled. The other options shown are not valid for this purpose.

236. A. The ip link set <device> up command attempts to bring an interface online. The other commands shown are not valid.

237. D. A - prefixed to a filename causes failure status codes to be effectively ignored and instead just recorded or logged. The other characters have no effect and would likely cause errors themselves.

238. A. The [Service] section is required within a systemd service unit file. The other options shown are not valid for use in a systemd service unit file.

239. B. The insults option, disabled by default, has been enabled in sudoers, thus causing the message when a user types their password in wrong. The other options shown are not valid within sudoers.

240. B. Using the -r option causes entries to be displayed in reverse order. The -a option displays all entries and the -t option is used to specify the syslog identifier to display. The -g option searches (greps) for the specified message.

241. A. The -I option changes the inode size. The -i option changes the interval between checks. The -s and -v options are not used.

242. D. The file /aquota.user indicates that quotas have been enabled on this filesystem. The other options are not valid to indicate that quotas have been enabled.

243. A. The ExecStopPost= configuration option is recommended for these situations. The other options are not valid.

244. A. Systemd requires special naming for filesystems managed through the systemd process. In addition to needing .mount file extensions, the name of the file itself needs to reflect the mount point but have dashes. Though there could be other reasons for the filesystem not mounting, making systemd happy is the first issue to address.

245. C. The two behaviors aside from panic are continue and remount-ro. The other options shown are not valid error behaviors.

246. D. A setting of 1us for the AccuracySec= option is the best accuracy setting with a systemd timer. The other options are less accurate than 1us.

247. B. The $MAINPID variable contains the process ID of the primary process associated with the service. The other options are not valid.

248. A. The x-systemd.requires option is used within /etc/fstab and parsed into systemd as Requires=. The other options are not valid.

249. B. The ExecStart configuration option is used to provide the command line of the service that should be started. The other options shown are not valid.

250. A. The /etc/mtab file contains currently mounted filesystems. Note that /etc/fstab contains filesystem information but not about which filesystems are currently mounted.

251. A. The tune2fs command displays a lot of information about filesystems, including the number of times the filesystem has been mounted. The number of mounts is not shown in /etc/fstab and mount -a simply mounts all filesystems shown in /etc/fstab. There is no /etc/fsmnt file.

252. A. Nonzero values for the DISC-GRAN and DISC-MAX columns indicate that trim support is enabled. The remaining options do not contain valid column names for lsblk output.

Chapter 5: Practice Exam

1. B. Current interrupt (IRQ) assignments are contained in the file /proc/interrupts. Therefore, viewing the contents of the file with a command such as cat will work. There is no view command, thus making option A incorrect. Likewise, there is no /dev/irq file, making options C and D incorrect.

2. D. Configuration files for udev are found in /etc/udev, which makes option D correct. The other options do not exist.

3. A. The modprobe command loads the module and its dependencies, if applicable. The lsmod command is used to list currently loaded modules, making option B incorrect. The insmod command will load a given module but not its dependencies. Option D, rmmod, is used to remove a module from memory.

4. A. The Shift key, if pressed when control has first been handed to GRUB, will cause the GRUB menu to be displayed.

5. D. The dmesg command displays the contents of the kernel ring buffer. On many Linux distributions, this log is also saved to /var/log/dmesg. The other options shown for this question are not valid commands.

6. A. The listing shows a symbolic linked file located in the current directory, linked to .configs/fetchmail/.fetchmailrc. The file is owned by the root user and root group and was created on July 8, 2014.

7. B. The systemctl command is used to work with services and targets. The list-units command is used to list targets. The other commands are not used for this purpose or do not exist with the required option.

8. C. The −nn option displays both numbers and device names, thus making option C correct. The −n option (option B) displays only numbers. The other two options do not exist.

9. C. Out of the options given, the systemctl status command and option are the most appropriate. The telinit and sysctl commands are not used for this purpose. Likewise, the −−ls option is not valid for systemctl.

10. D. The partition containing /var should be the largest for a mail server because mail spools are stored within this hierarchy. The /etc/ hierarchy is usually small, as is /usr/bin. The /mail directory does not exist by default.

11. B. The deplist option displays the dependencies for the given package. The list option displays information about a specific package, while the other two options are not valid.

12. A. The −ivh options will install a file using rpm, displaying both verbose output and hash marks for progress. The other options presented do not exist or do not accomplish the specified task.

13. A. The apt-cache command is used to work with the package cache, and the search option is used to search the cache for the supplied argument, in this case zsh. The apt-get command is used to work with packages themselves, while the apt-search command does not exist.

14. A. The −V or −−verify option will check the files in a given package against versions (or check-sums) in the package database. If no files have been altered, then no output is produced. Note that output may be produced for files that are changed during installation or for other reasons. Note also the use of an uppercase V for this option as opposed to the lowercase v for verbose.

15. D. The top command is used to continuously monitor things like CPU and memory usage, and the −p option monitors a single process. By using the runquotes with the pidof command, the process ID is provided as input to the −p option. It's worth noting that this only works if there's a single instance of the process.

16. A. The −g option displays the progress of the dump. The other options listed do not exist.

17. C. The debugfs command can be used for this purpose. When the filesystem is opened with −c, it opens in catastrophic mode, meaning that it will be read-only and will not read inodes when opening.

18. C. The xwininfo command displays information about a given window within an X session. The other commands listed are not valid.

19. C. The file /etc/localtime, which can be an actual file or a symbolic link, is used to indicate the local time zone. The other files listed as options do not exist.

20. D. Within the /usr/share/zoneinfo hierarchy, you will find information on the various regions and time zones available. The files within this hierarchy can be symlinked to /etc/localtime.

21. A. The /etc/skel directory contains files that are automatically copied to a user's home directory when that user is created. The other directories listed for this question do not exist by default.

22. B. The `atq` command shows a list of jobs that have been scheduled with the `at` command. The other commands don't exist, with the exception of option D, which shows the `at` command but with an invalid option (`--jobs`).

23. B. UTF-8 provides multibyte character encoding and is generally accepted as the standard for encoding moving forward. ISO-8859 is single-byte encoded. The other options are not valid.

24. C. LDAP over SSL (LDAPS) operates on port 636. Port 53 is used for DNS; port 389 is used for normal, non-SSL LDAP; and port 443 is used for HTTP over SSL.

25. B. The `chage` command can be used for this purpose, and the `-E` option accepts days since 1/1/1970. There is no `-e` option to `passwd`, and `-l` for `usermod` will not perform the action described. There is no `chguser` command.

26. A. The `-i` option for SSH is followed by the private key to use for authentication. Doing so implies that the public key is in the `authorized_keys` file on the remote host. The `-k` option disables the sending of GSSAPI credentials, while `-f` is used to request backgrounding of SSH. There is no `--key` option.

27. A. The `-n` option facilitates the scenario described and will exit nonzero rather than prompting. The `-i` option sets the login name and is not valid for this scenario. The `-q` and `--noprompt` options do not exist.

28. A. Single-user mode is typically runlevel 1. In runlevel 1, no network services are started, and it is known as `rescue.target` in systemd. Runlevel 2 has networking but typically not services. Runlevel 5 is full multiuser with networking, and runlevel 6 is reboot.

29. B. The `free` command shows current memory usage for both RAM and swap space, including total available, current amount used, and current amount free. The other commands shown as options do not exist.

30. A. The `df` command displays information on disk usage and can help with planning disk utilization over time. For example, if you note that the disk utilization is increasing significantly, preparations can be made to bring more disks online or even to change the log-rotation schedule such that logs are rotated faster, thereby freeing up space.

31. A. The `sar` command can be used for this purpose and, when provided with numbers in the format displayed, will update every X seconds for Y executions.

32. C. The `-m` option causes the disk-related statistics to use megabytes as the scale rather than the default kilobytes.

33. A. The `mkinitrd` command is used on older systems to create the initial RAM disk. The initial RAM disk is used to load, some might say preload, essential modules for things like disks and other vital components needed for booting.

34. D. A bzImage can mean that `bzip` was used to compress the image but can also mean simply "Big zImage" and compressed with `gzip`. bzImage is typically used for kernel images that can go above the 512 K limit that normally applies to a zImage.

35. A. The `-r` option repairs the filesystem, while the `-y` option causes `fsck` to assume Yes instead of prompting. The `-v` option is verbosity. There is no `-m` or `-x` option for `fsck`.

36. A. The `default.target` is the default target unit that is activated by `systemd` on boot. The default target then starts other services based on the dependencies.

37. B. The `mkswap` command is used to format a swap partition. The other commands are not valid.

38. B. A filesystem with the word `defaults` for its mount options will be mounted read-write (`rw`), `suid`, with the ability to have executables (`exec`). The filesystem will be auto-mounted (`auto`), but users will not be able to mount it (`nouser`). Character and block special devices will be interpreted (`dev`), and operations on the disk will be performed in an asynchronous manner (`async`).

39. C. The `fstrim` command is used to remove blocks that are not in use. The `fstrim` command is frequently used in a SAN configuration to give back unused storage to the SAN. The `fstrim` command can also be used with solid-state drives for the same purpose. The other commands shown are not valid.

40. A. The `--create` option enables creation of a RAID array that will use md. The typical argument is the `/dev/mdN` device. The other options listed are not valid for `mdadm`.

41. B. The `lvcreate` command is used to create a logical volume from previously created physical devices and volume groups. Using `lvcreate` is the final of three steps in the process for using LVM prior to actually using the logical volume.

42. A. The `ss` command provides many of the same functions as `netstat` but can show some extended information, such as memory allocation for a given socket. The `free` command shows memory usage but not by socket, and the other two commands do not exist.

43. D. The `-f` option is a flood ping. This will effectively cause the interface to send and receive large amounts of traffic, usually making it easier to find on a switch. The `-a` option is an audible ping, emitting a sound on `ping`. The `-c` option sends a certain count of pings, and there is no `-e` option.

44. C. The `bs` option is used to specify block size. Various suffixes are possible, such as `M`, which is equivalent to megabytes, and `K`, which is equivalent to kilobytes.

45. B. The `--size-only` option examines whether the files being synchronized are the same size. This can be helpful for situations where there may be significant time skew or other issues preventing the normal differencing mechanisms from working properly. The other options shown are not valid for `rsync`.

46. A. The lowest-priority number wins for MX records, thereby making 0 the highest-priority MX record for the domain.

47. D. DNS typically uses UDP port 53 except for zone transfers, in which case TCP port 53 is used due to the size of the request for most zones.

48. D. The `axfr` type can be used with `dig` to request a zone transfer. The client from which you request the zone transfer will need to be authorized to initiate a transfer.

49. D. The file `/etc/exports` contains definitions of filesystems to be shared using NFS. The other files are not valid for use with NFS.

50. B. The `max-lease-time` directive, followed by the number of seconds, specifies the amount of time that a given host can have a lease before it is purged. The other options shown are not valid in a `dhcpd.conf` configuration file.

51. A. Within `nsswitch.conf`, the `passwd` line contains information about authentication. The format is as shown in the correct answer. Local authentication is accomplished using the `files` keyword for the normal `passwd` file. There is typically a similar line called `shadow`, assuming that the server is using shadow passwords. The `shadow` line follows a similar format.

52. D. The `ssh-keygen` command generates a public and private key pair that can be used for user authentication between a client and server. The other commands shown are not valid.

53. D. The file `authorized_keys` contains keys that can be used for authentication when the corresponding private key is sent by the client. The other files are not valid.

54. D. A logical location to begin troubleshooting is within the system BIOS or firmware to ensure that the drive is being detected by the computer.

55. B. The `export` command is used for this purpose and accepts a `name=value` pair, as shown in the answer. The other commands are not valid, with the exception of the `echo` command, which will simply echo the argument to the console.

56. C. The `HISTFILESIZE` option configures the number of commands to keep in the history file. The other variables are not valid within Bash.

57. C. The `awk` command shown can be used for this purpose. The `-F` option sets the field separator, and the `OFS` option sets the output field separator.

58. B. The `git clone` command will clone into a different directory if that directory is passed on the command line, as shown in option B. The other options shown are not valid `git clone` syntax.

59. A. The `export` command is necessary so that any variables that are manually defined in your current session become available to child processes. The `source` command executes the file and can be used for the purpose described but requires an additional argument. The `let` and `def` commands are not valid.

60. C. The `source` command is the functional equivalent of a single dot (`.`). The `set` command exists but is not used for this purpose. The other commands are not valid.

61. A. The correct syntax is as shown. Note that a semicolon is required when the commands are included on one line, as shown in the correct answer.

62. B. The `-f` option sets the days between expiration and disabled for an account. The `-g` option is used to set the group ID, while `-e` is used to set the overall expiration date.

63. C. The `-r` option to the `crontab` command removes all cron entries for a given user. The `-l` option lists cron jobs, while the `-e` option edits the `crontab`. There is no `-d` option.

64. D. The `journalctl` command is used to view and parse log file entries on `systemd`-based systems that maintain logs in a special format. The `logger` command can be used to create log entries, and the other commands shown do not exist.

65. C. The `lpr` syslog facility sends messages from the `lp` subsystem to syslog. The `auth` facility is used for security-related messages. The other listed options are not syslog facilities.

66. D. Standard LDAP traffic is TCP port 389 on the server. TCP port 25 is SMTP, 443 is HTTPS, and 143 is IMAP.

67. C. When connecting to an alternate port, you can use the `-p` option to set the port or use a colon to separate the host from the port.

68. D. The `-p` option preserves permissions. The `-x` option extracts while `-z` unzips with `gzip`. The `-v` option is `verbose`.

69. B. The `-i` option tells `patch` to ignore white space. This might be necessary when the patch file doesn't match exactly what's needed. The `-p` option sets the level of directory for the patch, while `-e` informs `patch` to interpret as an ed script. There is no `-w` option for `patch`.

70. C. LUKS encryption is the default mode for the `dm-crypt` command. Other modes include plain, loopaes, and tcrypt.

71. B. The `-r` option reverses the journal, displaying the newest entries first. The `-n` option shows the most recent N events, `-f` is `follow`, and `-b` tells `journalctl` to show a message from a specific boot ID.

72. D. The `emergency` target can be used in situations where rescue mode cannot recover the system. The other targets are not valid.

73. A. As specified in the question, you need to remove both group and user ownership, therefore both `-g` and `-o` are needed. The other options are not valid, although you can remove individual options from an archive process with `--no-g` and `--no-o`, which would be equivalent to removing the `-g` and `-o` options from the command.

74. B. The `-r` option bypasses the routing tables and enables sending packets directly using an interface. The `-A` option is adaptive `ping`, while `-b` enables sending pings to a broadcast address. The `-q` option is quiet output.

75. B. The `-b` option makes a copy of the original file before patching. This can be particularly useful in a scripted scenario where several files are patched in succession. The `-d` option causes a change directory prior to patching, while `-c` tells `patch` to interpret the patch file as a normal diff file. The `-s` option causes `patch` to work in silent mode.

76. C. Orchestration software can use an agent, which is described as part of the question, or the orchestration software could also be agentless, not requiring special software to be installed on each client machine.

77. B. The `\r` escape sequence is a carriage return, and `\n` is newline. The `\c` sequence invokes a control character and is not related to this question.

78. A. The -f file test checks to see if the file exists and is useful in a scripting scenario as described.

79. C. By invoking a shell specifically for the commands in the script, you can execute the contents of the script. Option A requires the execute bit to be set. The other options won't work.

80. A. The ls-files command will be used for this purpose, and -i or --ignored will be used, along with a required exclusion pattern, thus making option A correct. Option B is missing the required exclusion pattern.

81. A. Redirecting input from a file uses the less-than sign. Option B takes the output from script.sh and sends it to file.txt. Option C tries to use file.txt as input but without any way to send the contents to STDOUT. Option D executes script.sh and sends the contents to file.txt, which is opposite of the scenario.

82. B. The -c option sets the maximum mount count. The -C option sets the current number of mounts. The -b and -a options do not exist.

83. D. The -f option, also known as fake, is helpful for situations where you need to debug the mount process or when you need to add an entry to /etc/mtab for a previously mounted filesystem. The -l option shows labels, and -v is verbose. There is no -q option.

84. A. The netstat command can be used for this purpose, and the -r option displays the current routes. The addition of -n prevents DNS lookups, which can help with performance.

85. A. The ps command provides information on processor and memory usage for individual processes. You can use this information to predict capacity.

86. C. The wa statistic shows time spent waiting for I/O and can be used to measure or find a bottleneck related to disk. The us statistic is time spent on userspace processes, while sy is time spent on kernel processes. There is no statistic called io within vmstat.

87. A. Load average with the uptime command is displayed in 1-, 5-, and 15-minute increments.

88. A. The -a option displays all values and their current settings for sysctl. The -b option is binary and displays values without any newlines. The -d option is an alias for -h, which displays help. There is no -c option.

89. B. The SIGTERM signal is the default signal sent with the systemctl kill command.

90. C. The ldconfig command is used to work with the library cache, and the -p option prints the directories and libraries in the cache. The -C option informs ldconfig to use a different cache. The ldd command prints the library dependencies for a given command, but the options given don't exist for ldd.

91. B. The vmx flag is an indication that hypervisors will be supported on the host. The other options shown are not relevant flags for this purpose.

92. A. The -n option disables name resolution, including hostnames and service names. The other options shown are not relevant flags for this purpose.

93. B. The `get-default` option shows the current target runlevel to which the system will boot. Of the other options, `show` displays information about configuration but not the target runlevel.

94. D. The `-s` option displays the output of `free` every N seconds in order to track memory usage over time while troubleshooting. The other options are not relevant for this scenario.

95. B. The `inspect` command shows detailed information about a Docker container. The other options are not relevant for this scenario.

96. C. The `lsinitrd` command shows information about an image created with `dracut`. The other options are not real commands.

97. B. The `chronyc tracking` command shows information about the current status of time synchronization. The other options are not real commands.

98. D. The `whois` command shows information about domains and IP block ownership and would be appropriate in this scenario. Of the other options, there is an `ip` command but no `info` subcommand. The other options are not real commands.

99. A. The `-j` option returns output in JSON format. Of the other options, `-i` is used for interactive command-line interface, `-s` shows statistics, and there is no -m option.

100. D. The `-6` option to the `ss` command displays IPv6 connections. The other options shown are not valid.

101. C. The configuration files for Postfix are stored in `/etc/postfix` on a Debian server. Of the other answers, none of the directories exist by default.

102. B. Given the Forbidden error and the permissions shown, `chmod 644` will change the permissions to allow the file to be world-readable. Of the other options, the scenario did not describe the directories; thus there isn't enough information and also the `mv` command shown is incomplete. Option C cannot be true based on the scenario showing the permissions for the file. Option D might be correct but renaming a file in Linux requires the use of the `mv` command.

Index

Online Test Bank

Register to gain one year of FREE access after activation to the online interactive test bank to help you study for your CompTIA Linux+ certification exam—included with your purchase of this book! All of the chapter review questions and the practice tests in this book are included in the online test bank so you can practice in a timed and graded setting.

Register and Access the Online Test Bank

To register your book and get access to the online test bank, follow these steps:

1. Go to www.wiley.com/go/sybextestprep.
2. Select your book from the list.
3. Complete the required registration information, including answering the security verification to prove book ownership. You will be emailed a pin code.
4. Follow the directions in the email or go to www.wiley.com/go/sybextestprep.
5. Find your book on that page and click the "Register or Login" link with it. Then enter the pin code you received and click the "Activate PIN" button.
6. On the Create an Account or Login page, enter your username and password, and click Login or, if you don't have an account already, create a new account.
7. At this point, you should be in the test bank site with your new test bank listed at the top of the page. If you do not see it there, please refresh the page or log out and log back in.